LIBRARY OF HEBREW BIBLE/
OLD TESTAMENT STUDIES

712

Formerly Journal for the Study of the Old Testament Supplement Series

Editors
Claudia V. Camp, Texas Christian University, USA
Andrew Mein, Durham University, UK

Founding Editors
David J. A. Clines, Philip R. Davies and David M. Gunn

Editorial Board
Alan Cooper, Steed Davidson, Susan Gillingham, John Goldingay,
Norman K. Gottwald, James E. Harding, John Jarick, Tracy Lemos,
Carol Meyers, Daniel L. Smith-Christopher, Francesca Stavrakopoulou,
James W. Watts

NARRATIVE AND OTHER READINGS IN THE BOOK OF ESTHER

Else K. Holt

LONDON • NEW YORK • OXFORD • NEW DELHI • SYDNEY

T&T CLARK
Bloomsbury Publishing Plc
50 Bedford Square, London, WC1B 3DP, UK
1385 Broadway, New York, NY 10018, USA
29 Earlsfort Terrace, Dublin 2, Ireland

BLOOMSBURY, T&T CLARK and the T&T Clark logo
are trademarks of Bloomsbury Publishing Plc

First published in Great Britain 2021
This paperback edition published 2022

Copyright © Else K. Holt, 2021

Else K. Holt has asserted her right under the Copyright, Designs and Patents Act, 1988, to be identified as Author of this work.

Cover design: Charlotte James

All rights reserved. No part of this publication may be reproduced or transmitted in any form or by any means, electronic or mechanical, including photocopying, recording, or any information storage or retrieval system, without prior permission in writing from the publishers.

Bloomsbury Publishing Plc does not have any control over, or responsibility for, any third-party websites referred to or in this book. All internet addresses given in this book were correct at the time of going to press. The author and publisher regret any inconvenience caused if addresses have changed or sites have ceased to exist, but can accept no responsibility for any such changes.

A catalogue record for this book is available from the British Library.
Library of Congress control number: 2020951549.

ISBN:	HB:	978-0-5676-9761-5
	PB:	978-0-5676-9764-6
	ePDF:	978-0-5676-9762-2

Series: Library of Hebrew Bible/Old Testament Studies, ISSN 2513-8758, volume 712

Typeset by: Trans.form.ed SAS

To find out more about our authors and books visit www.bloomsbury.com and sign up for our newsletters.

CONTENTS

Acknowledgements	vii

Chapter 1
THEOLOGY AND RELIGION — 1
1. Placing Esther in Theology—An Introduction — 1
Excursus: Luther and Esther — 4
2. God and Religion in the Book of Esther — 8
3. Concluding Remarks of Introduction — 14

Part I
BACKGROUND

Chapter 2
DATE, COMPOSITION, RECEPTION — 18
1. The Transmission of Esther — 18
2. Dating the Biblical Books of Esther — 20
3. The Composition and Ideology of the Books of Esther — 24
   3.1. The Hebrew Esther — 24
   3.2. The Greek Esthers — 28

Chapter 3
CHARACTER, GENDER, AND POWER PLAY — 31
1. Exscription and Inscription — 31
2. The Hebrew Esther — 33
3. The Greek Esthers — 39
4. Conclusion — 46

Part II
READINGS

Chapter 4
NOW ESTHER WAS ADMIRED BY ALL WHO SAW HER—
OR: HOW TO UNDERSTAND ESTHER 2/TOO? — 51
1. Intertextuality — 51
2. The Story of Esther — 53

3. Exscribing the Queen	54
4. Preparing the Bride	56
4.1. The Male Gaze	57
4.2. Initiation	62
4.3. The Perfume	65
Excursus: Made-up Jezebel	67
5. Conclusion	68

Chapter 5
DRESSING UP ESTHER: THE FUNCTION OF CLOTHES IN THE ESTHER NARRATIVE

	70
2. Exegesis	72
2.1. Vashti's Crown and Esther's: Esther 1:10-12; 2:17	72
2.2. Haman and the King's Signet Ring, Esther 3:10; 8:2	76
2.3. Mordecai in Sackcloth and Ashes, Esther 4:1-17	78
2.4. Esther Meets the King, Esther 5:1	82
2.5. Dressing Up Mordecai, Esther 6:6-11	85
3. Conclusion and Outlook	87

Chapter 6
HAMAN, THE SCAPEGOAT

	90
1. Rivals and Brothers, Scapegoats and Violence	91
2. The Shared Object—Power in Persia	93
3. Violence and Society	96
4. The Individual and the Collective Scapegoat	98
5. Conclusion: Of Scapegoats and Carnivals	101

Part III
IDEOLOGIES

Chapter 7
THERE IS A CERTAIN PEOPLE—
OR: HOW THE JUDEANS BECAME THE JEWS

	107
1. The Use of *yᵉhûdîm* in Esther	108
2. Are the Judeans in Esther Jewish? Or: How to Define Ethnicity?	109
3. There Is a Certain People	114
4. Purim and Tradition	118
5. Purim and Genocide	122

Chapter 8
THE SMALL SPRING AND THE DRAGONS:
READING THE BOOK OF ESTHER AS CHOSEN TRAUMA

	126
1. Chosen Trauma	126
2. Trauma and Collective Memory	127

3. We Shall Overcome 129
4. The Final Battle 135
5. Concluding Outlook 137

Chapter 9
GENOCIDE IN ESTHER?
A CONCLUDING DISCUSSION 139
   1. Violence in the Hebrew Bible: The Example of 1 Samuel 15 139
   2. The Problem of Violence in Esther 143
   3. Violence and Old Testament Theology 149
   4. The Authority of the Bible 155
   5. Is Esther a Bedtime Story? 156

Bibliography 159
Index of References 167
Index of Authors 171

Acknowledgements

Since 2010, studies in the book of Esther have been my diversion and beloved pastime, alongside my main research and teaching in the prophetic and poetic books of the Old Testament / Hebrew Bible. In February of that year, in the midst of a Georgia snowstorm, my husband and I arrived at the place that would be our home away from home for the next four months, Columbia Theological Seminary in Decatur, GA. By then, I had decided for a short period to exchange my trauma-hermeneutical studies in Jeremiah and Lamentations for something different, funnier and more colorful, and the book of Esther seemed to be the natural choice. I was never disappointed, and after our sabbatical I resumed to Esther studies whenever I got the chance. In the fall of 2018, we returned to CTS, where I got the chance of properly catching up on Esther, again reading and writing in the library and discussing my research with students and staff. My retirement in 2019 has given me the opportunity to conclude the present volume. My two sabbaticals were funded by Danish Council for Independent Research, Culture and Communication (2010) and the Faculty of Arts, Aarhus University (2010). I am grateful for their support for my project.

Books are never the work of a single person. In the case of the present volume, lots of people have been of immeasurable help: My BA-students in Aarhus, who were the first with whom I shared my fascination with Esther; my colleagues and friends at the departments of Biblical Studies at the universities in Copenhagen and especially Aarhus, who introduced me to theories of sociology and anthropology and patiently listened to and discussed my ideas and drafts; the faculty and students at CTS, with whom I discussed my exegetical, ethical, and theological finds "on the road." Here, I can only mention a few: Professors Kathleen O'Connor, Christine Yoder, William P. Brown, and Brennan Breed from the Department of Biblical Studies. The students with whom I was always on first-name terms: Rose, Katie, Kati, Wylie, Bob, Joe, Laura, Kibaya, Drew, and especially James. The staff in the John Bulow Campbell Library, especially Erica Durham and Mary Martha Riviere, whose kind help and interest in my project—and lots of other library users'—are far beyond what one could wish for. Reverend Kim LeVert at the international office, who showed us the practical and emotive ways of sisterly hospitality. And finally, my husband, Reverend Anders Holt, who has read every page of this book, discussed it with me over and again, and encouraged and challenged me to dive deeper into and think smarter about the book of Esther. It goes without saying that I take the full responsibility for all flaws and failures in the book. I am so grateful for your help and support, all of you.

I dedicate this volume to Anders and to all the fabulous people of the CTS community without whose help and interest it would never have been written.

Else K. Holt
Aarhus, July 2020

Chapter 1

THEOLOGY AND RELIGION

1. *Placing Esther in Theology—An Introduction*

"What is it, Queen Esther? What is your request? It shall be given you, even to the half of my kingdom" (Est. 5:3).[1] This is the repeated question of the mighty King Ahasuerus of Persia to his Judean queen in this fairy tale narrative about how to survive in the Diaspora. What do Esther and her compatriots want, what is their request for survival in a foreign world? And this question is also the question of the book of Esther, one of the less discussed but not least interesting of the books in the Old Testament/Hebrew Bible.

The book of Esther is the tale of a beautiful young Judean[2] girl, Esther, who becomes queen of the vast Persian Empire and who, by her influence on the king, averts the annihilation of all Judeans living in the Persian Diaspora. Other main protagonists are Esther's guardian, the good Judean courtier Mordecai, and his opponent, the evil vizier Haman who, because he is offended (or insulted?) by Mordecai, makes the foolish and irresolute king Ahasuerus sign an irrefutable decree of annihilation of all Judeans in the empire. As in all good fairy tales, everything ends well: Haman falls in his own snare, the Judeans are allowed to fight their enemies among the Persians (to put it neutrally—in fact, no fewer than 75,311 Persians are executed or slaughtered at the event!), the celebration of Purim is

---

1. All translations from the Hebrew Bible are according to the NRSV, unless otherwise indicated. All translations from the Septuagint and the Alpha-text are according to *A New English Translation of the Septuagint and the Other Greek Translations Traditionally Included under That Title* (NETS), ed. A. Pietersma and B. G. Wright (New York/Oxford: Oxford University Press, 2007.

2. I use the term 'Judean', not 'Jew/Jewish' when possible, since this is a more valid translation of the Hebrew *yᵉhûd/yᵉhûdî* in the Hebrew book of Esther; see the discussion in Chapter 7.

established, and Mordecai becomes vizier in Persia, beloved by all his fellow Judeans.

In other words, the book of Esther is about political power and who is to decide the destiny of the Judean people in the diaspora. Esther is, among many other things, first and foremost a book about power play, and we shall follow this red thread through the various readings of the book.

In scholarly and religious writings, the message of the book of Esther is understood as pointing in very different directions. This is no wonder, since, to quote the Jewish scholar Jon Levenson:

> the book of Esther is so entertaining, so comical, and so subtle that to speak of its "message" can be profoundly misleading. Like all great literature, it demands at least that the term be in plural: a book whose structure is amenable to many angles of vision surely has more than one message.[3]

In my reading, the book of Esther—like so many other books in the Hebrew Bible—is about life and death, survival and continued living for the exiled after the destruction of the Judean capital and temple in 587 BCE. But unlike all other books in the Hebrew Bible, God is not its main protagonist or among them, God is not even mentioned. The book is not about the sinfulness of Judah and its kings, not about righteousness and penitence, it does not lament the fate of the chosen people, and it is not an upfront instruction about how to live in this world as in wisdom literature. Esther is something different, something of its own together with the Joseph narratives (Gen. 37–50*, the Testament of Joseph, and Joseph and Aseneth), Tobit, Daniel, and Judith in the small genre named Diaspora novellas. Esther is about living in the Diaspora for better and for worse. Esther is also an entertaining book, a carnivalesque, maybe even burlesque, book which renders its message through literary means very distant from the serenity of most of the books in the Hebrew Bible.[4] This festive mood bears the whole tenor of the book, the joy of living, the carnivalesque one (or two) day(s) off when everybody dresses up in

---

3. Jon Levenson, *Esther: A Commentary*, OTL (Louisville/London: Westminster John Knox, 1997).

4. Rebecca S. Hancock describes the Esther narrative as "exceptionally complex and, thus, it is difficult to identify one episode as the interpretive lens for the whole." Rebecca S. Hancock, *Esther and the Politics of Negotiation: Public and Private Spaces and the Figure of the Female Royal Counselor*, Emerging Scholars (Minneapolis: Fortress, 2013), 11; contra Timothy K. Beal, "Tracing Esther's Beginnings," in *A Feminist Companion to Esther, Judith, and Susanna*, ed. Athalya Brenner, FCB 7 (Sheffield: Sheffield Academic, 1995), 87–110 (103).

fancy and funny outfits, disguising themselves as the wicked Haman, the triumphant Mordecai on the king's horse, or the lovely queen Esther; and even serious Hasidim drink themselves merry in wine and dance in the streets of Jerusalem and Brooklyn.

So, Esther is a very Jewish book, maybe the most Jewish of all the books in the Hebrew Bible. But it is more than that; it is also a book of resistance and courage for everybody. We can so to speak be Esthers, all of us. Let me illustrate with an example: When I first started working on the book of Esther during a sabbatical in 2010 at Columbia Theological Seminary in Decatur, Georgia, I heard a testimony from a middle-aged African-American woman who sang in a gospel choir from Georgia State women's prison one day at the daily chapel service. She was just about to leave prison to go on probation after serving 15 years, presumably for murder. She talked and talked. Very long and very eloquently, far beyond my European, Lutheran limits of religious embarrassment, she presented her testimony of her conversion, and she thanked the female minister and choir leader for her guidance. "You have been Esther to me," she said, meaning, "You were the right person in the right place, and you showed me the way." Is that what the book of Esther talks about: Being in the right place and taking responsibility? Or is the message: Even the most unlikely persons have the possibility and responsibility of taking charge?

The book of Esther is a book of many questions and messages. It has fostered many diverse responses during its time of transmission and reception, and it has not been universally popular, neither in Jewish nor Christian circles.[5] The rabbis discussed whether Esther should be included in the canonized Hebrew Bible; the question was whether Esther, together with Ecclesiastes and Song of Songs, "defiled the hands," that is, was holy enough to be included in the Canon.[6] In the end it was. Due to its clear character of being a Jewish book it remained almost uncommented upon by the Church Fathers. In the Renaissance, Martin Luther in one of his *Table Talks* famously said: "I am so hostile to this book and to Esther that I wish they did not exist at all, for they Judaize too much, and have much heathen impropriety."[7]

---

5. A valuable introduction to the reception of Esther is found in Jo Carruthers, *Esther Through the Centuries* (Malden: Blackwell, 2008).

6. On this discussion, see Michael J. Broyde, "Defilement of the Hands, Canonization of the Bible, and the Special Status of Esther, Ecclesiastes, and Song of Song," *Judaism* 44 (1995): 65–79.

7. "Ich bin dem Buch [2 Makk] und Esther so feind, daß ich wollte, sie wären gar nicht vorhanden; denn sie judenzen zu sehr, und haben viel heidnische Unart." Martin Luther, *D. Martin Luthers Werke. Kritische Gesamt-Ausgabe, Tischreden*, 1.

Excursus: Luther and Esther

Luther's assault on the book of Esther—historical or anecdotal—has had an undue influence on Protestant reception of the book. Thus, it has also been countered by recent scholarship, and rightfully so, especially if it would have been the only comment from his side. However, as usual with Luther, there is more to be said.

In 1964, the German Lutheran Old Testament professor Hans Bardtke published an essay on the topic,[8] in which he offered a thorough and informative analysis of Luther's use of Esther, one which sought to incite to a more balanced view: Luther translated, but never commented on the book *in extenso*, but he referred to its characters as examples in his commentaries etc. on biblical texts, with reference both to the Hebrew Esther and the Greek additions. He quoted the book in no fewer than 48 instances, most often in the affirmative (*im bejahenden Sinn*). These quotes are present in writings spanning the entirety of his career, writings on exegesis, theology, and edification, sermons and letters,[9] and this invites a more broadly based understanding on Luther's position to the book.[10] Bardtke comments on the infamous remark in the *Table Talk*, that Luther's approach is connected with his wish for the Jews to convert to Christianity, and that the book of Esther is of no help in that effort. "The fierce demand for self-reliance that runs through the book of Esther is in the way of the acknowledgement of sin and recognition of Christ."[11] He concludes: "'Luther and the book of Esther,' was the question of the present work. The answer that the detailed analysis sought to find gave a manifold image, much more manifold than could be expected from the generally known critical utterances by Luther. All in all, however, the positive attitude to the book is dominating, and the emphasis on Esther as piisima regina as late as in 1542 shows that he did not give up on his positive stance on the book. It is clear, on the other hand, that the sharp criticism of the book is linked up with his attitude to the Judaism of his age."[12]

Band (Weimar: Hermann Böhlaus Nachfolger 1912), 208 (A534); English translation in Timothy K. Beal, *The Book of Hiding: Gender, Ethnicity, Annihilation, and Esther*, Biblical Limits (London/New York: Routledge, 1997), 6.
  8. Hans Bardtke, *Luther und das Buch Esther* (Tübingen: J. C. B. Mohr [Paul Siebeck], 1964).
  9. Ibid., 50.
  10. Ibid., 86.
  11. Ibid., 72 (my translation from German).
  12. Ibid., 85–6 (my translation from German).

Likewise, Elias Bickerman[13] draws attention to the context of the quote as critical for the understanding of Luther's remark: "...the second reproach [*viel heidnische Unart*] is directed against the imagery of the Oriental court and its intrigues. The first one means that Esther cannot be applied to forward the doctrine that the Old Testament foreshadows the life of Jesus." Under the superscription, *Encomium mulierum*, Luther writes: "*Spiritus Sanctus laudat mulieres. Exempla sunt Iudith, Esther, Sara*" ("The Holy Spirit lauds women. Examples are: Judith, Esther, Sarah"). Bickerman also points out that in the introduction to his German translation of Esther, Luther says that the book contains "...much that is good." And finally, that Luther, in his work *On the Duties of Christian Spouses* (*"Vom ehelichen Leben"*) names Esther as a model to follow.[14]

Commentators of the modern era have also distanced themselves from the book of Esther, primarily because of its alleged hatred towards the gentiles. It is no surprise that some of this distaste belongs to the cultural milieu in Northern Europe in the beginning of the twentieth century. We note, for example, L. B. Paton's verdict: "There is not one noble character in the book... Morally Est. falls far below the general level of the OT, and even the Apocrypha."[15] But also later Christian, especially Protestant, scholarship has had its problems with the book; exemplary is the description of Esther by Bernard W. Anderson: "[T]he Book of Ester

---

13. Elias Bickerman, *Four Strange Books of the Bible: Jonah / Daniel / Kohelet / Esther* (New York: Schocken, 1967), 212–13.

14. According to Bardtke, this is in contradistinction to the scandalous Vashti; he comments: "Here, Esther appears as the typos of the devoted wife. This is never explicitly said in the book of Esther, but Luther has very rightfully recognized Esther's attitude of obedience toward Mordecai and her readiness to sacrifice herself for her people, and he has drawn this line further in Esther's total personality" (Bardtke, *Luther und das Buch Esther*, 58 n. 32). Bardtke joined the German *Bekenntniskirche* in 1934. He expresses his personal stance to the book of Esther in his closing paragraph: "The book of Esther is also present before the current generation in the church. The assessment of it surely would orientate itself to Luther's 'Yes.' In a time period which has put the twelve years' period that began in 1933 with all its bitter encounters and experiences behind it, it can hardly be different. But for the sake of the truth of the Cross the 'No' to the book must also be expressed. The redemption of the Cross of Golgotha also applies to the people who acted bravely in the book of Esther, but in their pursuit of self-help was subsumed by their wish for a second day of retribution" (ibid., 88, my translation from German).

15. Lewis Bayles Paton, *A Critical and Exegetical Commentary on the Book of Esther*, ICC (Edinburgh: T. & T. Clark, 1907), 96.

was inspired by a fierce nationalism and an unblushed vindictiveness which stand in glaring contradiction to the Sermon on the Mount."[16]

The status of Esther has also been volatile from the point of view of Jewish sages and scholars. On the one hand, Esther is the beloved legend that forms the background of the feast of Purim; on the other hand, its place among the scriptures has been debated. As mentioned above, already during the canonizing period, the sages discussed whether it "made the hands unclean," that is, whether it should belong to canon or not. One interesting example of a much later, modern, Jewish critique is from the Reformed Jewish journalist and scholar Shalom Ben-Chorin, who in 1938 published his "theologische Streitschrift": *Kritik des Estherbuches*. He stated his purpose in the opening sentence of the pamphlet: "I propose to remove the feast of Purim from the Jewish calendar and leave out the book of Esther from the canonical Holy Scriptures. Feast and book are unworthy for a people wishing to procure its national and moral regeneration under immense sacrifices."[17]

It is "no wonder" then, as emphasized by Wolfram Herrmann in his book about the ideological clash of understandings of Esther, that W. J. Fuerst in 1975 began his commentary on Esther with the words: "No book in the Old Testament has occasioned more antipathy for some readers, and more enjoyment for others, than the book of Esther."[18]

The motivation for the present volume is first and foremost the questions raised by the book's aforementioned obvious divergences from "mainstream" Hebrew Bible ideas. So many of the theologies and ideologies that inspire and drive the books of the Hebrew Bible/Old Testament, especially the Deuteronomistic History and prophetic literature, present life in the Diaspora as a struggle—many metaphorical harps seem to be hanging on the willows by the river of Babylon—for the only agreeable

---

16. Bernard W. Anderson, "The Place of the Book of Esther in the Christian Bible," *JR* 30 (1950): 32–43 (32). Michael V. Fox comments: "He might have found less of a contradiction had he chosen to compare Esther with the book of Revelation (e.g. 14:10-11, 20!)" (Michael V. Fox, *Character and Ideology in the Book of Esther*, 2nd ed. [Grand Rapids: Eerdmans, 2001], 221 n. 11). The heritage of Luther and Anderson's article is discussed at length in Beal, *Book of Hiding*, 8–12. On the academic reception of Esther in modern scholarship, see further Wolfram Herrmann, *Ester im Streit der Meinungen*, BEATAJ 4 (Frankfurt am Main: Peter Lang, 1986).

17. Shalom Ben-Chorin, *Kritik des Estherbuches: Eine theologische Streitschrift* (Jerusalem: "HEATID" Salingré & Co., 1938), 5 (my translation).

18. Wesley J. Fuerst, *The Books of Ruth, Esther, Ecclesiastes, The Song of Songs, Lamentations: The Five Scrolls*, CBCO (Cambridge: Cambridge University Press, 1975), 32, cf. Herrmann, *Ester im Streit der Meinungen*, 15.

place for a Judean to live is Jerusalem and Judah. Large parts of these books display the thought world of and literature for the traumatized, as rightly emphasized again and again in recent years.[19] But the Diaspora novellas disagree by and large on this view. These books present inspiration for living as foreigners in nations outside the promised land, and the most important thought is not "Next year in Jerusalem." Surprisingly, the Diaspora thought world is already presented in a brief passage in the book of Jeremiah. In Jer. 29:5-7 the prophet tells the exiles to settle down in their new country, build houses, marry off their children, multiply, and "seek the welfare of the city where I have sent you into exile, and pray to the LORD on its behalf, for in its welfare you will find your welfare."[20] In the Diaspora novellas, thoughts about life together with foreigners are in full flower. The book of Daniel, including the additions in the Septuagint, offer a picture of the shrewd young Judean who upholds the religious dietary regulations and at the same time retains the goodwill of the emperor. In the book of Tobit the focus is never on Jerusalem but unfolds the life of a wealthy Judean/Jewish family of merchants. The more belligerent book of Judith shows that the enemy can be defeated, even by a woman. And the Joseph novella in Genesis 37–50, the narrative closest to Esther in scope and storyline, illustrates how a diasporic Judean should behave at the royal court and towards his fellows and family.[21] It was curiosity about this presentation of life in Diaspora that from the outset launched my interest in Esther—and it was not long before I lost my heart to this simultaneously straightforward and enigmatic book. No wonder that so many fine books have been published on Esther, bearing such titles as *The Book of Hiding* and *Esther: The Outer Narrative and the Hidden Reading*.[22] To me as to

---

19. For an overview of and references to the abundant literature on trauma hermeneutics and the Bible, see Elizabeth Boase and Christopher A. Frechette, eds, *Bible Through the Lens of Trauma* (Atlanta: SBL, 2016), 1–26. For a reading of the book of Esther as trauma literature, see Chapters 7 and 8 below.

20. This message is surprising in Jeremiah, since the overall tone of the book is that of remorse and pain, close to Deuteronomistic theology.

21. Cf. Bernhard Lang, "Joseph the Diviner: Careers of a Biblical Hero," in his *Hebrew Life and Literature: Selected Essays of Bernhard Lang* (Farnham: Ashgate 2008), 93–109 (especially 102–9). Lang emphasizes the dichotomy between Moses who leaves Egypt—and brings the people out of the foreign land—and Joseph who remains and makes it possible for his family to settle down: "Moses stands for separation, law, and priestly religion in a barren desert setting where existence is reduced to its essentials; Joseph for openness, reconciliation, friendship and benefaction in a country known for its treasures and luxury, its lush pastures and fat cattle…" (107).

22. Beal, *Book of Hiding*; Jonathan Grossman, *Esther: The Outer Narrative and the Hidden Reading*, Siphrut 6 (Winona Lake: Eisenbrauns, 2011).

many others, Michael V. Fox's monograph *Character and Ideology in the Book of Esther*[23] has been an immense inspiration, and the questions I pose in what follows may be considered parallel to Fox's.

My approach to these questions, however, is different from Fox's. I am more interested in the hidden meanings of the book than in the intended message. While taking my point of departure in a standard historical-critical quest for date, background, genre, and transmission, I shall continue with readings searching for hidden motives and themes, such as power play, gender, and nationalism, before moving on to deal with theological-ethical questions. These, I believe, are the channels for the fascination raised by the book of Esther, and these questions, too, might mitigate the tension between the antipathy and the enthusiasm cultivated by the book and its protagonists, its heroes and villains.

However, questions of power, ideology, and theology cannot be properly pondered without a discussion of the puzzling question of the alleged absence of God in the book of Esther.

2. *God and Religion in the Book of Esther*

In Est. 4:14, one of the arguments that persuade Esther to change her mind and go and entreat with the king for the fate of her people is Mordecai's reference to "relief and deliverance [that] will rise for the Jews from another quarter (*mimmāqôm 'aḥēr*)." Which quarter is never openly indicated; but this is the place in the book where most commentators discuss a possible reference to an otherwise "absent" God.

David Clines openly denies the "other quarter" any religious meaning: "Contrary to common opinion, we should remark, it is not likely that 'from another quarter' is an indirect way of referring to God; for deliverance through Esther and deliverance from God cannot be contrasted."[24] Sidney White Crawford is also skeptical:

> The lack of religiosity in Esther is indeed striking. The book does not mention God even once. In addition, there is no prayer, no mention of the Temple, and no clear indication of religious activity on the part of Esther or Mordecai.[25]

---

23. Fox, *Esther: Character and Ideology.*
24. David J. A. Clines, *The Esther Scroll: The Story of the Story*, JSOTSup 30 (Sheffield: Sheffield Academic, 1984), 36.
25. Sidnie White Crawford, "The Book of Esther: Introduction, Commentary, and Reflections," in *NIB* 4 (Nashville: Abingdon, 1999), 853–972 (866).

Others, especially Jewish commentators, argue that the quarters indeed point to God's presence. This understanding is exemplarily voiced by Abraham D. Cohen. On the backdrop of his understanding of the casting of *pûr* as Haman's mistaken belief in chance-fate (Est. 3:7), he argues that God is present in Esther as the hand behind the events:

> *the "pur" is nothing less than the intentional symbol of chance-fate*, which at once conceal and appear to govern, these very same events… This interpretation proceeds from the only accurate reading which *Esther* allows, viz. that God acts behind the veil of causality and chance, on behalf of the people of Israel. It is specifically to accentuate this point that the name of God is not mentioned in the megillah, while all the events are "cast" to give the appearance of chance-occurrences, or, *purim*. For the author of *Esther*, this position is at once a statement of history and of everyday reality.[26]

Levenson develops A. D. Cohen's exposition:

> In light of the complete helplessness of the Judeans at that moment, the "other quarter" can only be the heavenly realm… It is not chance (*pûr*), but providence which ultimately accounts for the reversal of Esther's fortune and, because of her, of Israel's as well. The transformation which the Scroll of Esther celebrates is thus an example of God's *haṣṣālâ*, "salvation," "deliverance" (4:14).[27]

This understanding goes well with Shemaryahu Talmon's ground-breaking, now classic, analysis of the theology in Esther as wisdom literature and Esther as *a historisized wisdom-tale*.[28] Talmon renders it plausible that "the other place" is a substitute for the divine name,[29] and understands the covert presentation of God as a part of the story's intellectual background.

26. Abraham D. Cohen, "'Hu Ha-goral': The Religious Significance of Esther," *Judaism* 23 (1974): 87–94 (89, original emphasis).
27. Jon D. Levenson, "The Scroll of Esther in Ecumenical Perspective: ('How can we sing a song of the Lord on foreign soil?' Ps. 137:4)," *JES* 13 (1976): 440–52 (448). In his commentary, Levenson discusses the concept of "coincidence" at length. According to Levenson, the coincidences are not coincidental, as urged by Michael J. Fox. "It is more reasonable to assume that the author endorses the old saw that 'a coincidence is a miracle in which God prefers to remain anonymous'… One need not see the term 'quarter' (*māqôm*) as a name of God (which it will become in the rabbinic period) to suspect that the source of deliverance and retribution to which Mordecai alludes is indeed the Deity…" (Levenson, *Esther*, 19).
28. Shemaryahu Talmon, "Wisdom in the Book of Esther," *VT* 13 (1963): 419–55 (426, Talmon's emphasis).
29. Ibid., 429.

The author of Esther is a court-scribe, the "typical product" of international wisdom education who paints his male protagonists in his own image.[30] Talmon identifies wisdom-motifs in Esther, for instance, the relationship between the wise Mordecai and the orphaned Esther.[31] In essence, the main protagonists exemplify the traditional wisdom-triangle: the powerful, but witless dupe Ahasuerus, the righteous wise Mordecai, and the conniving schemer Haman.[32] Even if we do not accept all of Talmon's proposed parallels to wisdom thinking or embodiment of wisdom characteristics in Esther,[33] it is obvious that the God of Esther is different from the God of, for example, the historical traditions or prophecy; what characterizes wisdom theology is precisely its lack of interest in nationality or history, as shown by Talmon. God in Esther represents quite another image of God than what has normally been understood as "real, normative" Hebrew Bible/Old Testament theology. In Esther, God is not the unconcealed deity who interferes openly in the lives of the patriarchs; God is not the one who leads his people through the desert by the hand of his chosen servant Moses; God is not the one who thunders from the desert; God is not the one who speaks to the people through his prophets and punishes them through his servants, the foreign kings. God in Esther is not the national God of war who interferes and saves Jerusalem as in the days of Hezekiah, or the personal deity who takes care of the individual, like Jacob and the supplicant in the psalms of trust and petition. God is the God who works in the background through "ordinary" people like Esther and Mordecai, or Joseph in Egypt. Sandra Beth Berg describes God in Esther as a hidden God: "Because Yahweh's control of history is neither overt nor easily discerned in everyday events, the determination of the shape and direction of history shifts to human beings."[34] Or, in the words of Levenson: "Esther's God is one who works behind the scenes, carefully

---

30. Ibid., 434.
31. Ibid., 437–40.
32. Talmon claims that in Esther these types come in pairs, Mordecai and Esther, Haman and Zeresh, Ahasuerus and Queen Vashti, who is "introduced for the sole purpose of establishing an equilibrium of the couple-arrangement which is peculiar to our narrative" (ibid., 440).
33. "What the Esther narrative in fact does is to portray *applied* wisdom. The outline of the plot and the presentation of the central characters show the wise man in action, with the covert, but nevertheless, obvious implication, that his ultimate success derives from the proper execution of wisdom maxims, as set forth, e.g. in Proverbs and to a certain degree, in Ecclesiastes" (ibid., 427, Talmon's emphasis).
34. Sandra Beth Berg, *The Book of Esther: Motifs, Themes and Structure*, SBLDS 44 (Missoula: Scholars Press, 1979), 178.

arranging events so that a justice based on the principle of 'measure for measure' will triumph and the Jews will survive and flourish."[35]

According to Crawford, "quarter" (*māqôm*) "is not a circumlocution for God."[36] This does not mean, however, that religion is totally absent from the book in her view. It is present in the understanding of the importance of coincidence (as already emphasized by A. D. Cohen, Berg, and Levenson). "Therefore, for the author of Esther, there must be a God, and God must want the Jews to survive... [Esther and Mordecai] must act, with profound hope that they are thereby participating in the divine scheme."[37]

This God, in my opinion, is the God of the *māqôm aḥēr*, the other quarter. He is not Yahweh or El Shadday or El Elyon; if he is any known type of God, he is El, the wise creator of the world who made humans his stewards (Gen. 1:28-29), and he is the God of wisdom thinking, "an impersonal supernatural power," known from Ecclesiastes and the Job dialogues, as emphasized by Talmon.[38] Such a belief in divine providence and sustenance fits well with the situation in the Diaspora, far away from a Jerusalem-based Zion theology or a theology of sacral or God-guaranteed kingship. Those theologies apparently failed to sustain the religious beliefs of some exiles,[39] for whom God was less approachable, active, and present, less the God of the Covenant, and more to be searched for in everyday life and struggle. This is where Gerleman's understanding of Esther and Purim as a contradistinction to Moses and Passover becomes most convincing and inspiring.[40] For the implied author and audience of Esther, returning to Jerusalem and Judah is not the answer; it is the survival and influence in their new adopted country. For them, openness to the possibility of providence, even when history seems to weigh against its likelihood, becomes a posture of profound faith.[41]

---

35. Levenson, *Esther*, 21, with reference to Berg, *The Book of Esther*, 178. For Talmon, the concept of retribution lacks any religious motivation (Talmon, "Wisdom in the Book of Esther," 446).

36. Crawford, "The Book of Esther," 867.

37. Ibid.

38. Talmon, "Wisdom in the Book of Esther," 430.

39. Although obviously it was very meaningful for many others, since the God of history and national punishment and salvation is the dominant image of God in the Hebrew Bible.

40. See Chapter 7, below.

41. Cf. Crawford, "The Book of Esther," 868. Interestingly, according to Crawford, this type of faith "speaks to the skeptical end of the twentieth century" (ibid.).

Esther 4 also contains the first references to religious *practice* in the book of Esther—the Judean's fast together with Mordecai in 4:3, and Esther's call to a fast in 4:16. The Judean's fast is part of their mourning ritual, cast in a conventional semantic combination with lamenting, tearing of the clothes and dressing in sackcloth and ashes, Esther's fast is in preparation for her visit with the king.[42] Interestingly, there is no description of how this fast is supposed to be practiced or why it would help Esther in her effort to convince the king to save her people. Crawford understands it as the possible exception to the absence of religion, even if it "is not explicitly directed to God and seems to have no purpose beyond communal solidarity." That it works as community building is beyond dispute, as is its function as a marker of Esther's "conversion" to community leader. But it is more than that. Having a fast without having a God to impress seems meaningless, so Esther's fast is also an indication of religiosity in the book.

Fasting is a non-cultic religious practice and as such points to the non-cultic quality of Purim later in the book.[43] Purim *is* community building, consisting of celebrating communal festivities, sending food to friends and family, and giving presents to the poor (Est. 9:20-28). No cultic activities are mentioned, only the call to celebration.[44] The regulations for Purim in Esther describe a public holiday that can be celebrated without priesthood or temple—and as such also with no connection to the other peoples of the land and their religious institutions. Purim segregates the Judeans from all the other peoples of the Persian empire through a religious holiday that can be celebrated no matter where they live in the Diaspora.

From this perspective, Purim is reminiscent of another holiday of the Persian period, the reading of the Torah by Ezra the Scribe in Nehemiah 8. Here, the public reading of the Torah is followed by the instruction to the people to stop crying:

---

42. Berg sees the two fasts as a narrative pair but understands their qualities to be slightly different. Both are signs of mourning, but Esther's fast also represents hope that her mission will be successful (Berg, *The Book of Esther*, 38–9).

43. Fast and Purim are two obverse, non-cultic religious manifestations. Fasting is a manifestation of penitence and abstinence from eating, while Purim is full of joy and (over-)indulgence of eating and drinking.

44. Interestingly, in the confirmation of Mordecai's decree on Purim in Est. 9:29-32, the focus is not on the happier parts of Purim, but on "regulations concerning their fasts and their lamentations" (Est. 9:31). This confirmation seems to be especially focusing on Esther's authority, since she plays no role in the formulation of the (first?) decree, and thus connects to her initial fast in Est. 4.

> [9] And Nehemiah, who was the governor, and Ezra the priest and scribe, and the Levites who taught the people said to all the people, "This day is holy to the LORD your God; do not mourn or weep." For all the people wept when they heard the words of the law. [10] Then he said to them, "Go your way, eat the fat and drink sweet wine and send portions of them to those for whom nothing is prepared, for this day is holy to our LORD; and do not be grieved, for the joy of the LORD is your strength." [11] So the Levites stilled all the people, saying, "Be quiet, for this day is holy; do not be grieved." [12] And all the people went their way to eat and drink and to send portions and to make great rejoicing, because they had understood the words that were declared to them. (Neh. 8:9-12)

There are indeed differences between the two holidays, of which the most important are the following:

1. The reason for the celebration in Esther is the saving of the Judean people from genocide, that is, an external threat, while in Nehemiah it is the reading of the Torah that reveals an internal threat to the Israelites, namely their own transgression of the Torah.
2. The location of the holiday in Esther is Persia, while in Ezra it is Jerusalem.
3. The worship of God is emphasized in Nehemiah, while there is an "absence" of God in Esther.
4. The participation of the Levites is highlighted in Nehemiah, while all the participants are lay persons in Esther.[45]

Yet, the resemblances are also remarkable and instructive:

1. Both of the celebrations are "new," not part of the pre-exilic holidays and not mentioned in the cult calendars of the Torah. Even if in the following pericope of Nehemiah (Neh. 8:13-18), the Torah-celebration is connected to the re-invention of Sukkoth on the following day, it is most clearly emphasized that this celebration is something new to the participants who need to be instructed regarding how to build the booths (Neh. 8:14-15); "for from the days of Jeshua son of Nun to that day the people of Israel had not done so" (Neh. 8:17).
2. The participants are the entire people in both Nehemiah and Esther. In Nehemiah the people are described as "all the people as one man" (Neh. 8:1 NJPS), while in Esther we find a reference to "all

---

45. It should be noted, though, that the Levites in Nehemiah do not serve as cultic personnel but as instructors or teachers.

the Judeans," defined as "themselves and their descendants and all who joined them" (Est. 9:27).
3. Both books make reference to eating and drinking and the "sending of portions,"[46] presumably portions of the holiday food, as an important part of the holiday.
4. In both cases a written document plays an important role, in Nehemiah it is the Scroll of the Torah, brought back by Ezra to Jerusalem from Persia, while in Esther it is the Letters of Purim, written in Persia.

In conclusion: Although not a surface characteristic in Esther, the book indeed represents a religious world view. Anything else would be surprising considering its time. God in Esther is the God of wisdom, a God who might not be the epitome of a *deus otiosus*, but nevertheless a hidden God who works through the hands and cunning of humans. The religious practice in Esther is not cultic but takes place in the public sphere as a kind of civil religion, independent of priests and holy script, but concrete in its practice and serving as community building in a foreign country.

3. Concluding Remarks of Introduction

Having roamed the religious background of the biblical book(s) of Esther, we now turn our attention toward close readings of texts and themes in this fascinating novella. The work will be guided by the questions formed by the ideological critical curiosity, touched upon in the introduction to this chapter, and illuminated by the historical critical background that I have outlined above. The texts will mainly be taken from the Hebrew Esther; a thorough exegesis of all "the Esthers" is scarcely possible within the frames of a readable volume, and often the results would hardly be changed by the inclusion of the Greek versions. Yet in Part I, *Background*, after the present introduction, we shall briefly touch upon the historical location and transmission of the book(s) of Esther (Chapter 2), and then analyze the development of the literary figure of Esther on the surface level of the Hebrew and Greek variants (Chapter 3). In Part II, *Readings*, I turn my attention to the more subtle or deconstructive reading of themes, hidden in the depths of literary artistry under surface levels. Chapter 4 is the first example of such a reading of structures and themes below the surface of the Esther narrative; it discusses Esther's initiation into her role

---

46. *mišlôaḥ mānôt*, Est. 9:19; *wᵉšilḥû mānôt*, Neh. 8:12 (cf. Neh. 8:10).

as Persian queen in Esther 2 in intertextual conversation with two much later texts, *Arabian Nights* and the French erotic novel *Story of O*. Chapter 5 analyzes the importance of the changing of clothes as a "quasi-semiotic" marker, "the vestimentary code," at points in the narrative where a significant change of roles takes place, though without openly applying structuralist or semiotic theory. Chapter 6 discusses the relationship between Mordecai, the Judean, and Haman, the Agagite, as a matter of mimetic doubling and mimetic violence, leading to the intended pogrom on the Judeans and their vicious counterattack on their Persian enemies.

In Part III, *Ideologies*, the interest changes in Chapter 7 to the understanding of the sociological concept of ethnicity and ethnicity-construction as the backdrop for perceiving the importance of the instigation of Purim in Esther 9 and the violence connected to it. This story about manslaughter and a new religious beginning, then, will be discussed in Chapter 8 as an example of trauma literature, that is, literature that seeks to remedy traumatic memories, "real" or "constructed," for the sake of community-building. In the concluding Chapter 9, we return to the critical question of violence and the moral quality of the book of Esther, asking the question: "Is Esther a bedtime story?"

The goal of this volume is not to be complete but to insert probes into issues that have (and have not) been discussed among scholars and in communities of faith. First and foremost: How are the protagonists described in Esther? Fine and learned volumes have already been published on this subject; what I will do in the following chapters is to read less on the surface level of the texts than has often been done, thus not asking for the message of the implied author. I shall rather ask the whimsical questions, inspired not by the intention of the implied author but by the book's intriguing subtext of sex, jealousy, violence, and identity. This also leads to the final questions of ideology in the book which have divided opinions on Esther since the era of the Rabbis. Is this book a carnivalesque satire or is it a nationalistic book, glorifying bloodshed between two ethnic groups, one of which claims to be the suppressed underdog and thus having the moral right to strike back?

Part I

BACKGROUND

Chapter 2

DATE, COMPOSITION, RECEPTION

1. *The Transmission of Esther*

The book of Esther led a vivid and varied life in antiquity, and it is a fine example of the variability and adaptability that characterizes antique literature. It is located at the Persian court under King Ahasuerus.[1] Nevertheless, to use it as a source for historical events at the Persian court in the fifth century BCE would be not only incautious but directly against the tendency of the text, a tendency which is subtly communicated in the ironic literary style of the book. Even so, earlier scholarship sought to mine the text for historical information.[2] Yet the book is not meant to be a historical account—it is an educational and entertaining book containing advice for the Judean Diaspora that uses storytelling for the conveyance of its message. Moreover, the transmission of the book of Esther also offers a fine example of "Rewritten Scripture," understanding "Scripture" as "any Jewish composition to which a particular group of people imputed a particular authority."[3] Esther is transmitted in several

---

1. According to some, mainly earlier scholars, Ahasuerus might be identified as Xerxes I, known in the Septuagint as *Artaxerxes*, and in the Alpha-text as *Assyeros*. Josephus uses the name *Xerxes*. Fox discusses whether Xerxes I, who was king of Persia 485–465 BCE, serves as a point of departure for the king in Esther without taking it as an attempt of making a historically credible presentation (Fox, *Esther: Character and Ideology*, 14–15). Since I do not consider the book of Esther to be an account that is historically accurate, identification with any historical king of Persia is superfluous in the present context.

2. An outstanding example of early historical-critical interest in the historicity of Esther is Paton, *Commentary on the Book of Esther*.

3. Anders Klostergaard Petersen, "Rewritten Bible as a Borderline Phenomenon—Genre, Textual Strategy, or Canonical Anachronism?," in *Flores Florentino: Dead Sea Scrolls and Other Early Jewish Studies in Honour of Florentino García Martínez*, ed. Anthony Hilhorst et al. (Leiden/Boston: Brill 2007), 285–306 (287).

variants, the Hebrew (MT), the Targum, two Greek versions, as well as a Latin, a Coptic and an Ethiopian Esther. Moreover, it appears in Josephus' *Antiquitates*. The rewriting of Esther is an example of the intertextual activity present in antique texts—the joy of telling and retelling, again and again re-actualizing the existing material.[4] It is the underlying basis of the present volume that the two Greek Esthers, the *Septuagint* (Esther LXX) version and the so-called *Alpha-text* (Esther AT),[5] are re-actualizations of the Hebrew Esther (Esther MT). This is also the case with Josephus' re-writing in his *Antiquitates*, which again has its own characteristics.[6] Below, I shall present and discuss the three oldest variants, Esther MT, Esther LXX and Esther AT, which I name "the biblical books of Esther," with a special focus on identifying the ideological (or theological) variations between them.[7]

4. Cf. the discussion in Petersen, "Rewritten Bible as a Borderline Phenomenon," 294–7.

5. Esther AT is published in Hanhart's critical edition, *Septuaginta: Vetus Testamentum Graecum Auctoritate Academiae Scientiarum Gottingensis editum VIII.3: Esther* (Göttingen: Vandenhoeck & Ruprecht, 1966). There, AT is labeled *L* (Lucian) since it is preserved in manuscripts that contain the Lucian recension of Samuel and Kings. The text is no longer perceived as belonging to the Lucian group of texts, see further Karen H. Jobes, *The Alpha-Text of Esther: Its Character and Relationship to the Masoretic Text*, SBLDS 15 (Atlanta, GA: Scholars Press, 1996). On Esther AT and its relation to Esther MT and LXX, see also Kristin de Troyer, *The End of the Alpha Text of Esther: Translation and Narrative Technique in MT 8:1-17; LXX 8:1-17, and AT 7:14-41*, SBLSCS 48 (Atlanta: SBL, 2000), and the discussion below.

6. Josephus, *Ant.* 11.184-296. The text is published in English translation in Flavius Josephus, *Judean Antiquities* Book 11, in *Josephus Flavius: Translation and Commentary*, vol. 6A, trans. and commentary by Paul Spilsbury and Chris Seeman, ed. Steve Mason (Leiden/Boston: Brill, 2016), 59–87. See also L. H. Feldman, *Studies in Josephus' Rewritten Bible* (Leiden: Brill 1998), 513–38.

7. The later books of Esther can also be characterized as *fan fiction*, a term that has entered the world of biblical studies during the past 15 years. Fan fiction has been presented as "a type of writing produced by fans of an already existing story universe—be it a novel, a movie, or a television series—in which the fans, rather than the original creators, develop the original work by, for instance, expanding, reshaping, mending, relocating, or twisting the initial story" (Kasper Bro Larsen, "Fan Fiction and Early Christian Apocrypha," *ST* 73 [2019]: 43–59 [43]). This type of writing activity is not limited to modern times but is well known in antiquity and also in biblical writings. To mention but one example, Hebrew Bible exegetes have for many years identified *Fortschreibungen/re-lecture* in the book of Psalms. These *Fortschreibungen* actualize and "repair" or mend the original texts, the so-called hypo-texts, adding issues to the text which seem to be missing, for example, the concern for the

The variations between the biblical Esthers are most noticeable in the six so-called additions in the Greek versions, Additions to Esther A–F (Add Est. A–F), which are often printed as apocryphal, almost independent books in modern Bible translations. This, however, could not be more mistaken, for the additions are parts of the books proper and do not represent independent work.[8] The variations between Esther MT and the Greek versions are also present in additions and minor details outside Add Est. A–F, and these variations must be taken into consideration as well, since they contribute to the radical change of ideology and characterization of the literary characters in the Greek versions compared to the MT.

2. *Dating the Biblical Books of Esther*

Before turning to the literary development of the characters, however, we need a short look at the location and relative dating of the books of Esther. Much time has been spent and much ink has been used—though not spilled—discussing the question of the dating of the biblical books of Esther, both in terms of absolute dating and of the relative dating of the three versions. This is indeed an area for specialists, and, in the end, one must choose to trust the scholar whose arguments are the more reliable. Basically, there are two different, but also interrelated questions to be considered about the dating—on the one hand the traditio-historical development of the Esther-narrative, and on the other the literary interrelatedness of Esther MT, Esther LXX, and Esther AT.

For obvious reasons, modern commentators often place the *location* of the composition of the Esther MT in Persia, although it has also been seen as a "Judean text that is critical of strategies of Diaspora living."[9] The *date* of the composition of Esther MT is much discussed and more uncertain. Some commentators propose a date in the fifth and fourth centuries BCE, that is the early Persian period,[10] while others opt for the time of John

---

poor or the righteous vs. the sinner. For a thorough introduction to the world of fan fiction in biblical studies, see Larsen, "Fan Fiction and Early Christian Apocrypha."

8. According to Jobes, "[t]here is no manuscript evidence that the six additional chapters found in the Greek versions ever existed in Hebrew or Aramaic" (Karen H. Jobes, "Esther: To the Reader," in Pietersma and Wright, eds, *A New English Translation*, 424).

9. Elsie R. Stern, "Esther and the Politics of Diaspora," *JQR* 100 (2010): 25–53.

10. Thus, e.g., Adele Berlin, *Esther*, The JPS Bible Commentary (Philadelphia, PA: The Jewish Publication Society 2001), xli–xlii.

Hyrcanus, the Hasmonean High Priest, who reigned 135–104 BCE, a period in which the emphasis on Jewish sovereignty makes good sense.[11] I shall return to this discussion in Chapters 6 and 7.

What, then, about the date of the two Greek versions, Esther LXX and AT? The closing of Esther LXX, Add Est. F, mentions that this translation was taken to Egypt in the fourth year of Ptolemy and Cleopatra, which according to Michael V. Fox "probably refers to Ptolemy XII Auletos, making the date 73 B.C.E."[12] This date is partly substantiated by Kristin de Troyer, who proposes 164 BCE as a *terminus post quem*, and as the *terminus ante quem* "the time of Ptolemeus XII Auletos and Cleopatra V,"[13] that is, September 12, 78 BCE–September 11, 77 BCE. The reason for de Troyer's proposal is the affinity of Esther LXX to 2 Maccabees. There, a decree by Antiochus IV Epiphanes (c. 215–164 BCE) is quoted, in which this Seleucid king shortly before his death withdraws a very anti-Jewish decree which is later confirmed and re-instated by his successor. Esther LXX clearly makes use of these decrees.[14] In her introduction to the *NETS* translation of Esther LXX and AT, Karen H. Jobes adds the possibility of a dating as late as 48 BCE, though without discussing it.[15]

So much for the specific dating of Esther LXX. The dating of Esther AT, however, depends on the relative dating of the two Greek versions. Which of them is the elder?[16] For this question we must turn to the textual history of the three books. In his ground-breaking monograph from 1984, *The Esther Scroll: The Story of the Story*, David J. A. Clines presented a narratological analysis of the book of Esther and proposed a textual history in five steps based on this analysis:

---

11. On the discussion of the dating, see Lawrence M. Wills, *The Jewish Novel in the Ancient World* (Ithaca and London: Cornell University Press, 1995), 99–100.

12. Fox, *Character and Ideology*, 139.

13. De Troyer, *End of the Alpha Text*, 398, refers to Elias J. Bickerman, "Notes on the Greek Book of Esther," *PAAJR* 20 (1950): 101–33; repr. in *Studies in the Book of Esther* (New York: KTAV, 1982).

14. "The terminology of 8:11 LXX exhibits a striking resemblance at the level of content with the words of the amnesty decree of Antiochus IV Epiphanes (2 Macc. 11:27-33), and the letter of Antiochus V Eupator to his people (2 Macc. 11:22-26) which can be dated prior to and after the death of Antiochus IV Epiphanes in the autumn of 164 respectively" (de Troyer, *End of the Alpha Text*, 276).

15. Jobes, "Esther: To the Reader," 424.

16. Esther AT is only preserved in four, very late manuscripts; see de Troyer, *End of the Alpha Text*, 5–9.

- the Esther (and Mordecai) stories, hypothetical sources for
- the pre-Masoretic story, witnessed to by the Greek AT, and expanded into
- the proto-Masoretic story, itself expanded by various appendices to form
- the Masoretic story, translated and supplemented by major Semitic and Greek additions to form
- the Septuagint story.[17]

This tradition- and redaction-critical suggestion was typical for the time of Clines' monograph, and was more or less followed by Linda Day, Michael V. Fox, and many others.[18] Since then, however, scholars have become less and less confident in the possibility of tracing the tradition history of the Hebrew Bible texts in general; and when it comes to the tradition- and redaction-history of Esther MT, there is not much hope that we will ever be able to ascertain the written sources behind the book without any reasonable, scholarly doubt.

Regarding the dating of the Greek versions, philological and translational scholarship has pointed to a much simpler textual history of Esther than the one suggested by Clines. In opposition to him and many others, both Karen H. Jobes and Kristin de Troyer have claimed that Esther MT is the direct *Vorlage* for the Greek versions. Not only by applying philological methods but also by establishing the translation technique of Esther LXX and Esther AT, Jobes and de Troyer assess the relation between the two Greek versions. As mentioned, their results indicate that Esther MT is the *Vorlage* of Esther LXX and Esther AT, yet from this point their conclusions part ways.[19] Jobes maintains that "[t]he AT is a translation of a Hebrew *Vorlage* that was a direct ancestor of the MT and quite similar

---

17. Clines, *Esther Scroll*, 137; see his graphic presentation of the development of the text, p. 138.

18. Linda Day, *Three Faces of a Queen: Characterization in the Books of Esther*, JSOTSup 186 (Sheffield: Sheffield Academic, 1995), 15–18; Fox, *Character and Ideology*, 254–73; Levenson, *Esther*, 27–34. See also Charles V. Dorothy, *The Books of Esther: Structure, Genre and Textual Integrity*, JSOTSup 187 (Sheffield: Sheffield Academic, 1997).

19. Jobes proposes the following possibilities: AT is "(a) translation of another revision of the o′ text [Old Greek = LXX], (b) a second, independently made translation of the MT, (c) a translation of another Hebrew text of Esther of uncertain relationship to the MT, or (d) a midrashic re-write of the Esther story." Jobes, *Alpha-Text*, 424.

to it in its content and extent,"[20] and she claims that the "AT preserves the older form of additions A, B, C, E, and F."[21] De Troyer, on the other hand, asserts that the longer version, Esther LXX, is the backdrop of the shorter Esther AT. She suggest that the AT is "a rewritten form of the LXX with one specific person and one specific historical context in mind," Agrippa, grandson of Herod the Great and son of Aristobulos IV, who "championed the case of the Jews in Alexandria and managed to convince Claudius [the Roman emperor] to confirm their ancient rights and even add a further edict thereto."[22] This dating, of course, is speculative and can hardly be confirmed.

Nevertheless, and even if de Troyer's exhaustive study only covers the closing of Esther AT, that is, the text we find in MT Est. 8:1-17, her results in my opinion allow for drawing of conclusions concerning the internal relations between the full texts of the three textual variants.[23] I propose to follow de Troyer's relative dating of the Greek versions, primarily because Esther AT in my opinion often "solves" narratological problems already present in the Hebrew text or created through the additions in Esther LXX.[24] In what follows, my comprehension and presentation of the development of the characters in the rewritten books of Esther are based on this relative dating of the three variants, the Hebrew, the Septuagint and the Alpha-text. I will discuss each of the three variants from a synchronic perspective without further discussion of which literary or oral traditions might predate them. It is very probable that independent Esther and Mordecai narratives existed before Esther MT as Clines and others

---

20. Ibid., 221.
21. Ibid., 193.
22. De Troyer, *End of the Alpha Text*, 401. She proposes that "the AT would appear, moreover, to have been written in Rome around 40–41 CE by a Jewish author who addressed himself to non-Jews. This individual was familiar with the Esther narrative in its LXX form, which he rewrote with Agrippa, the new deliverer of the Jewish people, in mind" (ibid., 402).
23. On the textual history of the Greek versions, see also Jill Middlemas, "The Greek Esthers and the Search for History: Some Preliminary Observations," in *Between Evidence and Ideology: Essays on the History of Ancient Israel Read at the Joint Meeting of the Society for Old Testament Study and the Oud Testamentisch Werkgezelschap Lincoln, July 2009*, ed. Bob Becking and Lester L. Grabbe (Leiden: Brill Academic, 2010), 145–63.
24. André LaCocque refutes for literary reasons that Esther LXX and AT can be older than Esther MT; see André LaCocque, *Esther Regina: A Bakhtinian Reading* (Evanston: Northwestern University Press, 2008), 103–7.

presuppose, and the two Hellenistic Esthers might very well have circulated in a number of independent variants.²⁵ Nevertheless, I regard the three books of Esther to be the results of the implied authors' intentional selection and/or de-selection of the material, that is, as the representation of a narrative and/or ideological strategy. It is this narrative—and sometimes these three narratives—that is the subject of my readings in this volume.

3. *The Composition and Ideology of the Books of Esther*

3.1. *The Hebrew Esther*

The ideology of the three biblical books of Esthers can be traced through analyses of their composition. The most important feature is the principle of peripety, and Fox—among others—points to peripety as governing the structure of Esther.²⁶ Peripety is prevalent in Esther MT, and even more so in the Greek versions where it is accentuated by the additions. According to Aristotle's *Poetics* (1452a, 24-26) peripety is "the circumstance in which an action or state of affairs intended or expected to produce a certain result yields the opposite one."²⁷ Fox adds to this definition that although Aristotle "regards peripety as an essential component of tragedy, it is not limited to that genre. If the reversal is in the direction of happiness, peripety is comic. Peripety in all cases is ironic."²⁸

Ironic peripety is the governing literary vehicle in Esther.²⁹ Fox describes the central, climactic chapters, the core-drama, as a thesis–antithesis series beginning in Esther 3 "after the preparatory episodes, and ending in 8:17, just prior to the discursive concluding matters in chapters 9 and 10."³⁰ According to Sandra Beth Berg, the turning point is 4:13-14, that is, Mordecai's words that persuade Esther to take charge of the situation.³¹ According to Fox, "the plot takes *its* sharpest turn in 6:10," where the king orders Haman to direct the honoring towards

---

25. Wills, *Jewish Novel*, passim.
26. Fox, *Character and Ideology*, 153–63.
27. Ibid., 251.
28. Ibid.
29. Berg, *The Book of Esther*; cf. Stan Goldman, "Narrative and Ethical Ironies in Esther," *JSOT* 47 (1990): 14–31.
30. Fox, *Character and Ideology*, 162 (original emphasis).
31. Berg, *Book of Esther*, 110.

Mordecai instead of himself. That is a sign of Haman's humiliation and Mordecai's elevation, as emphasized by Haman's wife, Zeresh (6:13).[32] I prefer to see the words of Zeresh in 6:13 as *one* important marker of this turn, but not as *the* turning point proper. Zeresh points to the fundamental problematic of the entire book—how can the Judeans prevail? Like other foreigners in the Hebrew Bible, the prostitute Rahab from Jericho in Joshua 2, the Assyrian Rabshakeh in 2 Kings 18/Isaiah 38, and Ebed-melech the Ethiopian eunuch in Jeremiah 38, she hits the nail on the head with her words: "If Mordecai, before whom your downfall has begun, is of the Judean people, you will not prevail against him, but will surely fall before him" (Est. 6:13). We shall return to the role of Zeresh below.

Scholars such as Yehudi T. Radday, Jon D. Levenson, and Lawrence M. Wills have proposed a chiastic structure for the entire book of Esther.[33] Yet it is only possible to demonstrate the existence of the perfect chiasm if—to borrow the method used by Cinderella's sisters—"a toe or a heel are cut," and the abundance of divergent chiasms identified by scholars in the book of Esther further illustrates the problems. To me, it seems obvious that the book of Esther has not one, but multiple turning points[34] and the structure is not strictly chiastic. However, if a semi-chiastic structure lies beneath the Esther narrative, it need not necessarily be the result of deliberate authorial choice but probably as the result of the overall theme of reversals.

In my view, the pivot or turning point of the plot is not one single point but the sequence of narratives in Esther 4, 5, and 6, which all relate a radical shift. These chapters present a chain of incidents that lead to the ultimate solution and release of suspense in Esther 9. First, in

---

32. Fox, *Character and Ideology*, 162 (original emphasis).

33. Yehuda T. Radday, "Chiasm in Joshua, Judges and Others," *LB* 27/28 (1973): 6–13; Levenson, *Esther*. Wills identifies two plot lines in Esther, the Mordecai and the Esther plot lines. The Mordecai plot is actually a double plot, consisting of two narratives of threat, against Mordecai and against the Jews, "marvelously interwoven… but still progressing along two tracks." Its "double threat–and–deliverance structure an *a–b–b–a* pattern…with chapter 6…as the crux of the reversal of action." This plotline seems to be the most important to Wills. However, parallel to this runs the Esther plot line, the tale of the beautiful young virgin who wins the king's admiration and becomes the queen of the empire (Wills, *Jewish Novel*, 93–5).

34. Cf. Fox: "[If] we think of a plot-line as a curve, there can be more 'turning points'" (Fox, *Character and Ideology*, 162 n. 14).

Esther 4, the balance of influence shifts between Mordecai and Esther. In a complicated exchange of requests between the two protagonists the initiative moves from the elder male superior to the younger subservient and passive female, who—at least for a limited time—becomes the moral leader of the Jewish people. Esther 5:1–5, Esther's audience of the king, is the resolution to the crisis instigated and announced in ch. 4. The first minor difficulty is overcome as the king accepts to listen to Esther. Esther 5:5-9, then, lays the foundation for the second major crisis and inversion, the humiliation of Haman and the raising of Mordecai in Esther 6, when the king honors and raises up Mordecai at Haman's expense. This turning point is foregrounded by the remark made by Zeresh, Haman's wife, in 6:13, as discussed above. This turning point in ch. 6 presages and predicts the final fates of the two antagonists in Est. 7:1–8:2: Haman is executed on his own gallows, while Mordecai is elevated to be the vizier of Persia in Haman's place. Thus, it can be concluded that the two major protagonists each have their own turning point in relation to their narrative "twin":[35] Esther takes (or receives) the initiative from Mordecai in chs. 4 and 5, while Mordecai takes the political upper hand from Haman in ch. 6.[36]

Around this cluster of turning points or crises, Esther 2–3 prepare the complications that lead to the crisis, and the narrative dénouement in Esther 7–8 relates the actual reversal of the status of the characters and prepares for the ultimate conclusion in Esther 9, the victory over the—almost anonymous—enemies and the institutionalization of Purim.[37] Finally, the introductory presentation of the splendor of the Persian court in ch. 1 is mirrored by and lends significance to the concluding triumphant proclamation of the raising of Mordecai, the Judean, to the position of second-ranking person in the Persian kingdom.

Figure 1 succinctly presents my understanding of the structure of the MT version of Esther:

---

35. On Mordecai and Haman as mimetic twins, see Chapter 5 below.

36. The discussion in this chapter about turning points works within a narrative framework. We shall return to Est. 4 as an ideological/theological turning point in Chapters 5 and 8 below.

37. Many commentators claim that an original Ester–Mordecai narrative ended at Est. 8:17; see, e.g., Clines, *Esther Scroll*, 39–49. This might be correct, though unprovable. However, Esther MT as we have it now surely presents the double solution, the victory, and the instigation of Purim as the goal of the story, presenting Mordecai's high status as a logical consequence and side effect thereof.

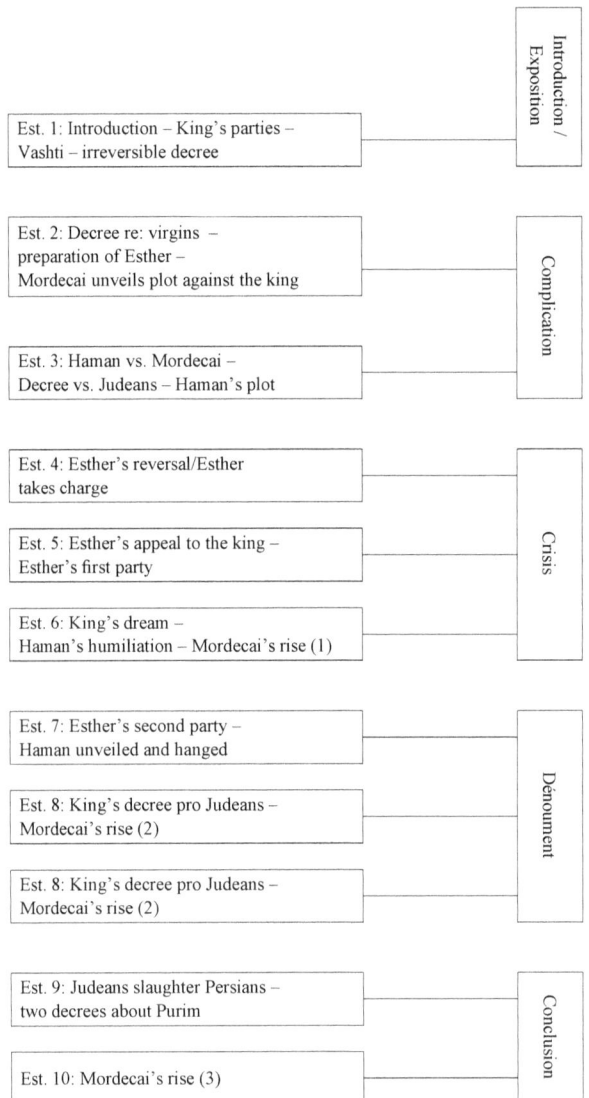

Figure 1. *The Structure of Esther MT*

3.2. *The Greek Esthers*

Let us turn now to the composition of the Greek variants, Esther LXX and AT. The most visible difference between the Hebrew and the Greek variants, of course, are the additions in the Greek variants (Add Est. A–F). Their place in the composition are almost identical in the LXX and the AT, with only minor differences.

Figure 2 shows how the additions interact with the elements found in the MT version of Esther:

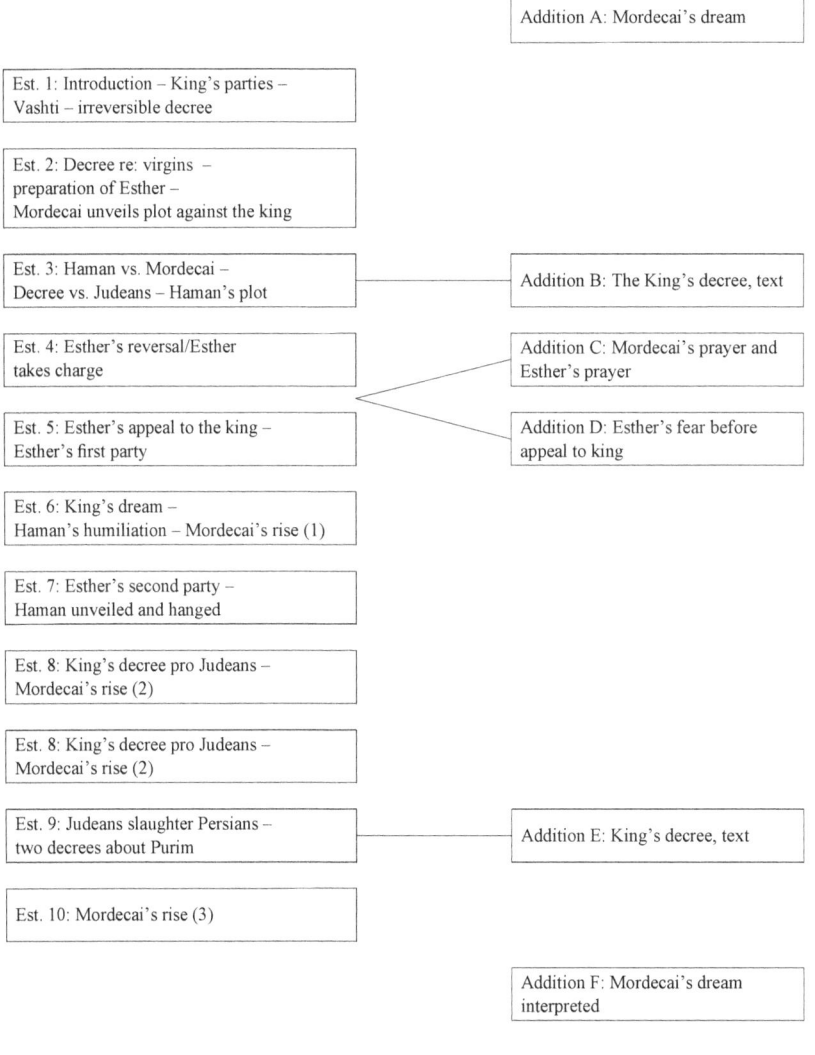

Figure 2. *The Structure of the Greek Books of Esther*

The additions come in pairs, scanning the Hebrew text, and accentuating the chiastic substructure in the text. Addition A, the record of Mordecai's dream, is interpreted by Add Est. F. Additions B and E, respectively, convey the "missing" texts of the royal decree *against* the Jews in ch. 3, and *for* the Jews in ch. 8. The first of these decrees (Add Est. B) ignites the crisis, and the second (Add Est. E) calls it off. Additions C and D pinpoint the center of the crisis: Add Est. C relates Mordecai's and Esther's long penitential prayers before Esther goes to entreat Ahasuerus in ch. 5, while Add Est. D is an expansion of the record of Esther's uninvited visit to the king's court. I shall return to this episode below. All in all, the four middle additions do not change the structure of the Hebrew Esther; they rather accentuate its semi-chiastic structure.

Considering composition, then, the main difference between the Hebrew and the Greek Esthers is the inclusion of Additions A–F, which create a new literary framework for Esther. Addition A presents a new beginning, placed before the Hebrew ch. 1. It relates a prophetical dream, dreamed by Mordecai. "Look! Shouts and confusion! Thunder and earthquake! Chaos upon the earth! Look, two great dragons came forward, both ready to fight… And the whole righteous nation was in chaos… Then they cried out to God, and from their cry, as though from a small spring, there came a great river…and the sun rose…" (Add Est. A, 4-10*). Addition F closes the Greek Esther with Mordecai's interpretation of his dream. Esther is the river; Mordecai and Haman are the two dragons; the nations are "those that gathered to destroy the name of the Judeans." The conclusion is that "the Lord has saved his people…" (Add Est. F, 3-6*). First, these additions bring about a change in the relative importance of Esther and Mordecai since Mordecai adds an important title to his CV as a prophetic dreamer in the Joseph–Daniel league. This early presentation is balanced by the status of Mordecai as a royal vizier at the end of the book. Moreover, from the outset of the story in the Greek versions Mordecai enters the story with an impressive lineage while Esther is pushed further behind and simply disappears before the closing of the story.

Secondly, the vision and its interpretation add importance to the events in the Esther story by connecting them to world-shattering phenomena. The text of the framing additions, which most scholars claim to be a Greek translation of an originally Hebrew text, seems to be a meek variant of the genre of ancient Near Eastern apocalyptic, though it "knows" the formulaic language of the Hebrew Bible. Lawrence M. Wills points out that Mordecai's dream differs from the apocalyptic visions of contemporary, that is, late Hellenistic, Jewish literature. It is shorter than the Jewish visions and "the symbols do not cover a whole range of history."[38] He labels Add Est. A "a flourish of mock-apocalyptic" and "an artificial apocalypse" that "gives notice of the rousing adventures to come and serves the same function as do dreams and oracles in Greek novels."[39] According to Wills, several of the Greek novels, for example, Xenophon's *An Ephesian Tale* (1.6), "contain dreams or oracles at the beginning of the story, to foreshadow the dangers, and in some cases, to predict a happy resolution as well."[40] I find Wills' clarifications very helpful, and I follow him in his description of the literary function of Mordecai's dream as a foreshadowing emphasizing of the importance of the Esther narrative.

The characterization of the main protagonists and the description of their relation in Esther gives the final form of each of the three variants each their own focus. The difference between Esther MT and Esther AT is substantial, while Esther LXX and AT are closer, especially due to the additions but probably also as the result of their interdependency. Nevertheless, the minor variations between the two Greek texts also give them different foci. Generally speaking, in Esther MT it is difficult to decide who is the true main protagonist, Esther or Mordecai,[41] while Esther LXX adds importance to Mordecai. This becomes even clearer in Esther AT, where Mordecai succeeds Ahasuerus/Assyeros as king of Persia after his death.

Thus, a comparison between the biblical Esthers shows variations in the description of the main protagonists in the versions, and this insight helps us to understand the characteristics of the individual versions and pinpoint issues of interest for the modern reader. In the following chapter, we shall track the construction of the gendered character Esther in her connection to the male characters, Mordecai, Ahasuerus, and Haman.

38. Wills, *Jewish Novel*, 116.
39. Ibid., 116–17.
40. Ibid., 117.
41. Jobes recounts anecdotally how in an informal survey among a class of Hebrew students 13 identified Esther as the main character while six chose Mordecai and eight were undecided (Jobes, *Alpha-Text*, 185 n. 7).

Chapter 3

CHARACTER, GENDER, AND POWER PLAY

1. *Exscription and Inscription*

Gender and gender related questions have always played a significant role in the exposition of the book of Esther. Many of the comments, ancient and modern, approving or disapproving, on the Esther and Vashti characters have been based on rigid, primarily male notions of "decent feminine conduct" and the lauding (or condemnation) of the wise man Mordecai. In feminist exposition, from the early days of Elizabeth Cady Stanton's *The Woman's Bible* in the late 1800s, over the first feminist wave in the 1970s and 1980s, till today's feminist exegesis the book and its presentation of the women in it have been discussed with different outcomes. Briefly stated, Esther has been either applauded for her courage and vigor or criticized for being too deferential and obedient to men. Vashti, the first queen of the Persian king Ahasuerus, has also been a matter of discussion, but she is generally considered more of an unquestionable role model than is Esther.[1]

---

1. For Luther, Vashti is "in general, the typos of the disobedient and wrongheaded woman (*ungehorsame und halsstarrige Frau*) who can rightfully be cast-off" (Bardtke, *Luther und das Buch Esther*, 58, my translation). On the reception of Esther and Vashti, see Chapter 2, "A Pair of Queens," in Elliott Horowitz, *Reckless Rites: Purim and the Legacy of Jewish Violence* (Princeton: Princeton University Press, 2006), 46–62. I shall not discuss the vast feminist exegesis here; the question will surface from time to time throughout the book, but due to the number of excellent volumes already written on the subject and on gender hermeneutics, gender will not be an issue to be discussed *per se* in this book. Timothy Beal treats the discussion at length in *Book of Hiding*, especially in Chapter 3, "The Bible as Moral Literature." There, he calls attention to the phenomenon that "this scholarship falls into the

So, there is no doubt that gender is important; and so is the matter of power and to whom it belongs, the power play. Gender criticism and power criticism go hand in hand—he who holds the power is from the outset (and per definition) male. The power play in Esther, then, is staged in the shape of male–female gender play, as well as in the male–male rivalry between Mordecai and Haman.[2] The tale of the expulsion of Vashti in Esther 1 presages ironically the general swapping of male and female roles that takes place in the subsurface of Esther, when Esther for a period gains/takes over political influence, and thus seems to grasp the political power over the Persian empire. Esther seduces Ahasuerus and Haman so that she can get her way politically; the king assigns Haman's house to Esther, who hands it over to Mordecai, but from the outset it becomes Esther's; and especially in the Hebrew Esther she has her share of the political power as we shall discuss below. The image of Haman's wife Zeresh is also interesting. Despite being a minor character in the book, or maybe *especially* because she is a minor and in principle dispensable person—her advice and later words could as easily have been uttered by Haman's friends—she is interesting, since she is the one to predict a decisive incident in the story-line, Haman's downfall in Est. 6:13. In this capacity she resembles other "foreign" persons, who tell an unpleasant truth in an important situation: Rahab, the harlot in Jericho (Josh. 2:9-13), the Assyrian Rabshakeh (Isa. 36), and Nebuzaradan, the Babylonian captain of the guard (Jer. 40:2-3). Also, as emphasized by Linda Day, Zeresh like Vashti flouts Persian law; in spite of the royal decree that all men are to be masters in their own households, Zeresh seems to be the one to tell Haman what to do, and he does it (Est. 5:14).[3]

It is worth considering whether a trail of changeovers is already laid out in the description of Queen Vashti's refusal to obey her king and master in ch. 1 and her subsequent removal from her position. The point of departure for Timothy Beal's intriguing reading of the book of Esther is the "writing out" of Queen Vashti from the book. On the surface level, Vashti is not that important; she is merely the one who must disappear to make way for the new queen, the main female protagonist, Esther. But her story is more than that. Beal understands the book as a

---

category of what Toril Moi and others have called 'images of Women' criticism" (Beal, *Book of Hiding*, 41). In the present volume I am less interested in moral deliberations on the Esther character than in narratological.

2. See Chapter 6, "Haman, the Scapegoat," below.
3. Linda Day, *Esther*, AOTC (Nashville: Abingdon, 2005), 113.

kind of "palimpsest": a story is written, then erased, and then the other woman is written over by the story of the other Jew. Vashti is erased, and in different ways Esther and Mordecai will each occupy the blank spaces she leaves behind.[4]

Vashti is "abject"[5] and "exscribed" (written out of the story) and replaced by Esther and Mordecai. But Vashti remains at the beginning of the book as the lens through which the story must be read: "Vashti will survive her own end in the narrative. She will haunt the rest of the story."[6] Vashti does not disappear, for her insubordination is written and broadcast to the whole empire as a compelling warning to married women (and their husbands as well). Or as strikingly formulated by Beal:

> Yet, insofar as her [Vashti's] exscription is a reinscription of the law, it is compelling also as an inscription of her transgressions, thereby enforcing memory of her as a threat. As a result, her exscription exposes insecurities in the sexual-political order being presented and opens that order to its own destruction… As a way into the narrative of Esther as a whole, the story of the other woman's exscription opens to critical reflection on the problematics of identity-coded politics and the possibilities of political subversion and transformation introduced by those problematics.[7]

Against this background, let us turn our attention to the very much inscribed female main protagonist, the Judean virgin Esther as she is described in the Hebrew and Greek versions. What will become apparent in this comparison is that—as is often the case—gender and power play intermingle in the narrative of the rise and fall of a Judean heroine. The more feminine, the less powerful.

2. *The Hebrew Esther*

The Hebrew Bible only randomly describes "round" or full-fledged characters, that is, characters described with different emotions and even personal considerations, about whom, to use Adele Berlin's typology, "we

---

4. Beal, *Book of Hiding*, 29. Beal (12–14) uses the term "other" as a designation of the person or gender (i.e. woman) that serves as a defining counterpoint to yourself (i.e. male) with reference to Simone de Beauvoir's seminal work *The Other Sex*.

5. "Vashti has become, quite literally, *abject*: she can be neither subject nor object within the social and symbolic order, and therefore she must be repulsed, pushed outside its boundaries" (ibid., 24, original emphasis).

6. Ibid., 29.

7. Ibid., 32 (original emphasis).

know more than is necessary for the plot."⁸ This reticence in the texts has often inspired—or even provoked—readers, including academic readers, to compensate for the "lack" of information. Gap-filling is commonplace, being part of theological or exegetical, historical-critical or post-modern approaches.⁹ This can hardly be avoided since it seems to be part of any involved reading. Gap-filling fulfills a psychological need for involvement in most readers. The mere fact that biblical narratives often have become parts of a larger biblical and extra-biblical network of re-readings and re-writings, points to creative reading as a universal phenomenon. As part of any modern reading strategy, gap-filling, though, should be handled with as much hermeneutical self-discipline as any other scholarly methodology. This call for scholarly self-discipline in the exposition of personal emotions among biblical characters also counts for the book of Esther.

In the book of Esther, we find literary *personae*, characterized not only through their actions but also through an authorial description of their inner emotions. This is a characteristic for the literary genre to which, according to Wills, already the Hebrew Esther comes very close, namely the antique, Greek novella.¹⁰ But still, even if Esther resembles modern literature in its interest in the inner life of the protagonists more than, for example, the narratives of the matriarchs in Genesis, much is still left aside by the author, and the characterization is closer to biblical style than to contemporary literature. Like its elder biblical prototypes, Esther MT does not relate much more information than needed for the flow of the storyline, and much of the psychological information given by the text seems to be part of literary conventionalism.¹¹ Therefore, it seems recommendable to follow Susan Niditch and take the insights of folk-lore studies into consideration along with speculations about the psychologies of the literary *personae*. When, for instance, Esther postpones the uncovering of Haman, it is not only because she from the outset is a shrewd or manipulative woman, but also as a result of a literary technique of delay to heighten the suspense, and of the rule of narrative *trislegomena*, the threefold repetition of a narrative motif, which invites the audience

---

8. Adele Berlin, *Poetics and Interpretation of Biblical Narrative*, Bible and Literature Series 9 (Sheffield: Almond, 1983), 32.

9. For fine examples of character reading in Esther, see Day, *Three Faces of a Queen*, and Fox, *Character and Ideology*.

10. Wills, *Jewish Novel*, 3. Linda Day discusses the relationship to the contemporaneous literature, including the Ancient Greek novella; see Day, *Three Faces of a Queen*, 214–32; and cf. Chapter 1 above.

11. This is even more prevalent in the Greek versions to which we shall return below.

to active interaction with the story.[12] This interaction, then, gives the audience the *impression* of Esther as a shrewd and manipulative woman. Saying much more than that would be to take the exposition further than the evidence of the text can bear.

Esther in the Hebrew version is first and foremost described as a beautiful, modest, well-bred, and well protected, that is, almost perfect, young Judean woman.[13] She is presented through her family relation to her elder cousin and guardian, Mordecai. She is never asked if she wants to partake in the royal beauty contest, and she never protests. This part of the tale is obviously not important enough for the narrative flow to attract an attention-drawing exposition. Likewise, there is no mention of her feelings when she leaves the royal harem to go to the king's chambers. The information given is that she does not ask for more than what the eunuch offers her, though the text informs us that she has a special relationship to him, and thus could have asked for more. What is important is the communication that she is likeable and sexually attractive—thus, the perfect female spy. Being a secret Judean in a non-Judean context, an ignorant but very useful tacit undercover agent in a potentially hostile, superior environment seems to be her most important role. Independent enterprise, on the other hand, is not one of Esther's inborn characteristics in Esther MT. Complications are piling up around her, but Esther is not part thereof. Having been introduced, she is unimportant for the first part of the narrative—Esther is portrayed as a "sleeping" agent.

The turning point in the characterization of Esther is the communication between Esther and Mordecai in Esther 4. Here, she is presented as developing from an ignorant teenager to a responsible, adult woman. This reversal of personality is communicated through a meticulously constructed series of exchanges of tacit and verbal information which in the end leads Esther to take over the ultimate responsibility for the salvation of the Judeans. Mordecai is temporarily transformed to a subordinate character. This exchange moves Esther from being part of the Persian royal court and under the influence of her husband, the king, and her kin, Mordecai, into being an influential, independent woman bonded with her Judean compatriots. From now on she can act on her own. The text

---

12. Cf. Berg, *Book of Esther*, 110.

13. As mentioned in the introduction to this chapter, scholars—not least feminist scholars—discuss whether Esther is a role model for women. Mary Gendler's comment is interesting in this connection: "Esther is certainly the prototype—and perhaps even a stereotype—of the ideal Jewish woman, an ideal which I find restrictive and repressive" (Mary Gendler, "The Restoration of Vashti," in *The Jewish Woman*, ed. Elisabeth Koltun [New York: Schocken, 1976], 241–7 [242]).

does not give the reader any direct information about Esther's thoughts or emotions. It relates only facts, the brute fact about the dangers of approaching the king uninvited, Mordecai's words of persuasion, Esther's order of fasting to Mordecai and every Judean in Susa, and her promise of taking action. Moreover, the text stresses the unimportance of Esther as a person; it is Esther as the clandestine Judean who is going to be the vehicle in the salvation of the Judeans. "Perhaps you have come to royal dignity for just such a time as this," Mordecai says (4:14). Esther's role, not her personal fears or feelings of responsibility, is of narrative importance. Indeed, her last words to Mordecai in Esther 4, "I will go to the king, though it is against the law; and if I perish, I perish" (4:16), present her as a courageous woman, but the focus of the text is more on Esther as a role model than as a person. The author does not describe Esther's very reasonable fear, nor her mastering of such fear of her emotions; we only have hints of these through her arguments and actions. Esther does not say that she is afraid of going to the king; she only mentions the reason for her reluctance.

Likewise, the presentation of Esther's banquets with Ahasuerus and Haman in Esther 5 and 7 is far more concerned with narratological patterns than with psychological probability; the narratives convey nothing about her deliberations or motives. I understand the two parties as primarily necessary for prolongation and delay, which serves to emphasize Haman's stupidity.[14] His boasting before the first party is perfectly balanced by his wife's ominous words before the second (6:13). Even if one cannot follow Fox and enter into speculations about "Esther's undoubted need for cunning and circumspection," his remarks, that this portrait "justifies the interpretation of her speeches and actions as being formulated with careful thought and control, rather than as indecisive and haphazard," remain valid.[15] In my opinion, though, it is the author, not his leading lady, who shows careful thought and control. The author's interest lies *beyond* the literary character's psychology and *within* the ideology he wants to

---

14. However, Fox might be right that the Esther character is smarter than imagined by most commentators: "Commentators who condemn her circuity do not pause to think what would have happened if she had immediately made bold demands. Would the king have done away with his prime minister with no further ado? He himself was implicated in the scheme. Esther is more subtle than that. Her delays pique the king's curiosity and elicit from him a repeated promise to fulfill her wish, whatever it may be" (Michael V. Fox, "Three Esthers," in *The Book of Esther in Modern Research*, ed. Leonard J. Greenspoon and Sidney White Crawford, JSOTSup 380 [London: Continuum, 2003], 50–60 [53]).

15. Fox, *Character and Ideology*, 201.

convey, the ideology of Judean perseverance and survival. To achieve this goal, he must paint a portrait of a woman able to take charge of her responsibility.

Fox discusses the portrait of Esther in chs. 5 and 7 and calls her "indirect, self-effacing, and manipulative." He continues: "Some commentators find these qualities morally unappealing or offensive as an image of the feminine," and Fox speculates that the author himself almost anticipates such reproaches by showing, via the example of Vashti's expulsion, that the king dislikes strong-willed women. This and other preemptive rebuttals suggest, according to Fox, that "the author is salving Jewish sensitivities by showing that indirection, cunning, and at least some show of subservience are necessary stratagems in such circumstances and should not offend Jewish pride." The Jews cannot afford an entire nation of Mordecais, people who refuse to bow to their superiors like Mordecai does to Haman. "Mordecai himself must call upon another type of person for help."[16] Sidney Ann White[17] describes Esther as the perfect role model for the "weak" and "subordinate" Judeans in Diaspora, who had to adjust to "their lack of immediate political and economic power and learn to work within the system to gain what power they could." As a woman, Esther's role in society is "constantly precarious…[and she] must learn to make her way among the powerful and to cooperate with others in order to make herself secure."[18] I concur with Fox's later conclusion, that Mordecai needs a partner, but not necessarily his first, that the author makes his choice of storyline to "salve Jewish sensitivities." The narrative plot itself calls for a person who can complement Mordecai. Esther is the perfect match, as a woman and thus as an easily placed "mole" at the royal court, and as a person who without losing any pride at all can appeal for mercy to the foreign king. This is the social role of a woman, as described by White, and of a trickster in a patriarchal society.[19]

In Esther 8, after Haman is hanged the king gives his house to Queen Esther. Mordecai is called to the king, too, because he is Esther's kin, and he receives the royal signet ring which had been in Haman's position up till now. Esther sets Mordecai over Haman's house. In these two verses, 8:1-2, the narrative prepares the return of direct influence from Esther

---

16. Ibid., 201–2.
17. Sidnie Ann White, "Esther: A Feminine Model for Jewish Diaspora," in *Gender and Difference in Ancient Israel*, ed. Peggy L. Day (Minneapolis: Fortress, 1989), 161–77.
18. White, "Esther: A Feminine Model for Jewish Diaspora," 167.
19. On the concept of tricksters, see Susan Niditch, *Underdogs and Tricksters: A Prelude to Biblical Folklore* (San Francisco: Harper & Row, 1987).

to Mordecai; no overt, intra-narrative explanation of this judicial development is given, and one might speculate that it is due to Mordecai's legal role as Esther's original guardian. From a literary perspective Fox offers the interesting proposal that by being able to turn stewardship of Haman's house to Mordecai, Esther "stands in the role of donor to Mordecai."[20] Moreover, by setting Mordecai over Haman's house, Esther shows respect for Judean mores and traditions—she might be the queen of Persia but at the same time she is Mordecai's ward, so she spans both worlds. Her "modesty" also compares well to the image of her as a modest young woman in Esther 2, where she did not take more with her from the harem than any of the other girls, even if she had a special friend in the overseer of the women, Hegai the king's eunuch (2:15). Following this incident, she uses her female influence on the king once again. Weeping, she pleads with him to avert Haman's decree against the Judeans, and stressing her ties with the people she makes it a personal cause, "for how can I bear to see the calamity that is coming on my people? Or how can I bear to see the destruction of my kindred?" she says (8:6). The tacit Judean has become the outspoken Judean and thus a role model for a new, self-assured people.

The king informs Esther and Mordecai—and reminds us, the readers—about the prerequisite of the whole drama, the irrevocability of a royal decree. He puts Mordecai in total control over Persia, not because he saved his life earlier or because he has been a trusted civil servant, but because he is Esther's cousin (8:7); yet, her position as an independent leader of the Judean people is declining. It is Mordecai alone who finds the way to outdo the Haman/Ahasuerus decree; when the writers on Mordecai's command and in the name of the king write the decree that allows the Judeans to defend themselves from their enemies, a legitimate Judean "defense" is at hand without the participation of Esther (8:9-14).

So, this is the end of Esther's grandeur, and even though she is not as totally exscribed as Queen Vashti, she loses the role of being an active protagonist and main character. The final outcome of the story is that Mordecai is back in office as the patriarchal guardian, not only of Esther but of all Judeans in Persia, and in ch. 9 he, not Esther, writes the first decree of Purim. She is conspicuously absent in the second half of ch. 8, and she returns only twice in Esther 9. The first time is the strange second permission of the extra killings in Susa on the 14th Adar (9:11-15), a passage which must have been composed to explain differing dates for Purim.[21] As opposed to the previous conversations, this time it is the king

---

20. Fox, "Three Esthers," 53.
21. See, e.g., Levenson, *Esther*, 122–3.

who takes the initiative, thus keeping him in the dominant position, too. After this short encounter, Esther disappears once again, only to return as a co-author of a second decree about the celebration of Purim (9:29-32). This decree puts Esther back in the story for a short period and helps keep the narrative balance between the two protagonists, Esther and Mordecai. However, the story ends with the celebration of Mordecai's status in ch. 10, where he is appointed as vizier of Persia and as the beloved leader of all the Judeans. Queen Esther has disappeared as quietly as she arrived.[22]

Let me recapitulate briefly. Esther MT presents a picture of Esther that is more vivid than most, but definitely not all, characterizations in the Hebrew Bible. The psychological details are primarily conveyed indirectly through her actions and her interactions with others,[23] not through her thoughts or emotions. The relative importance of Esther and Mordecai is mainly communicated through the structure of the book. Its communicative strategy, with its semi-psychological information, invites the reader to gap-filling. Gap-filling, however, often leads to readings of the text which are more telling of the reader and interpreter than of the text and author. This is also the case of the two Greek rewritings of Esther in the Septuagint and the Alpha-text, where gaps certainly are filled.

3. *The Greek Esthers*

When it comes to character in the Greek Esthers—Esther LXX and AT— the discourse is very different from the account in the Hebrew Bible. These late texts resemble the antique Hellenistic novella in many ways, one of them being the emphasis on the emotions of the protagonists. What, then, are the differences between the Hebrew and the Greek images of Esther?[24]

---

22. Talmon, analyzes the core of the book of Esther as wisdom literature and sees Esther as the most influential character: "In the canonical Book of Esther, especially in the chronistic summary, Mordecai occupies the center of the stage. But in the last count it is the wise Esther who dominates the scene. In the course of events she ascends from the role of Mordecai's protegee to become her mentor's guardian. In fact, she completely overshadows her uncle and outclasses his adversary Haman in the art of crafty planning and successful execution. In the end it is Esther's superior cleverness which saves the day" (Talmon, "Wisdom in the Book of Esther," 449).

23. Cf. Day, *Three Faces of a Queen*, 22–5.

24. Day (ibid.) offers a meticulous analysis and comparison of the portraits of Esther in MT, LXX, and AT. She follows Clines' relational dating of the texts and understands AT to be the elder version.

Both the additions A-F proper and other minor additions in the text add Jewish piety to the Hebrew Esther. One of the curious and defining hallmarks of Esther MT is the apparent absence of God or of any religious praxis, even though both ancient and modern commentators tend to find implied and unspoken references to the divine, for example, in Esther's fasting in ch. 4.[25] This lack of overt piety is scrupulously remedied in the Greek versions, where large paragraphs of religious discourse are added. Most important is Add Est. C, the prayers of Mordecai and Esther before she approaches King Ahasuerus, in Esther LXX named Xerxes, in Esther AT Assyeros (Est. 5). These prayers resemble the Second Temple period genre of penitential prayer.[26] Mordecai's prayer follows directly after Esther has accepted to plead for the Jews[27] with Ahasuerus (4:17). Following the characteristics of penitential prayer, he first invokes the Lord, the King of all powers (LXX), creator of the universe, and then affirms his innocence: it was not out of pride that he refused to do obeisance "to this prideful Haman"[28] whereby he ignited the conflict between Haman and the Jews. Finally, he calls upon God to intervene and save his people, just as he did in Egypt (Add Est. C:1-11).

Esther's prayer (Add Est. C:12-30) is much longer and more elaborate than Mordecai's, furnished with details of her emotions. She was

> seized with the agony of death. Taking off her garments of glory, she put on the garments of distress and mourning, and instead of costly perfumes she covered her head with ashes and dung, and she utterly humbled her body; every part that she loved to adorn she covered with her tangled hair. (Add Est. C:12–13)

---

25. As opposed to especially Dan. 1–6, the book of Esther mentions neither Shabbat nor dietary rules. God is only indirectly present in Esther MT, as discussed in Chapter 1, above. For God as a character in Esther, see Fox, *Character and Ideology*, 235–47.

26. For an introduction to penitential prayers, see *Seeking the Favor of God: Volume 1, The Origins of Penitential Prayer in Second Temple Judaism*, ed. Mark J. Boda et al., Early Judaism and its Literature (Atlanta: SBL, 2006), in which see especially William Morrow, "The Affirmation of Divine Righteousness in Early Penitential Payers: A Sign of Judaism's Entry into the Axial Age," 101–17.

27. Following the considerations by Cohen and others on the best translation of the term *Ioudaios* in the late Second Temple period, discussed in Chapter 7 below, I translate this and cognate words "Jew, Jewish, Judaism" in LXX and AT.

28. This assertion of virtue offers an explanation to the puzzling incident Est. 3:2-5, where Mordecai refuses to bow down to Haman, the scene that triggers Haman's hatred and request to the king for a pogrom.

This description of her emotional acts is followed by her prayer: she is alone, "her danger is in her own hand." She has heard from her birth how God took care of Israel; yet now they have sinned, "because we honored their gods." But these gods do not exist; the Lord shall make himself known, and most importantly: the Lord knows that she abhors the bed of the uncircumcised and abhors the sign of her glorious position "like a menstrual cloth," and that she has not eaten at Haman's or the king's tables (Add Est. C:14-28).[29]

This prayer paints the picture of a devout Jewish woman, who keeps the rules of what to eat and what not to eat, how to and how not to behave, and who knows the genre of petition. It expresses eloquently Esther's fears, hopes, and hates so that nothing is left to further gap-filling. Mordecai's and Esther's prayers also change the underlying message of the book; where Esther MT is positive toward living in the Diaspora, the Greek versions are more reluctant: the Judeans might have to and be able to live together with the gentiles, but they must keep their distance and abide to the Law. Thus, a new theological strand is inserted into the elder narrative, a theology much closer to Second Temple piety, resembling, for example, the piety of the Psalms of the Righteous.[30]

In the final chapters of the book of Esther, we shall see how the Esther character lessens in importance, while Mordecai grows, so that the "power balance" between them is reversed again, especially in the AT. This relative "thinning" of the Esther character and "growing" of Mordecai in Esther AT as compared to Esther LXX and MT is already present, in fact, in the record of their dialogue in ch. 4 about whether she should approach the king uninvited or not. Here, at the first turning point of the narrative, the roles of the two are inverted for a while;[31] Esther's role is downplayed while Mordecai's is enhanced. In the AT, the initiative of the interchange lies with Mordecai, while in MT and LXX it is Esther who takes the initiative and approaches Mordecai with her offer of better and more appropriate clothing. Also, her proclamation of the fast—in the AT of "a religious service"—is much shorter and less impressive in Esther AT than it is in Esther LXX. We shall return to Esther 4 in Chapter 4 below.[32]

---

29. There are only minor, insignificant differences between the LXX and AT versions of Addition C.

30. See Else K. Holt, "'Let the righteous strike me; let the faithful correct me': Psalm 141 and the Enclave of the Ṣaddiqîm," *SJOT* 33 (2019): 185–202.

31. See on the inversion pp. 35–36 above.

32. For the impact of Mordecai's dream and its exposition (Add Est. A; F) on the relative power balance between Esther and Mordecai in LXX and AT as opposed to MT, see pp. 29–31, above.

Having come this far, the Greek texts continue with a heart-breaking account of Esther's fearful meeting with Ahasuerus/Xerxes. Before the added prayers (Add Est. C) she had said to Mordecai (Est. LXX 4:11):

> All the nations of the empire know that every man or woman who shall go to the king inside the inner court uninvited—there is no deliverance for him. Only if the king holds out the golden rod to someone, will that person be safe. And I myself have not been called to go to the king for these thirty days.[33]

Now, after the prayers, she must approach the king, and this she does with articulate fear and trembling (Add Est. D).[34] She takes off her mourning garments that she has worn during her fasting and puts on her garment of glory (AT). Then, when she has become majestic (Add D:2) she goes to the king, praying and accompanied by two attendants; "on one she leaned gently for support, while the other followed, holding up her train" (Add Est. D:3-4, AT).[35] The two maids point indirectly to her internal and external manifestations, fear and royal glory. The text is expressive and moving:

> She was radiant with the full flush of her beauty, and her face looked happy as if she were cheerful, but her heart was in anguish from fear. When she had gone through all the doors, she stood before the king. He was seated on the throne of his kingdom, clothed in the full array of his splendor, all covered with gold and precious stones. And he was most terrifying. And when he raised his face inflamed with glory, he gazed at her in the full flush of anger. The queen staggered, her color turned pale from faintness, and she collapsed on the head of the attendant who went before her. (Add Est. D:5–7, LXX)

The description of Esther's mixed feelings is especially interesting; on the surface she is radiant, but her heart is filled with fear. A disproportion between inward and outward appearance is closely connected to the intense interest in emotions in the antique novellas. In the older Hebrew Bible narratives, there is most often a direct proportion between

---

33. The Septuagint text is close to MT. Esther AT presents a shorter version of the same information, while, on the other hand, it is the only text to pinpoint the dangers of going to the king, adding the question: "How can I go now not being invited?"

34. Esther MT presents a much shorter version of the incident in Est. 5:1-5.

35. There are minor differences between the LXX and AT presentation of the episode. For at detailed analysis, see Day, *Three Faces of a Queen*, 45–63.

appearance and emotion,[36] but not here. The subsequent conversation between Esther and the king demonstrates the feelings of the two persons. The king's anger is turned to gentleness: he jumps "alarmed" from his throne, he takes her into his arms, and he keeps comforting her with soothing words (Add Est. D:7-8, LXX). Esther's emotions, though, outdo the hefty feelings of the king. After being quieted after her faintness she tells the king about her fear of his glory; he was like a divine angel, she says. "And while she was speaking, she fell from faintness"—this time so violently that the king calls all his servants to reassure her.

The AT inserts an even more detailed description of this scene. The king raises his face inflamed with glory, gazing right at her like a bull in the full flush of his anger. And the queen is terrified and faints. However, she faints only once in Esther AT; in accordance with its more economic narrative style, the AT simply mentions that upon her face is a measure of sweat, while she tells him how scary he looks (5:12, AT).[37]

As mentioned above, the composition of the Greek Esthers lends greater importance to Mordecai at Esther's expense than the MT, and the AT even more so than the LXX. Chapter 9 of the AT is shorter than the Masoretic and the LXX variants, leaving us with a smoother and more economical text, one without the repetitions of the Hebrew and the LXX texts, but also with a text that "exscribes" Esther from the book.[38] The LXX follows the MT portrayal in 9:1-12, presenting Esther's petition to the king that he revoke Haman's decrees of annihilation of the Judeans. One interesting difference between the MT and LXX is that while Esther is the one to approach the king in both accounts, in the MT Mordecai is the sole author of the decree while in LXX the king allows the two of them to have the letter written, and in the end the king seals the letters himself.[39] This, however, only moves the balance between Esther and Mordecai a little.

In Esther AT, on the other hand, the words of the king turns the readers' attention away from Esther to Mordecai, right after Haman has been executed: "He [Haman] even planned to kill hang Mardochaios who

---

36. Cf. Berlin, *Poetics and Interpretation*, 37–9.

37. A similar example of emotions being added in AT is Est. 7:2, "Esther struggled with her reply, because the adversary was before her eyes, and God gave her courage as she called upon him". MT / LXX, by contrast, read "Then Esther/she answered…"

38. For a diligent analysis of the last chapters of Esther in the MT, LXX and AT, see de Troyer, *End of the Alpha Text*.

39. The Greek translator seems to have overlooked the irrevocability of the king's decrees,

saved me from the hand of the eunuchs," he explains (7:14 AT).[40] Then he gives Haman's belongings to Mordecai (not to Esther), asks what he (not Esther) wants, and Mordecai (not Esther) replies: "That you revoke Haman's letters." The king entrusts Mordecai to the affairs of the kingdom (7:15-17 AT) while Esther asks for permission to have her enemies and especially Haman's sons killed (7:18-21 AT). Then she virtually disappears, only to return briefly in ch. 9.

After this conversation follows Add E, the text of the king's letter that condemns Haman in harsh words, revokes his decree, allows the Jews to follow their traditions and threatens their opponents with annihilation. After the letter the two Greek versions each take their own direction. Broadly speaking, LXX keeps the long and repetitious storyline from the MT about the killing of the enemies in the countryside and in Susa, including not least Haman's sons. After this is reported to the king, he asks Esther for the final time what she wants, and she replies by asking for a repetition of the Susa killings the following day and for the corpses of Haman's sons to be hanged on public display (9:1-15 LXX). Then she disappears for a while; Esther is nowhere mentioned in the following long and meticulous presentation of the first authorization of Purim (Est. 9:16-19, 20-28 MT, LXX); Mordecai is the authoritative voice in the legalization of the holiday. When Esther does return in 9:29, almost as an aside, she writes the second letter of Purim together with Mordecai, presumably to match and confirm the second day of Purim. In Esther 10, the LXX version retains Mordecai's status as second to the Persian king. Queen Esther never acts again.

While the LXX largely follows the MT, the AT offers a much shorter version that collapses the events. After Add E, Mordecai is presented in his new authority (AT 7:33/8:14),[41] writing a letter to the Jews about Haman's death. This is followed by a short report of the killing of the enemies (7:42-45/9:3-11) among whom are a few named persons and Haman's ten unnamed sons. This contrasts with the MT and LXX, where

---

40. With reference to the episodes Est. 2:21-23; 6:1-3 MT. In LXX and AT the episode where Mordecai uncovers and reports the two servants who plan to kill the king is told already in Add Est. A, after the report of Mordecai's dream; it serves as the reason for Mordecai's position as a servant at the court and for Haman's jealousy. The AT version of these events is more unfolded than in the LXX, presenting Mordecai's importance to the king in a way that matches the waning role of Esther in ch. 8.

41. The numbering of the last part of AT is complicated. I follow the double numbering in the NETS version.

the Jews even take spoil. A dialogue follows between Esther and the king concerning a (repeated) killing throughout the country (7:45-46/9:12-16). After the king has given his consent, the text reports that "they killed seventy thousand one hundred men." This is the last reference to Esther in AT; she is never mentioned in connection with Purim. Day comments on Esther's brutality:

> A [AT] presents Esther as both desirous of control and extremely violent. Whereas in B [LXX] and M [MT] she asks the king to do the action which will fulfill her request, to revoke Haman's decree, here Esther herself demands to bring about the result she desires ('allow me', Δός μοι). The action she envisions performing is savage.
>
> In the other two texts [MT and LXX], the last we see of Esther is her constructive and peaceful action of informing the people about Purim. In the A text, the last we see of Esther, except for the brief identification in Mordecai's dream interpretation, is her violent and destructive action in Persia.[42]

The two short episodes in AT, Esther's requests for revenge (7:18) and for a second day of destruction and plundering (7:45-46/9:13), call for consideration, for how do they add to the image of the emotional and frail young woman presented in the previous chapters? The report of the instigation of Purim is much shorter in the AT than in MT and LXX, and, as remarked by Day, the text exscribes Esther totally from the instigation of the holiday. Esther's role is restricted to the warfare. Maybe this exonerates Mordecai from responsibility, leaving to him the role of the solemn lawgiver (7:47-49/9:20-26), then archivist, and ultimately king of Persia (7:50-52/10:1-3)—in other words, the perfect Torah-abiding leader of the righteous ṣaddiqîm in early antique Judaism. If this is the case, then the feast of Purim is also exonerated from the atrocities of the killing of the Judean's Persian neighbors (enemies in Esther's opinion).[43] Is this the reason why Esther's concerns in AT 7:18-21 are less about the fate of her Judaic kin, more about punishing her enemies? Is the burden of and responsibility for the slaughtering of the Persians taken away from Mordecai and put only on Esther's shoulders in AT? Did she lose the power but earn the blame?

---

42. Day, *Three Faces of a Queen*, 143, 195; strictly speaking, the remarks concern Esther's first request in AT 7:18-21.

43. See Chapters 7 and 8, below.

4. Conclusion

A comparative reading of the Hebrew and Greek versions of Esther shows that the Esther character changes during the redactional-translational *Fortschreibung* of the narrative, especially with reference to construction of gender characterization. Over time, Esther becomes more concordant with a masculine-normative, androcentric description of the Jewish woman of the Hellenistic era—more emotional, more obedient, more Law-abiding, in short, more feminine than the Hebrew Esther. Shaye Cohen describes the role of the woman in Second Temple Judaism, and in antiquity as such, with a quotation from Josephus:

> A wife, says the Law, is in all things inferior to a husband. Let her accordingly be submissive, not for violent ill-treatment, but that she may be directed; for God has given authority to the husband.[44]

"Men act; women are to be acted upon. Men dominate; women are to be dominated. A woman's role is to assist her husband," Cohen concludes.[45] How much more does this not apply to the younger cousin of a mighty courtier at the Persian court? Thus, the Greek Esther lives up to the restrictions of early, Torah-fearing Judaism. As we have seen, she also suits the literary norms of the Hellenistic novella. Only one stain can be placed on Esther's character in the Greek Esther: her belligerent attitude as the sole person responsible for the killings in AT 7, as discussed above. Here, however, she resembles another Jewish heroine, Judith, who beheads the enemy general Holofernes and thereby leads the way for her fellow "sons of Israel" to beat his panicking army of Assyrians. There are many similarities between the two books, but also important differences, the most suggestive in this context presumably being the location of the narrative—Esther in Persia, Judith in Israel. For if de Troyer's suggested dating of Esther AT in the first century CE is correct, and Esther AT was conceived as a book that makes it "abundantly clear that God's punishment will ultimately catch up with those who harm his people,"[46] then there might be a need of yet another unlikely violent feminine savior of the subdued Jews in the Roman Empire of the first century BCE.[47]

44. Shaye J. D. Cohen, *From the Maccabees to Mishna*, 3rd ed. (Louisville: Westminster, 2014), 74, with reference to Josephus, *Against Apion* 2.24 §201.
45. Cohen, *From the Maccabees to Mishna*.
46. De Troyer, *End of the Alpha Text*, 402.
47. For a comparison of Esther and Judith, see Sidnie White Crawford, "Esther and Judith: Contrasts in Character," in Greenspoon and Crawford, eds, *The Book of Esther in Modern Research*, 61–76.

It remains to be discussed whether any of the three Esther characters could and should serve as a model for our time; she certainly should for her own. What cannot be discussed is that her narrative is the story about a woman who was in the right place at the right time and who conquered her fears and used the means of persuasion available to her as a young woman in a world of powerful men. This image of Esther is present throughout the three biblical portraits of her. In that capacity, Esther retains her place in the league of biblical women who have a decisive role in the Judean salvation history, together with Sarah, Tamar, Rahab, Deborah, Ruth and Judith.

Part II

READINGS

Chapter 4

NOW ESTHER WAS ADMIRED BY ALL WHO SAW HER—OR: HOW TO UNDERSTAND ESTHER 2/TOO?

1. *Intertextuality*

> [Of the narratives in the Hebrew Bible,] the Book of Esther appears the most obvious candidate for folkloristic approaches. Its characters seem to be drawn from a veritable motif index of treacherous villains, fair maidens of lowly status who become wives of kings, upright and wise heroes, stupid and ineffectual kings. Its magiclike setting is plush with the trappings of court: servants, purple furnishings, fetes, food, and magnificent clothing.[1]

Susan Niditch, quoted above, reads the book of Esther together with the Joseph novel, looking for "shared literary form" and/or "direct interdependence through borrowing."[2] This search for shared literary form has led to suggestions of a shared "genre." The books of Daniel (including the Additions), Joseph, and Esther have been read through the lens of "The Jew in the Court of the Foreign King," the title of Lawrence M. Wills' influential Harvard dissertation.[3] In other words, there is a rich tradition for reading Esther intertextually, and what follows in the present chapter might be understood as a side track of this tradition for intertextuality. However, I shall find my textual interlocutors outside the genre of biblical court tales, in the classical folkloristic *Arabian Nights* and in the opening section of the French, erotic novel, *Story of O*.

An intertextual reading of the beginning of the book of Esther (Est. 1–2), the introductory narrative of *Arabian Nights*, and the opening

---

1. Niditch, *A Prelude to Biblical Folklore*, 127–8.
2. Ibid., 126.
3. Wills, *The Jew in the Court of the Foreign King*. For the *Forschungsgeschichte* of this vein of analysis, see his introductory Chapter 1, pages 1–12.

section of *Story of O* may seem puzzling or even absurd to some, and from the outset the most important question is: Can anything at all be gained from that kind of analyses? What from the outset triggered me to venture into this comparative reading was the openly erotic timbre of Esther 1–2 in light of its function as *rite-de-passage*, and its literary function of preparing the main corpus of the narrative. In my opinion, comparative intertextual analyses of these—from other perspectives diverse—texts can lead to new insights in the literary artistry of the book of Esther. Thus, the questions and methodologies applied in the following will not, and should not, be set within the historical-critical framework; rather, they are rooted in narrative analyses, intertextual reader response analyses, and studies of ritual.

What I want to demonstrate is twofold. First, that certain narratological motifs are common for *Arabian Nights* and the book of Esther, suggesting an intertextual connection. Secondly, that Esther 2 can be read as a rite-of-passage for the queen-to-be, comparable to the rites which convert the self-assured, independent protagonist of *Story of O* into a passive object for male sexual desire. These comparative analyses will help to reach a deeper understanding of the fascination of the Esther narrative and the literary means utilized by its antique storyteller(s).

Reading Esther 2 in the light of *Story of O* does not imply, of course, that Esther 2 should be labeled pornography. In my view, nobody—no matter how critical he/she might be toward pornography and no matter how he/she defines pornography—would consider Esther 2 pornographic. Yet, there is an irrefutably erotic timbre in Esther 2 which deserves to be examined. To do this is the aspiration of the following analysis.

From the outset, an intertextual analysis will take its point of departure from the reader's subjective associations, triggered by repetition of semantics or of narrative patterns; such associations, in their turn, trigger the curiosity and fuel the scholar's search for intertextual markers. The intertextual inquiry in the present context does not intend to demonstrate the existence of such textual links as provided deliberately—or by chance—by an original author, in other words as an intertextuality based on historical-critical examination. Rather, my inquiry follows the lead of readerly association, aiming to substantiate intertextuality from the point of view of readerly reception. In this connection, it should be remembered that intertextuality is not only established through repetition of sounds and words, sentences and texts or parts of texts; intertextuality is also based on transformation: "textual elements or patterns are both repeated and transformed in order to be assimilated into new text structures. Repetition and transformation are therefore intertextuality's characteristic features," as stressed by Ellen van Wolde.[4] This does not only apply to intertextuality created during text *production*, it also counts for intertextuality realized through text *reception*. Only when patterns of transformation are taken into consideration and appreciated, the intertextual connections between two or more texts divided by time, space, and meaning will be appreciated.

In this respect, reading Esther 1–2 not only activates associations to *Arabian Nights*, also known as *1001 Nights*, but also, as intimated above, to the *Story of O*. Can such intertextual connections be substantiated? Our study will proceed along two paths, the first being the appreciation of the simple correlation of a narrative motive, the relegation of the queen in a lush oriental kingdom and the subsequent gathering of beautiful virgins as substitutes of the queen, that is, a comparative reading of Esther 2 and the introduction to *Arabian Nights*. Then follows an analysis of the preparation of "the bride", Esther and O. And behind the readings, the question of who has the power rests once again.

2. *The Story of Esther*

Put succinctly, the book of Esther is about negotiating power. As an introduction to the power play, the *personae dramatis* are introduced in Esther 1–2. King Ahasuerus of Persia throws a party to display "the great wealth of his kingdom and the splendor and pomp of his majesty" (1:3). After six months of partying, "when the king was merry with wine" (1:10), he orders his eunuchs to bring his queen, Vashti, before the king, "wearing the royal crown, in order to show the peoples and the officials her beauty; for she was fair to behold" (1:11). Vashti, however, refuses to follow orders, and after some considerations among the leaders of the country it is decided to ban her from ever showing herself at the court again. Now, what to do when—after some time—the king misses a queen? The advice is to gather all the beautiful young virgins in the country to the harem, give them a cosmetic treatment, and let the girl who pleases the king be queen instead of Vashti (2:3-4). Among the beautiful young virgins is also Esther, the orphaned Judean girl whose guardian, Mordecai, happens to be a court official.

---

4. On the various types of intertextual analysis, see, representatively, Ellen van Wolde, "Texts in Dialogue with Texts: Intertextuality in the Ruth and Tamar Narratives," *BI* 5 (1997): 1–28.

Esther is taken to the harem, given the mandatory twelve-months beauty treatment, and "the king loved Esther more than all the other women; of all the virgins she won his favor and devotion, so that he set the royal crown on her head and made her queen instead of Vashti" (2:17). The drama can begin.

3. *Exscribing the Queen*

The frame narrative in *Arabian Nights* presents the background for the ingenious Shahrazad's storytelling. In the old days in the islands of India and China the Sasanian king Shahriyar invites his younger brother, Shah Zaman, to visit him. On his way, however,

> …at midnight he thought of something that he had forgotten and went back to the palace. When he entered his room, it was to discover his wife in bed with a black slave. The world turned dark for him and he said to himself: "If this is what happens before I have even left the city, what will this damned woman do if I spend time away with my brother?" So he drew his sword and struck, killing both his wife and her lover as they lay together, before going back and ordering his escort to move off.[5]

Arriving at his brother's palace and being in a very bad mood, Shah Zaman stays behind from his brother Shahriyar's hunting party, and he secretly witnesses how Shahriyar's queen and her slave girls entertain themselves erotically with male slaves in the palace garden, believing both brothers to be away. When Shahriyar returns from hunting, Shah Zaman of course informs him about the queen's shenanigans, and the two kings plan another surveillance of the queen and her girls, with the expected outcome, the disclosure of the women's misbehavior. Consequently, the two kings leave the kingdom, but after having met yet another poor male, this time a *jinni*, who is cuckolded even worse, they return to Shahriyar's city, "where they entered the palace and cut off the heads of the queen, the slave girls and the slaves. Every night for the next three years, Shahriyar would take a virgin, deflower her and then kill her," the narrative continues.[6] But in the end, the king is presented to the beautiful Sharazad, the elder shrewd daughter of the king's vizier. Allegedly in order to protect

---

5. Malcolm C. Lyons, *Arabian Nights: Tales of 1001 Nights*, Vol. 1, trans. Malcolm C. Lyons, with Ursula Lyons, introduced and annotated by Robert Irwin (London/New York: Penguin, 2008), 3.

6. Ibid., 7.

her father from the king's anger, she insists on marrying the king, knowing full well that it might cost her her life,[7] and through her storytelling she puts an end to the misery.

A parallel motif is staged in Esther 1–2. Here, Vashti holds the part of the unfaithful queen whose misdemeanor is to be disobedient, that is, not to fulfill her queenly duties to the king. Consequently, she is banished from the court and literally disappears from the narrative (Est. 1). In *Arabian Nights* the queen's misbehavior is much graver, of course, since she transgresses the boundaries of marital sexual fidelity. But both offences are against the implied codex of male honor, and thus comparable from an intertextual point of view. What we find, then, is a common motif of removing the queen from the narrative, modestly in Esther, since Vashti allegedly stays alive, and far more dramatically in *Arabian Nights*. Both Vashti and Shahriyar's first—nameless—wife are exscribed from the narrative, so to speak. The function of the exscription is dual: to inspire and substantiate the king's misogyny and to make room for the introduction of a new queen who will then be the main female protagonist, Shahrazad, the teller of the *Tales of 1001 Nights*, and Esther.[8]

Both women know that their interference might cost them their lives. In the case of Shahrazad, the motif is connected to the king's disposition of the "used" virgins. Shahrazad says to her father: "Father, marry me to this man. Either I shall live or else I shall be a ransom for the children of the Muslims and save them from him."[9] This motif mirrors Esther's legitimate concerns for her life in Esther 4, but in the end, the two queens reach the same goal, to save their people from the whimsicality of the king—Shahrazad "the Muslims," Esther the Judeans.

Moreover, there is a common interest in the opulence of the royal household in *Arabian Nights* and Esther, aptly emphasized in Esther, implied in *Arabian Nights* through the reference to forgotten jewels, lush palace gardens, and black slaves and slave girls. As pointed out by Adele Berlin, the detailed description of the opulent Persian court and its parties in Esther is atypical of biblical narrative, apart from late biblical and apocryphal literature from the Persian and Greek periods.[10] In Esther this interest can be understood as fascination with the luxury of the Persian

---

7. Ibid.
8. On the concept of exscription and its implications, see Beal, *Book of Hiding*, 25, and Chapter 3 above.
9. Lyons, trans., *Arabian Nights*, 5.
10. Berlin, *Esther*, 4

court, probably also mirroring the view of contemporary Greek literature on Persians—and the Persian court in particular—as "indulgent, decadent, and effeminate."[11]

Last but not least, the motif of the gathering of the virgins from all over the country is structurally identical in *Arabian Nights* and the book of Esther, even if in Esther there is no whiff of killing the virgins after their night with the king; in the biblical narrative the castoff virgins are simply collected in another harem, implicitly precluded from marriage with any other man, and thus so-to-speak dead from the world. Again, we can identify a transformation or parallel shift—and aggravation—of a motif in the later narrative of Arabian Nights.[12]

Consequently, the *ex*scription of Vashti and the subsequent *in*scription of Esther are not only preparation for the story to follow as discussed in Chapter 3, above, but also an important narrative motif, known and used for centuries. As an introduction to the narrative, it serves to add emphasis to the young woman who is supposed to be the leading lady of the story. We shall return to this motif below.

4. *Preparing the Bride*

Another thought-provoking aspect in Esther, the thorough and very lengthy preparation of the virgins before they are taken to Ahasuerus, is not present in the frame narrative of *Arabian Nights*. This, however, is a well-known motif, especially in modern erotic literature. The most famous—and academically acceptable—example is the French novel *Histoire d'O*, the *Story of O*, by the pseudonymous author Pauline Réage. This novel is generally associated with the sado-masochistic humiliations of the protagonist, the woman O, but it is opened with an extended description of how O is prepared for her ordeal.[13]

---

11. Ibid., xxvii–xxvii.

12. An interesting transformation of the motif, which mediates killing the virgins/ disposing of them in the harem, can be identified in the European fairy tale *Bluebeard*, in which a very rich man kills his unfaithful wives, one by one, and is only stopped by the cunning and courage of his last wife.

13. *Histoire d'O* was published in 1954 under the pseudonym Pauline Réage and was for a long time supposed to be written by the French writer, literary critic, and publisher Jean Paulhan (1884–1968). Now, the novel is known to have been written by the French journalist and author Anne Desclos (1907–1998), also known as Dominique Aury, who for many years was Paulhan's lover.

Analysis of these intertextual associations leads methodologically in two different directions which shall be followed separately in the following. The first is the analytical concept of "the male gaze," the second the concept of *rite-de-passage* and liminality, originally identified by Arnold van Gennep and Victor Turner.

4.1. *The Male Gaze*

The male gaze as a scholarly concept was introduced in 1975 in a famous article by the American cinematologist Laura Mulvey, "Visual Pleasure and Narrative Cinema."[14] Against the backdrop of a classical, Freudian psychoanalytical approach, Mulvey defined "Woman as Image, Man as Bearer of the Look":

> In a world ordered by sexual imbalance, pleasure in looking has been split between active/male and passive/female. The determining male gaze projects its phantasy on to the female figure which is styled accordingly. In their traditional exhibitionist role women are simultaneously looked at and displayed, with their appearance coded for strong visual and erotic impact so that they can be said to connote *to-be-looked-at-ness.*[15]

Mulvey analyses two classical Hollywood movies, *Only Angels Have Wings* from 1939 with Cary Grant and Jean Arthur, and *To Have and Have Not* from 1944 with Humphrey Bogart and Lauren Bacall in the leading roles. She writes about the female protagonist—not without a certain foreshadowing for the present study:

> She is isolated, glamorous, on display, sexualised. But as the narrative progresses she falls in love with the main male protagonist and becomes his property, losing her outward glamorous characteristics, her generalized sexuality, her show-girl connotations; her eroticism is subjected to the male star alone. By means of identification with him, through participation in his power, the spectator can indirectly possess her too.[16]

Mulvey's concept, the male gaze, became instrumental in the following decades, presumably because it was very easy to follow, not only in literature but also as experienced on an everyday basis, as in the influential

---

14. Laura Mulvey, "Visual Pleasure and Narrative Cinema," *Screen* 16 (1975): 6–18.
15. Ibid., 11.
16. Ibid., 13.

BBC television series *Ways of Seeing* from 1972.[17] A couple of remarks in the ensuing volume to this series are suggestive in our connection; in the introduction to Chapter 3 the author writes:

> According to usage and conventions which are at the last being questioned but have by no means been overcome, the social presence of a woman is different in kind from that of a man. A man's presence is dependent upon the promise of power which he embodies...
>
> By contrast, at woman's presence expresses her own attitude to herself, and defines what can and cannot be done to her... To be born a woman has been to be born within an allotted and confined space, into the keeping of men. A woman must continually watch herself. She is almost continually accompanied by her own image of herself.[18]

This is followed by a passage on surveillance of women by both men and women, and the paragraph ends:

> One might simplify this by saying: *men act* and *women appear.* Men look at women. Women watch themselves being looked at. This determines not only most relations between men and women but also the relation of women to themselves. The surveyor of woman in herself is male: the surveyed female. Thus she turns herself into an object—and most particularly an object of vision: a sight.[19]

The concept of the male gaze, of course, was introduced in feminist exegesis as well. Jennifer A. Glancy's remarks may serve as an example:

> Feminist scholars widely concur that gender is typically configured both in written texts and now in film in terms of subject–object relations, in which masculinity is associated with subjectivity and femininity with objectivity. In particular, man is conventionally represented as the subject of the gaze, and woman as the object of the gaze. To see is to control; to have one's vision represented is to have one's perception of the world ratified. To be seen is to be subject to control; to represent women solely as objects of others' vision denies women their subjectivity. A danger inherent in the definition of femininity as "to-be-looked-at-ness" is that while female characters are thereby denied subjectivity, they are simultaneously held responsible for exciting the desire of male viewers.[20]

---

17. Here, I refer to the volume that accompanied the series, John Berger, *Ways of Seeing: Based on the BBC Television Series with John Berger* (London: BBC and Penguin Books, 1972).
18. Ibid., 45–6.
19. Ibid., 47.
20. Jennifer A. Glancy, "The Accused: Susanne and her Readers," in Brenner, ed., *A Feminist Companion to Esther*, 288–302 (290). A partial list of relevant scholarship

Mulvey's rather robust understanding has been criticized, appropriately in my opinion, by later feminist scholars. Especially her Freudian psychoanalysis,[21] based on the classical concepts of phallocentrism, penis envy, and castration anxiety is *überholt* and one-dimensional. As candidly formulated in 2002 by the feminist cinematologist Linda Williams: "It *had* become boring and repetitious to see all the sensationalism of cinema motivated by castration anxiety."[22] But even if the Freudian approach to the phenomenon of the male gaze does not stand for a closer examination, its mere existence cannot be denied. The concept of the male gaze as an *only* analytical tool must be discussed, of course, but as an inspiration for textual awareness it proves to be efficient. So, let us apply the concept of looking to our texts:

In the book of Esther, the phrase *kî-ṭôbat mar'eh hî* ("for she was good to look at"[23]) is used four times in Esther 1–2, once about Queen Vashti, twice about the virgins, and once about Esther.[24] The gaze thus is a recurrent motif in these chapters. In the case of Vashti, whom the king wants to display for his guests in the same way as he displays his wealth and power (1:10), what triggers the narrative crisis is exactly that Vashti refuses to be looked at. Timothy Beal puts his finger right on the spot when he writes:

> Within the sexual political order, beauty and pleasure are associated with objectification—to be one of the objects by which the subject secures power publicly. Insofar as objectification is associated with presentability, moreover, the integration of proximity/distance and pleasing/displeasing as codes for locating ostensible power becomes particularly important. For Vashti in particular, to be pleasing will mean to remain accessible and presentable as object for the pleased male ogle.[25]

---

in Glancy's article includes: Mulvey, "Visual Pleasure and Narrative Cinema"; M. A. Doane, *The Desire to Desire: The Women's Film of the 1940s* (Bloomington: Indiana University Press, 1984); idem, *Technologies of Gender: Essays on Theory, Film and Fiction* (Bloomington: Indiana University Press, 1987).

21. Mulvey, "Visual Pleasure and Narrative Cinema," 6–8.
22. Linda Williams, "Why I Did Not Want to Write This Essay," *Signs: Journal of Women in Culture and Society* 30 (2004): 1264–71 (1268). See further Corinn Columpar, "The Gaze as Theoretical Touchstone: The Intersection of Film Studies, Feminist Theory, and Postcolonial Theory," *Women's Studies Quarterly* 30 (2002): 25–44 (31–3).
23. My translation; NRSV: "For she was fair to behold."
24. Est. 1:11; 2:2-3, 7.
25. Beal, *Book of Hiding*, 19.

As a direct consequence of her disobedience, her refusal of being looked at, Vashti is expelled from the royal palace. Beal understands her refusal as pointing to a relative ambivalence in the balance of power between genders at the Persian court. From a narrative perspective, Vashti's party for the women in the king's house is a parallel to the king's party, and this makes her an acting subject, however fleetingly (cf. Glancy's remarks above). Following Beal, then, one could speculate that Vashti's refusal turns the absent (but called for) Vashti into a most present (but bodily absent) threat to the king's power, a threat which is instantly understood by his advisors (1:16-18; cf. 1:22); consequently, they advise the king to make her permanently *un-present*, or—with Beal—making her an *abject:* "she can be neither subject nor object within the social and symbolic order, and therefore she must be repulsed, pushed outside its boundaries."[26] Beal continues:

> She was more than an object. Within the world of the narrative, then, the king's demand that she be brought into his presence and be the good-looking object of the male ogle aimed to settle and reduce that ambivalence and excess once and for all—to pin things down, and thereby to secure the king's own identity. Refusing to come and be looked at, thereby rejecting the status of fixed object (perhaps finding it objectionable, as Targum Sheni suggests), and being refused the status of full subject, she must be banished, abjected.[27]

Vashti's becoming un-seen/in-visible, absent and abject prepares the way for Esther to be visible, present, a newfound object for the king's sexual needs. In the text, Esther is seen, too: "The girl was beautiful in form and fair to behold" (2:7); "and she found grace from everyone who looked at her" (2:15, my translation). Moreover, the narrative style used in Esther 2 leads the audience to *see* what is going on; the language is sensual and creates images. As secret spectators, the audience is taken all the way through Esther's and the other virgins' preparations for the narrative's presumed pivot of their life, the night with the king. The communicator to the audience of the gaze is Hegai, the eunuch, who especially points to Esther as the main character (2:9). This main character, however, is still described as an object, not only for the king, but also for her cousin

---

26. Ibid., 24.
27. Ibid., 24 with n. 10 (p. 127): "It is intriguing that some rabbinic tradition understood her refusal to be due to the fact that 'leprosy had broken out on her' (noted in Rashi's commentary on 1:12 [in Schwartz and Schwartz 1983])." Beal refers to Avraham Schwartz and Yisroel Schwartz, *The Megillot and Rashi's Commentary with Linear Translation: Esther, Song of Songs, Ruth* (Jerusalem: Feldheim, 1983).

and guardian Mordecai's machinations. She is seen as an object, not as a subject as a Judean woman, for on Mordecai's demand she hides her Jewishness.

The frame narrative of *Arabian Nights* also draws on the concept of looking. The description in the frame narrative of the erotic activity of the queen and her company in the palace gardens has the king's younger brother, King Shah Zaman, as the voyeur through whose eyes the audience see the intimate details which are in no way concealed:[28]

> In the royal palace there were windows that overlooked Shahriyar's garden, and as Shah Zaman was looking, a door opened and out came twenty slave girls and twenty slaves, in the middle of whom was Shariyar's very beautiful wife. They came to a fountain where they took off their clothes and the women sat with the men. "Mas'ud," the queen called, at which a black slave came up to her and, after they had embraced each other, he lay with her, while the other slaves lay with the slave girls and they spent their time kissing, embracing, fornicating and drinking wine until the end of the day.[29]

Later, the two brothers watch the queen and the slave girl's action with the slaves "as Shah Zaman had described."[30]

The (male?) gaze also governs the introduction to *Story of O*,[31] where the female protagonist is taken by her lover to a big house, Roissy, outside Paris, which serves as domicile for a group of male masters. At Roissy, the woman O is placed naked in the care of "two young and beautiful women dressed in the garb of pretty eighteenth-century chambermaids."[32] They give her a thorough beauty treatment in front of a wall "covered from floor to ceiling with a large mirror, which was unbroken by any shelving," and in which "she could see herself, thus open, each time her gaze strayed to the mirror."[33] After the treatment "she was led into a room where a three-sided mirror, and another mirror behind, enabled her to examine herself closely."[34] The focus on the gaze, O's direct gaze and the

---

28. This was the reason why Payne's 1901 Victorian London edition of *Arabian Nights* from the outset was "Printed For Subscribers Only."
29. Lyons, trans., *Arabian Nights*, 4.
30. Ibid., 5. The scene is accentuated by the detailed, double description of what the two brothers saw. Note that a little later in the frame narrative, the beautiful woman, stolen on her wedding night, who cheats on her abductor, the *jinni*, is beautifully described in a poem, full of light metaphors (ibid.).
31. And the whole book at that!
32. Réage, *Story of O*, 6.
33. Ibid., 7.
34. Ibid.

reader's indirect, is obvious. Later, the more developed sado-masochistic parts of the novel focus on how O is shown to the men who use/abuse her. One of the rules of the house is that men can look at women, while women are ordered to keep their eyes to the ground, so that they cannot see the men—or rather: they cannot see the men's faces, only their exposed genitals.

Although it is much less a general rule than the author meant it to be, in the case of all these examples the BBC producer John Berger was right when he stated in his 1972 TV series, *Ways of Seeing*, that

> Men look at women. Women watch themselves being looked at. This determines not only most relations between men and women but also the relation of women to themselves. The surveyor of woman in herself is male: the surveyed female. Thus she turns herself into an object—and most particularly an object of vision: a sight.[35]

Thus, as stressed by Mulvey, the male gaze directs the implied audience's attention to the (lack of) power balance between men and women in these narratives. What the three, agreed, very different narratives hold in common is a focus on sexuality, conveyed through the focus of the male gaze. What can be obtained through this initial search for intertextual markers or motifs is the sharpening of the reader's focus on the importance of sexuality and seduction in the biblical text.[36]

4.2. *Initiation*

These observations lead to the next point of our investigation, the reading of Esther 2 and *Story of O* as descriptions of initiation rites. The anthropological concept of initiation rite is well known, also in biblical studies, as one of the rites-of-passage.[37] In the initiation rite a person, the so-

---

35. Berger, *Ways of Seeing*, 45–7; interestingly, Mulvey does not refer to Berger. A few years ago, a talkshow, "Blachmann," was presented on Danish public service television. Here, the host, a TV celebrity known from a talent show, and an invited male guest, while sitting comfortably in a sofa, discussed the aesthetics and sexual attractiveness of a naked woman, who stood in front of them. Other subjects were gender roles, the "new male," age, and the hosts' innermost feelings about themselves *vis-à-vis* women. The women, who had all agreed to participate, were primarily treated as objects of art, being spoken about, but almost never spoken to.

36. Other biblical and post-biblical narratives of the sexuality of the male gaze are the stories about David and Bathsheba (2 Sam. 11) and Susanna and the voyeuristic elders (Additions to Daniel A).

37. See Victor W. Turner, *Forest of Symbols: Aspects of Ndembu Ritual* (Ithaca: Cornell University Press, 1967), 93–111.

called *neophyte*, is transformed from one state in life through a liminal situation into another state. Briefly put, the liminal situation is defined as a situation at the boundary between two states of life as the preparation for a new status, where everything is totally different from the person's current status. This, of course, is most characteristic for "relatively stable and cyclical societies, where change is bound up with biological and meteorological rhythms and recurrences"[38] Here, however, I will use it in a broader understanding as a description of a situation in which the subject is placed between two stable positions, in an "innerstructural situation."[39] In Victor Turner's famous phrasing, the subject is "betwixt and between."[40]

According to Van Gennep and Turner, rites of transition "are marked by three phases: separation, margin (or *limen*), and aggregation,"[41] through which the subject is detached from her/his social group or status, going through a period in which the state of the subject is ambiguous,[42] to a new state of stability with "rights and obligations of a clearly defined and 'structural' type."[43] Moreover, due to their state as "non-persons," their role as a *neophytes* is described as passive, as being an object for a liminal treatment conducted by others, not as a self-relying subject. In my view, these definitions compare exactly to our two narrative women, Esther and O.

Both O and Esther are described as extremely passive. In both cases, the young woman is taken from one status to another through a liminal period. O is taken to a house, Roissy, outside Paris where she is to be turned into an object for the masters' lust.[44] In the case of Esther, the verb

38. Turner, *Forest of Symbols*, 93.

39. Ibid. This broader use of the concept is in accordance with Van Gennep's and Turner's taxonomy; see, e.g., *Forest of Symbols*, 95: "They [rites of passage] also concern entry into a new achieved status, whether this be a political office or membership of an exclusive club or secret society. They may admit persons into membership of a religious cult where such a group does not include the whole society, or qualify them for the official duties of the cult, sometimes in a graded series of rites."

40. Ibid., 93.

41. Ibid., 94.

42. The subject "passes through a realm that has few or none of the attributes of the past or coming state" (ibid.).

43. Ibid.

44. "If you hesitate about going in, they'll come and take you in. If you don't obey immediately, they'll force you to. Your bag? No, you have no further need for your bag. You're merely the girl I'm furnishing. Yes, of course I'll be there. Now run along" (Réage, *Story of O*, 5).

to take (*lāqaḥ*) is used twice in the chapter, both times in the passive, *she was taken*;[45] thus, through this being taken Esther changes from the status of an unknown, Judean, orphaned virgin to a chosen, "non-Judean," married woman.[46] In Est. 2:7 she is presented as belonging to Mordecai and as beautiful and lovely to see (cf. above), and she carries the Judean name Hadassah, Myrtle. She is then taken from this status and given—or rather taken—to the royal palace and put under surveillance of Hegai, the guardian of women. When she distinguishes herself in his eyes by her beauty, she is *taken* to "the best place in the harem" (Est. 2:9).

Both women are under surveillance by a male domestic slave, Esther by Hegai the eunuch (Est. 2:9), O by Pierre, the servant. Furthermore, Esther like O is monitored by her former guardian. In the case of O, René, her lover, pays her special attention during her first meeting with the masters of the house; in Esther we read: "Every day [for 12 months!] Mordecai would walk around in front of the court of the harem, to learn how Esther was and how she fared" (Est. 2:11). This is part of the "interstructural character" of the liminal. Here a social structure exists in which the relationship between the neophyte and the instructor (master/guide) is one of absolute obedience, while the relationship between the neophytes is characterized by equality.[47]

To sum up, Esther is taken twice from her original status and put into a liminal space, the room where the women receive the cosmetic treatment which shall make them ready (or: worthy) to take a new position as queen. Thus, liminality is coined *spatially* in her residence in the harem, *temporally* in the emphasis on the 12 months of cosmetic treatment as a preparation for the night with the king, which must be seen as the ultimate test at the end of the liminal period.[48] After that, the young women/Esther will be transformed from innocent virgin and be assigned two possible statuses, either as a rejected concubine or as queen.

O is taken to her private room, a special room with a very special, extravagant furnishing where she passively is treated by others for *a very long time* and from where she is taken to the room of her intended status as

---

45. Est. 2:8, 16. For *lāqaḥ* in connection with Esther, see also 2:7: *ûbᵉmôt 'abîhā wᵉ'immā lᵉqāḥā mordŏkāy lô lᵉbat*, "and when her father and her mother died, Mordecai had taken her as his own daughter"; 2:15: *mordŏkāy 'ăšer lāqaḥ-lô lᵉbat*, "Mordecai who had taken her as his own daughter" (my translations).

46. Cf. Turner's concept of state as a "stable or recurrent condition that is culturally recognized" (Turner, *Forest of Symbols*, 94).

47. Cf. Ibid., 99.

48. The longevity of the beauty treatment also intimates the exorbitant exaggerations, as in the description of the king's party in Est. 1.

object for her master's lust. Here, then, the spatial and the temporal codes are represented, as well. Common to the protagonists, moreover, is that they share the place of their liminal treatment with other—anonymous—women who might be their rivals but who, from a narratological point of view, function as the backdrop for the selection of the chosen objects, Esther and O.[49]

During the liminal period, the subject/object in Turner's words is "structurally, if not physically, 'invisible.'"[50] Does this compare to the focus on the male gaze stressed above? Actually it does, since the women are both segregated from the society, to which they used to belong, and—as shown above—placed in confined spaces to which only other *neophytes* and the guards, both slaves and masters, have access. Thus, the women are at the same time visible and invisible, seen and unseen.

4.3. *The Perfume*

The cosmetic treatments *per se* administered to Esther and O are interesting as a semantic code of liminality. In the case of Esther, she and the other virgins are treated under the regulations of women with "oil of myrrh and with perfumes and cosmetics" (Est. 2:12). O is also prepared,

> her eyelids pencilled lightly; her lips bright red; the tip and halo of her breasts highlighted with pink; the edges of her nether lips rouged; her armpits and pubis generously perfumed, and perfume also applied to the furrow between her thighs, the furrow beneath her breasts, and to the hollows of her hands.[51]

As before, the description in Esther is more modest and simpler than that of the intertextual parallel, *Story of O*. Nevertheless, the connection is viable and the intention of the perfuming obvious to the reader. In both cases, the aromatic code—the perfumes—disconnects the subjects from their previous status and transforms them to their new status as sexual objects.[52]

Apart from what can be substantiated from common everyday experience and habit, such as adding perfume before going on a date or to a party, the effect of aromatics as affiliated and leading to eroticism is duly

---

49. Cf. Turner about social equality among the initiands; see Turner, *Forest of Symbols*, 99.
50. Ibid., 95.
51. Réage, *Story of O*, 7.
52. The passage is also marked by change of clothes; for the vestimentary code, see Chapter 5 below.

corroborated in the Hebrew Bible as well as in classic Greek mythology. In his epoch-making volume *Les jardins d'Adonis* from 1972,[53] the French structuralist historian and specialist in Ancient Greece Marcel Detienne analyzes the importance of spices, including aromatics, as a way of understanding Greek mythology. "Spices are employed," Detienne contends, "in the ritual making of smoke and in sacrifices; but they are not used for these religious ends alone. In the form of ointments, perfumes and other cosmetic products they also have an erotic function."[54] Moreover, this eroticism has to do with seduction, not primarily with marriage. Detienne refers to the moralistic tradition of Plato, according to whom "the scent given off by perfumes at banquets and the seductive attraction of ointments rubbed on to limbs represent a kind of life given over to the delights and pleasures of the senses."[55]

In the Hebrew Bible, the erotic quality of aromatics, herbs and ointments is duly exemplified in the Song of Songs. In ch. 4, the beloved young woman is metaphorically described in the images of an abundant garden, of delicate fruit, and of aromatics,

> henna with nard,
> nard and saffron,
> calamus and cinnamon,
> with all trees of frankincense, myrrh and aloes,
> with all chief spices
> …Awake, O north wind, and come, O south wind!
> Blow upon my garden that its fragrance may be wafted abroad.
> Let my beloved come to his garden,
> and eat its choicest fruits.[56]

The Danish Old Testament scholar Hans J. Lundager Jensen has demonstrated how the code of aromatics, as one among several, facilitates the

---

53. The references are to the English translation: Marcel Detienne, *The Gardens of Adonis*, with an introduction by J.-P. Vernant, trans. Janet Lloyd (Princeton: Princeton University Press, 1994).

54. Ibid., 60.

55. Ibid., 62. The quote continues: "The very evocation of spices is, by itself, enough to conjure up a succession of images of luxury and sensuality—flowing dresses, exquisite dishes of relishes and sweetmeals, wreaths of flowers, courtesans and women of pleasure—in sum, all the refinements of life lived in the Persian manner, at least as the Greeks imagined it."

56. Song 4:13–14:16. A detailed analysis of the general coded language in the Song of Songs is presented by Hans J. Lundager Jensen, *Den fortærende Ild: Strukturelle analyser af narrative og rituelle tekster i Det Gamle Testamente* (Aarhus: Aarhus University, 2000), 192–7, 311–12.

separation of the young couple in Song of Songs from everyday life and responsibilities, work, marriage, time, pregnancy, childbirth, and parenting, all in all locating them, separated from "reality," in a phantasmatic space. This separation places the young lovers in a time warp "between childhood and adulthood, in a place where sexuality is present without sociality having closed itself around the person and having allocated the genders in their roles, the male in the field, the woman in the house."[57]

Excursus: Made-up Jezebel

Another, but this time unfavorable, example of the intertwining of make-up and sex is the Israelite queen-mother Jezebel (2 Kgs 21:30-37). When the conspirer Jehu comes to the capital Jezreel after having killed the king, Jezebel's son Joram, "she painted her eyes, and adorned her head, and looked out of the window," saying teasingly to Jehu: "Is it peace, Zimri, murderer of your master?" Jehu orders two of her eunuchs to throw her out of the window: "some of the blood spattered on the wall and on the horses, which trampled on her." Later, her body has dissipated, and this is understood as the fulfilment of the word of the Lord as spoken by the prophet Elijah: "In the territory of Jezreel the dogs shall eat the flesh of Jezebel; the corpse of Jezebel shall be like dung on the field in the territory of Jezreel, so that no one can say, This is Jezebel" (2 Kgs 9:36-37, cf. 1 Kgs 21:23). The reference to Elijah underscores the wickedness of the originally Phoenician queen (1 Kgs 16:31), who is blamed for seducing King Ahab to "go after idols," especially in the narrative of the battle between Elijah and the Ba'al prophets at Mount Carmel (1 Kgs 18:16-46).

In the text, Jezebel's make-up and her seductive wickedness are apparently two sides of the same bad coin. Cheryl Exum, however, states that Jezebel "met her death with characteristic audacity: she painted her eyes, adorned her head, and greeted Jehu from her window with a caustic insult."[58] Claudia V. Camp describes the presentation of Jezebel as a leader with remarkable strength, which "can also explain her final appearance at the window, painted and bedecked. If she is to have any hope at all at rallying people behind her, she must appear in all the glory of her queenship."[59]

---

57. Ibid., 194 (my translation). Jensen does not refer to Turner or Van Gennep here, but the theory of liminality is clearly operative. Note that Turner is present in the vast bibliography of this comprehensive Danish doctoral thesis.

58. J. Cheryl Exum, "Jezebel," in *Harper's Bible Dictionary*, ed. P. J. Achtemeier (San Francisco: Harper & Row, 1985), 489.

59. Claudia V. Camp, "1 and 2 Kings," in *The Women's Bible Commentary*, ed. Carol A. Newsom and Sharon H. Ringe (Louisville: Westminster, 1992), 96–109

Thus, like the young lovers in Song of Songs, Esther and O are separated from the living conditions of ordinary women, in a liminal space, from which they are taken into the phantasmatic room of absolute, eternal, and unlimited sexuality, while the young lovers are expected to return to a reality as adults beyond the time warp, the liminal experience of honeymooning.[60] O stays in this erotic confinement, even after she has been returned by her lover to her apparent everyday life as a photographer in Paris;[61] Esther, on the other hand, leaves liminality and becomes the Queen of Persia. From this position she disappears for a time from the narrative, however, and is given her role as a "mole" or "sleeping agent" for Mordecai, only to be re-activated in the exchange of gifts and demands between Esther and Mordecai in Esther 4.[62]

The coding of Esther and O through excessive use of aromatics, "oil of myrrh, perfumes and cosmetics," adds to the fairy tale atmosphere of the narrative and takes the reader out of his/her everyday world to a place where anything exotic and erotic might happen. His/her senses are awakened and thus his/her preparedness for listening to the main plot of the narrative, the conspiracy against the Judeans.

5. Conclusion

Let us sum up the outcome of this analysis. First, the reader's attention is turned to the description of Esther as a passive object. Only after the first turning point of the narrative, the dialogue between Esther and Mordecai in Esther 4, is she awakened from her status as "sleeping agent" or "mole" at the Persian court. In Esther 5, she can use her beauty as a means for her enterprise, the withdrawal of Haman's decree against the Judeans. The analysis also turns the reader's attention to the incontestably erotic twist

---

(103–4). On the generally negative understanding of Jezebel in exegesis, see Tina Pippin, "Jezebel Revamped," in *A Feminist Companion to Samuel and Kings*, ed. Athalya Brenner, FCB 9 (Sheffield: Sheffield Academic, 1994), 196–206.

60. Cf. Jensen, *Den fortærende Ild*, 186–92.

61. Phantasmatic, or at least unrealistic living conditions, labeled "separate utopias" by Linda Williams, are characteristic of hard-core pornography; cf. Linda Williams, *Hard Core: Power, Pleasure, and the Frenzy of the Visible* (Berkeley: University of California Press, 1989), 160.

62. In the case of the young wife in the fairy tale *Bluebeard*, liminality and seclusion in the house are intimated by the husband leaving home (cf. the kings in *Arabian Nights*), which allows her to cross the borders of obedience. In Esther, change of status is also indicated through change of clothing (the vestimentary code); I shall return to this theme in Chapter 5 below.

of the narrative which makes it entertaining and attractive, although it is neither as explicitly erotic as the later *Arabian Nights*, where no titillating details are withheld, nor as explicitly pornographic as *Story of O*. Yet the book of Ester does use narrative motifs that it has in common with erotica/ pornography. This, however, in no way makes the book of Esther pornography. What the present analysis has offered is a complementary reading which opens up complementary aspects of the book of Esther.

I do not claim that the author(s) and redactors of the book of Esther wittingly used the sado-masochistic subtext in the erotic material to trigger the attention of the audience; I believe that they would be both surprised and offended if presented with the idea. But the convergence of the themes is present and should not be overlooked. Does this have any significance in a gender-oriented context? The book of Esther is yet another example of fixed gender-roles being used in a biblical story as an unconscious premise for the communication of an important message. It might offend readers of Esther who demand the Bible to be "moral literature" (to quote Timothy Beal), be it for religious or for gender-hermeneutical reasons.[63] In my opinion, however, there is no reason to be offended. The average present-day reader outside a few, narrowly faith-based circles—at least in a northern European context—does not read the biblical narrative of Esther as particularly authoritative; rather, it is understood as a good and entertaining narrative.[64] He/she might be surprised, rather than offended, by the openly erotic ambience of the book, since he/she would expect the Bible to be less human, more faith-oriented.

If someone is on the look out for offensiveness in Esther, he/she should rather turn to the butchering of the 75,311 innocent Persians. There, at least, a deliberately offensive ideology is at work.

---

63. Beal mentions such voices as, on the one hand, The Christian Coalition movement, which "claims the Christian Bible as the sole univocal guarantee for the social order," and, on the other hand, "on the political and religious left, in feminist and gender studies in Esther." See further Beal, *Book of Hiding*, 40–9.

64. Cf. Else K. Holt, "'The Stain of Your Guilt is Still Before Me' (Jer 2:22): (Feminist) Approaches to Jeremiah 2 and the Problem of Normativity," in *Prophecy and Power: Jeremiah in Feminist and Postcolonial Perspective*, ed. Carolyn J. Sharp and Christl Maier (London: Bloomsbury T&T Clark, 2013), 101–16.

Chapter 5

Dressing Up Esther: The Function of Clothes in the Esther Narrative

1. *Introduction*

In his fairy tale, *The Emperor's New Clothes*, Hans Christian Andersen tells the story of the vain and stupid emperor who is fooled by swindlers. Two fake weavers persuade him to invest a fortune in invisible clothes that purportedly will help him know who among his people is a fool and unfit for his post. Those who cannot see the emperor's new clothes are such people, the weavers say. They weave and cut and sow the imaginative clothes, the emperor and his officials laud them highly, and the emperor walks in a procession through the city, greeted by his people, for nobody wants to confess that he cannot see the clothes. Until a little child says, "But he hasn't got anything on." First whispering, then crying out loud, the townspeople repeat the child's word,

> And the Emperor shivered, for he suspected they were right. But he thought, "This procession has got to go on." So he walked more proudly than ever, as his noblemen held high the train that wasn't there at all.

Andersen uses the emperor's clothes to disclose the foolishness of vanity and pride, individual and collective, and since an emperor's clothes are by definition a public affair, Andersen's choice of symbolic vehicle is a wise and in no way arbitrary choice. Clothes are an easily understood symbol of status, rank, and gender and thus an effective vehicle of communication.[1] Professional uniforms are a good example. The policeman's uniform

---

1. This of course requires that the persons involved share the knowledge of the cultural context. If you do not know what an emperor is or that an emperor has access to power, money and ceremonial clothes, you will not understand H. C. Andersen's

with its traditionally mono-coloring and symbols of the societal monopoly of violence, baton and often even firearms;[2] the nurse's white and easily washable clothes; the builder's practical clothes and safety boots; the minister's robe in catholic, orthodox and many mainstream protestant churches: all of them signal a special role that removes the person wearing them from their private sphere and into the public space. When the police officer, the nurse, the builder, or the minister changes his/her clothes, he/she also changes status and becomes—or at least signals that he/she wants to be perceived as—a private individual. As pinpointed by Susan B. Kaiser: "During the course of social interactions, clothes serve two primary functions with regard to communication: (1) the negotiation of identities and (2) the definition of situations."[3]

Therefore, it is no surprise that clothes and the change of clothes play a vital role as a semantic marker of importance in some of the significant scenes in the book of Esther, a "vestimentary code" pointing to a main character or conflict. It will also be evident that clothes are intimately connected to the semantic field of social honor, shame and disgrace as indicated by Jan Dietrich and others.[4] In the following, we shall read these

---

parable. In the words of Susan B. Kaiser: "[C]lothes provide cues toward which individuals can make indications allowing them to negotiate their identities or to fit their lines of action together in a manner that allows them to understand one another's identities in a given situation. Identity negotiation allows for interaction to proceed more smoothly" (Susan B. Kaiser, "Toward a Contextual Social Psychology of Clothing: A Synthesis of Symbolic Interactionist and Cognitive Theoretical Perspectives," *Clothing and Textile Research Journal* 2 [1983–84]: 1–8 [2]).

2. The American police officer's belt, with its many attached objects, is an especially impressive example of public display of the right to use violence on anyone who transgresses the law.

3. Kaiser, ibid. Cf. Ruth P. Rubinstein: "Exercising authority, wielding power, differentiating the sexes, and arousing sexual interest are all facilitated by the employment of categories of clothing signs" (Ruth P. Rubinstein, *Dress Codes: Meanings and Messages in American Cultures* [Boulder: Westview, 1995], 8).

4. "Honor, shame and disgrace of the body…always materialize as honor, shame, and disgrace of the *social* body: while they constitute themselves through the reputation [German: *Ansehen*, looking-at] of the individual in public life, they may not only appear on the body but also through clothing as the second, 'social' bodily skin, as well as in rituals which are carried out on the body or the clothing of the body: clothes point to the bodily exhibition [German: *Zurschaustellung*] of honor, shame and disgrace—they are thought of and imagined materially. 'Clothing was not mere body covering, but indicated one's role and status, as to it is best viewed in terms of the values of honor and shame'" (Jan Dietrich, *Der Tod von eigener Hand: Studien*

scenes exegetically with special emphasis on the function of clothes and accessories;[5] then we shall sum up and discuss our observations.

2. *Exegesis*

2.1. *Vashti's Crown and Esther's: Esther 1:10-12; 2:17*

> On the seventh day, when the king was merry with wine, he commanded Mehuman, Biztha, Harbona, Bigtha and Abagtha, Zethar and Carkas, the seven eunuchs who attended him, to bring Queen Vashti before the king, *wearing the royal crown*, in order to show the peoples and the officials her beauty; for she was fair to behold. But Queen Vashti refused to come at the king's command conveyed by the eunuchs. At this the king was enraged, and his anger burned within him. (Est. 1:10-12)

After establishing the place, time, and occasion, a long and overwhelming party for the ruling classes of the vast Persian empire under King Ahasuerus (1:1-5), the book of Esther begins with the description of the clothing of the banquet room that shall serve as setting for the opening of the story. The reader is invited into a room, covered in luxurious decoration, meant to "display the great wealth of [King Ahasuerus'] kingdom and the splendor and pomp of his majesty":

> There were white cotton curtains and blue hangings tied with cords of fine linen and purple to silver rings and marble pillars. There were couches of gold and silver on a mosaic pavement of porphyry, marble, mother-of-pearl, and colored stones. (1:6)

The Hebrew text is difficult to translate, and Levenson speculates that "[t]he author may be employing exotic terms to enhance the sense of extreme opulence."[6] The room is dressed up as a sign of the king's wealth

---

zum Suizid im Alten Testament, Alten Ägypten und Alten Orient, ORA 19 [Tübingen: Mohr Siebeck, 2017], 25, with reference to J. H. Neyrey, "Clothing," in *Handbook of Biblical Social Values*; ed. J. J. Pilch and B. J. Malina [Peabody: Hendrickson, 1998], 21–7 [22]; my translation from German). On the semantic value of honor and shame in the book of Esther, see Timothy S. Laniak, *Shame and Honor in the Book of Esther*, SBLDS 165 (Atlanta: Scholars Press, 1998).

    5. For a short introduction, see Jopie Siebert-Hommes, "'On the third day Esther put on her queen's robes' (Esther 5:1): The Symbolic Function of Clothing in the Book of Esther," http://www.lectio.unibe.ch/02_1/siebert.pdf.

    6. Levenson, *Esther*, 43.

and power over the entire world.⁷ The textiles are costly;⁸ the mosaic flooring is made of the most expensive stones imaginable. So, the room's interior is dressed up in the most luxurious way imaginable, suitable to display the king's great wealth. The furniture belongs to the dressing up as well, there are couches of gold and silver and the goblets are golden and of various design, all of it intended to show the king's bounty (1:7). Splendor is all around, setting the scene for the arrival of the king's most precious possession, Queen Vashti.

Vashti is supposed to be shown off as the king's trophy wife, but she refuses, and the king is enraged. The text of Est. 1:10-12 shows the difference between the king's request of Vashti as an *objet d'art* and Vashti's refusal as *a subject* to comply. Much has been said and written about Vashti's role in the book of Esther.⁹ Why would she not obey the king? The Babylonian midrash to Esther understood the command to wear the crown as a command to wear *nothing but the crown*, and thus considered her refusal morally good.¹⁰ Some of the Rabbis, on the other hand, saw her as "wicked" and even invented a story about how Vashti forced Jewish female slaves to work naked on the Sabbath—thus, her own purported naked appearance. Paton claimed that "it was not custom in Persia to seclude the women as in the modern Orient" and "surely a Persian queen must have been accustomed to the spectacle of drunken men." Accordingly, "the author of Est. apparently regards the refusal

---

7. In the book, the king has no internal enemies to fight, and no military personnel are mentioned; the war in the book is solely a war between civilians.

8. Purple (*tᵉkelet*) is not the name of a fabric but of a color (*pace* the translations). *Tyrian purple*, also known as Tyrian red, Phoenician purple, royal purple, imperial purple or imperial dye, is a distinctive dye color associated with royalty and wealth, produced in the coastal zone of Syria and Phoenicia. The dye was extracted from a mucous secretion from gastropod mollusks, and since the material was scarce and the production involved much labor, the dye was highly valued (Roger S. Boraas, "Purple," in *The HarperCollins Bible Dictionary*, ed. Paul J. Achtemeier [San Francisco: HarperSanFrancisco, 1996], 902–3). The cords that attach the white and purple linen/cotton, presumably used as flags or sun screens and as decoration, are made from byssus (*bûṣ*), an "exceedingly fine and valuable textile fibre and fabric known to the ancients; apparently the word was used, or misused, of various substances, linen, cotton, and silk, but it denoted properly…a kind of flax, and hence is appropriately translated in the English Bible 'fine linen'" ("Byssus," *Oxford English Dictionary*, online edition [accessed 2 April 2020])

9. See Chapters 3 and 4 above.

10. See Berlin, *Esther*, 11. On the Rabbinic understanding of Vashti, see Fox, *Character and Ideology*, 164–5.

as merely a whim, for which he offers no explanation." And with good reason, Paton continued: "The added words, *which he sent unto her by the eunuchs*, shows that the summons was delivered in the proper, formal way, and, therefore, enhance the disrespect of Vashti."[11]

Fox seems to have a positive view of the Vashti character; "[H]er independence and dignity are worthy of respect," he writes.[12] Levenson acknowledges Vashti's courage, but as compared to Esther, "queen Vashti's absolute and uncompromising refusal to comply with her husband renders her powerless and ineffective and ultimately sweeps her from the scene."[13] Conversely, Timothy Beal's post-structuralist, post-feminist reading understands the Vashti character as the foil or palimpsest for two of the protagonists in the book, Esther and Mordecai.[14] Beal sees correctly, that Vashti's insubordination paves the way to Esther's rise as political person and savior of her people.[15]

Historians can tell us that the queen's parallel party for the women in the palace (Est. 1:9) is historically unlikely; its rationale is purely literary. It paints the picture of two separate worlds, the men's ("The absence of women at Ahasuerus's banquets enhances the perception that these were really just overdone 'stag parties,' with all the licentiousness and disrespect the term implies," Levenson writes[16]), and the women's, incommensurable as they apparently are. Berlin quotes Plutarch:

> The lawful wives of the Persian kings sit beside them at dinner, and eat with them. But when the king wish to be merry and get drunk, they send their wives out and send for their dancing girls and concubines. They are right in what they do because they do not concede any share in their licentiousness and debauchery to their wedded wives.[17]

11. Paton, *Commentary on the Book of Esther*, 150 (Paton's emphasis).
12. Fox, *Character and Ideology*, 164–70.
13. Levenson, *Esther*, 48.
14. Beal, *Book of Hiding*. About Esther, Beal states, "There are also traces of Vashti in the one [Esther] who fills the space she leaves as queen… [T]he fact that they are similar both as subjects and as objects, moreover, suggests a third kinship: the ambivalence and excess of their place in the order of things." Regarding Mordecai, Beal says, "an astonishing identification of the newly introduced Jewish insurrectory hero, Mordecai, as the other Jew over against the law of Haman and the king, with the previous heroine, the non-Jewish insurrectory woman Vashti, as the other woman over against the law of Memuchan and the king" (ibid., 101 and 54, respectively). On "otherness" in Esther, see ibid., 60–9.
15. See further Chapters 3 and 4 above.
16. Levenson, *Esther*, 46,
17. Berlin, *Esther*, 11, with reference to Plutarch, *Moralia* 140 B 16.

5. *Dressing Up Esther*

It is against the backdrop of this incommensurability of male and female space, pinpointed by Plutarch, that Vashti's refusal should be understood. The king's command demands that the queen enters the male space; indeed, through his command the king himself transgresses the boundaries between female and male space, where only indecent women appear. The text does not indicate Vashti's nakedness, as implied by the Rabbis, but in all its indefiniteness the thought is not far away from it, and that points to the importance of clothes as a marker. It is as a queen, not as a concubine or dancing girl, that Vashti is commanded to appear before the drunken king and his equally drunken guests. Her high rank as a queen is indicated by her wearing the royal crown. However, as the highest-ranking woman in Persia, she cannot denigrate herself to the role of a concubine (who would not be wearing a crown), and thus she must rebuff the king's summons.

Yet, the crown also indicates that she is in a mixed position as a high-ranking queen *and* a wife, and it is this mixed position that sets the stage for the rest of the Esther story, as emphasized by Beal. The importance of the scene of Queen Vashti's "insubordination" is highlighted by the reference to the royal crown. Ahasuerus might have enormous treasures to display, but the crowned queen does not want to play the part of an exhibition piece.

Commentators rightly tend to compare the two queens, Vashti the abject and Esther the object-turning-subject. The remark about Esther's advancement to queen in Est. 2:17 underscores their opposed roles, and this remark again uses clothing—the crown—as vehicle of attention:

> The king loved Esther more than all the other women; of all the virgins she won his favor and devotion (*watissā ḥen wāḥesed lᵉpānāyw*) so that *he set the royal crown on her head* and made her queen instead of Vashti. (Est. 2:17)

Where Vashti refuses to adorn the crown and thereby forfeits her royal status, Esther accepts the crown and the status. Where Vashti is forbidden to "come before (*lipnê*, 'in the sight of') King Ahasuerus" and is reprieved of her status and crown (Est. 1:19), Esther receives the status and crown from the king himself, because she found (*watissā*) grace (*ḥen*) and admiration (*ḥesed*) in the sight of him (*lᵉpānāyw*). Her way to royalty was discussed in Chapter 4, above, and shall not be treated further here. It suffices to repeat that Esther's metamorphosis from orphaned, foreign virgin to adult, Persian queen happens through a *rite-de-passage*, a rite that marks a person's social and/or sexual transformation. This passage was extremely bodily oriented through the preparatory, lengthy cosmetic treatment, and now the passage is confirmed by the swift rite of crowning, that also marks the shift from Vashti to Esther as queen.

2.2. *Haman and the King's Signet Ring, Esther 3:10; 8:2*

> Then Haman said to King Ahasuerus, "There is a certain people scattered and separated among the peoples in all the provinces of your kingdom; their laws are different from those of every other people, and they do not keep the king's laws, so that it is not appropriate for the king to tolerate them. If it pleases the king, let a decree be issued for their destruction, and I will pay ten thousand talents of silver into the hands of those who have charge of the king's business, so that they may put it into the king's treasuries." *So the king took his signet ring from his hand and gave it to Haman son of Hammedatha the Agagite, the enemy of the Jews.* [11] The king said to Haman, "The money is given to you, and the people as well, to do with them as it seems good to you." (Est. 3:8-11)

The initiating turmoil in Persia is brought to a peaceful state of affairs at the end of Esther 2. Letters of women's obligation to domestic obedience have been delivered (and presumably read) all over the empire, the king has chosen himself a beautiful, compliant, and well-educated wife, and a *coup d'état* among some of the king's servants has been prevented by Mordecai, resulting in the first of many executions in the book (2:21-23). Esther 3:1-11 unleashes the major crisis in the book, the intended pogrom on all Judeans in Persia. Haman, who is presented as an Agagite hating all Judeans—the background for this hate is only hinted at[18]—is raised to the highest position in Persia, but Mordecai the Judean refuses to bow down for him. As often remarked, the author offers no explanation for this insubordination which has led to many scholarly and expository guesses. In my opinion there are two mutually supplementing explanations, one narratological-technical and one content-oriented "ideological." From the literary perspective, the narrative "needs" a conflict to trigger the main crisis, and Mordecai, who ends up as the symbol of the Judeans, serves the role as "trigger" very well, since—and this is the "ideological" explanation—his ethnicity is stressed time and again:

> When they spoke to him day after day and he would not listen to them, they told Haman, in order to see whether Mordecai's words would avail; for he had told them that he was a Jew. (3:4)

---

18. For a discussion of the ancient conflict between the Agagites and the Israelites, see Chapter 6 below.

The speakers quoted are two courtiers who seemingly want to stir up a conflict between Haman and Mordecai. They have tried to make Mordecai obey the king's command of bowing down for Haman, but to no avail. When they learn of Mordecai's ethnicity, they tell Haman of his disobedience—Mordecai's ethnicity is mentioned three times in vv. 4 and 6—and this inflames Haman's inherited hatred for all Judeans; to kill only Mordecai is too little for Haman, the arch-villain (3:6). Therefore, he bribes the king to let a decree be issued for the destruction of the Judeans (3:9) and the king *de facto* transfers his power to Haman and confirms it by giving his signet ring to Haman, since the signet ring will authorize Haman to sign any decree he would like. Again, we see how the transfer of an artefact of clothing, an accessory to the king's personal attire, marks the decisive moment in the narrative. The obtuse king gives up his power and hands it over in the shape of the signet ring to the sly enemy of the Judeans who sets the final solution to his trouble in motion, and thus the crisis of the book, the annihilation of the Judean people in Persia.

Transference of the royal signet ring returns as a motif towards the end of the narrative in Est. 8:2:

> Then the king took off his *signet ring*, which he had taken from Haman, and *gave it to Mordecai*.

This remark opens the door to the solution of the narrative crisis. Mordecai the Judean succeeds Haman the Agagite as the king's vizier, and the king allows him to overwrite Haman's murderous decrees, seal his decree with the signet ring,[19] and save the lives of his people. The scene is followed and completed by Esther's request for permission to write the decrees against the enemies (8:3-8) and their subsequent formation and release by the royal Persian mail (8:9-14). The scene ends in 8:15-17, where Mordecai leaves the king, "wearing royal robes of blue and white, with a great golden crown and a mantle of fine linen and purple, while the city of Susa shouted and rejoiced" (Est. 8:15), again a narratological marking of power shift through donning of clothes. The clothes are royal ($l^eb\hat{u}\check{s}$ $malk\hat{u}t$) and made from purple byssus ($b\hat{u}ṣ$ $w^e\,'arg\bar{a}m\bar{a}n$), identical to the fabric of the chords in the royal banquet area in 1:6, and Mordecai receives not only the signet ring and the royal robes but also a

---

19. Catching the semiotic importance of the signet ring, the Alpha-text (AT) adds to Haman's mortification by stating that "the king removed the signet ring from his [Haman's] hand, and his life was sealed with it" (7:13 AT).

golden crown (*ʿṭeret zāhāb*),²⁰ an open proclamation of his power. Thus, Mordecai's royal clothes can also serve as a sign to the general public: "The city of Susa shouted and rejoiced, and for the Jews there was light and gladness, joy and honor" (8:15-16).²¹ There is no need for the king or Mordecai to say anything; the royal clothes, the crown on his head, and the signet ring on his finger tells it all.

2.3. *Mordecai in Sackcloth and Ashes, Esther 4:1-17*

> When Mordecai learned all that had been done, *Mordecai tore his clothes and put on sackcloth and ashes*, and went through the city, wailing with a loud and bitter cry; he went up to the entrance of the king's gate, for *no one might enter the king's gate clothed with sackcloth*. In every province, wherever the king's command and his decree came, there was great mourning among the Jews, with fasting and weeping and lamenting, and *most of them lay in sackcloth and ashes*.
>
> When Esther's maids and her eunuchs came and told her, the queen was deeply distressed; she *sent garments to clothe Mordecai, so that he might take off his sackcloth*; but he would not accept them. Then Esther called for Hathach, one of the king's eunuchs, who had been appointed to attend her, and ordered him to go to Mordecai to learn what was happening and why. (Est. 4:1-5)

---

20. The term for the queens' crowns (or diadems) in 1:11 and 2:17; the royal crown on Mordecai's head in 6:8 is *keter*.

21. The city of Susa and its inhabitants play a peculiar role in Esther. It is the citadel of King Ahasuerus and as such serves as the location of the royal banquet (Est. 1), the royal household (Est. 2) and the issuing of both Haman's, and Esther's and Mordecai's decrees (Est. 3; 8). As a citadel it is also the location for Esther's and Mordecai's discussion at the royal gate in Est. 4. In these instances, the city is neutral. The citizens of Susa, however, seem to be especially friendly toward the Judeans: after Haman's decree is issued, he and the king celebrate the coming solution to the "Jewish" problem, "but the city of Susa was thrown into confusion" (3:15). Likewise, when Mordecai leaves the king after the issuing of the counter decree, dressed in royal attire, "the city of Susa shouted and rejoiced" (8:15), mirroring the light and gladness, joy and honor among the Judeans in the following verse. Nevertheless, Susa is the place for no fewer than two killings, on the first day of five hundred persons, including the ten sons of Haman, then a second, additional killing of three hundred (9:13-15). There is no reason given in the narrative for the second day of killing, and the reader cannot help wondering why the poor Susans are targeted. The only reason seems to be the need for an explanation of the two different days of Purim.

Mordecai's response to the threat of eradication of the Judeans is to tear his clothes and put on sackcloth and ashes (4:1);[22] this is an expression of fear, horror, lament, and despair, described throughout the Hebrew Bible as a response to the shock and terror of an actual or imminent disaster. Jephthah tears his clothes when he realizes that he must sacrifice his own daughter (Judg. 11), and when King Hezekiah's servants come to tell the king about the coming Assyrian attack on Jerusalem, they come with their clothes torn (2 Kgs 18:37).[23] Job 1–2 offer instructive parallels to Mordecai's reaction. When Job heard about the death of his sons and daughters, "he tore his robe, shaved his head, and fell on the ground and worshiped" (Job 1:20); when Satan "inflicted loathsome sores on Job from the sole of his foot to the crown of his head…he took a potsherd with which to scrape himself, and sat among the ashes" (Job 2:7-8); and when Job's friends came to visit him and saw him in this terrible state, "they did not recognize him, and they raised their voices and wept aloud; they tore their robes and threw dust in the air upon their heads" (Job 2:12). The reactions of Job and of the friends show that tearing the clothes, putting on sackcloth and throwing dust or ashes on one's head are powerful symbols of sorrow and despair, not only over a loss already experienced but also of a loss or a disaster yet to come. Moreover, the tearing of clothes and putting on sackcloth is part of the lamenting over a dead (cf. Jacob over Joseph, Gen. 37:34; David over Abner, 2 Sam. 3).[24]

In Esther 4, the tearing of clothes and the putting on of sackcloth has a double communicative meaning: (1) Mordecai is in despair and (2) the Judeans are already as good as dead. Mordecai's sackcloth serves in the same way as the prophetic use of the lament genre to proclaim the coming death of the people (e.g. Jer. 8:23 MT; 9:9; Amos 5:1-3, cf. the use of lament in Ezek. 27–28). His public appearance conveys a message of the upcoming death of the Judeans in Persia, both to the Judeans themselves and to Queen Esther. The Judeans follow Mordecai's

---

22. *wayyiqra' mordᵉkay 'et-bᵉgādāyw wayyilbaš śaq wā'eper*.

23. The tearing of clothes can also be a sign of despair over the Israelite's stupidity and defection, e.g. Num. 14; Josh. 7; Ezra 9; over defeat in war, e.g. 1 Sam. 4 and six times in 1 Maccabees; a sign of penitence, 1 Kgs 19; 2 Chron. 34. In 2 Sam. 13:19 Tamar puts ashes on her head and tears her long robe after her bother has raped her.

24. On tearing of clothing as a sign of emotion, see Winfried Thiel, "קָרַע *qārā'*; קְרָעִים *qerā'îm*," *TDOT* 7:175–80. On the use and meaning of sackcloth as "a mourning or penitential garment, worn either after or in anticipation of a disastrous event," see further Winfried Thiel," שַׂק, *śaq*," *TDOT* 14:184–9 (185–6).

lead, fasting, crying and lamenting, and "most of them lay in sackcloth and ashes" (Est. 4:3).[25] Esther, on the other hand, fails to understand the message and to respond adequately to Mordecai's tacit, symbolic information. Is this failure an oblique indication that after her initiation and marriage in ch. 2, she is now more assimilated to the Persian than to the Judean society? We shall return to this question below, but the conclusion seems to be right at hand.[26]

Knowing that it is prohibited to come near to the king's gate dressed in sackcloth, Esther sends replacement clothes to Mordecai. Since sackcloth is mainly worn as an undergarment and does not cover the whole body, Mordecai's appearance at the public space in front of the king's gate is not only a matter of communicating self-abasement as a part of "a larger ensemble of mourning and penitential rites";[27] it is also an indecent, half-naked appearance, embarrassing to viewers in general and especially to Esther. It is to this part of Mordecai's clothing that Esther—mistakenly—reacts, not to the message of despair he wants her to apprehend. Esther's mistake is an ironic reference to the importance of the vestimentary code.

Two further observations are relevant, (1) Esther's initial failure to understand serves as an indication of her unwillingness to engage in the conflict, and (2) Esther does not bring the clothes herself but sends a servant, Hathach, as a mediator. In Esther 2 it was emphasized that Esther and Mordecai were close; she hid her ethnicity as he had told her, and he kept an eye on her every day when she was in the king's harem. Now, they are separated by space and social situation, she being inside the palace and associated with the Persian king, he outside and related to the Judeans. She cannot and will not leave the palace; he cannot and will not enter it—which they both communicate via clothes. Mordecai has put on clothes that cannot be worn in the palace; Esther sends the replacement garments via an unidentified, anonymous channel.

Thus, the initial communication between the two is done by proxy via the messages of the clothes, which are supposed to be intelligible. But in the case of Esther and Mordecai, the communication via clothes fails. This is striking, for it is the only time in the book of Esther that the vestimentary code is misunderstood by anybody. What the implied

---

25. It remains a mystery why not all the Judeans lie in sackcloth and ashes.
26. The consequences of understanding the change of clothes and the associated dialogue in Est. 4 as an ideological-theological turning point in the book of Esther will be discussed in Chapter 8 below.
27. Thiel, "śaq," 186.

author tells the reader is a story of a relationship gone wrong and consequently that the Judeans will fall victims of Haman's machinations. The two protagonists who in the end are meant to solve the crisis have never been farther away from each other than in this time of peril; unrest and agitation are rising.[28] What Esther and Mordecai need is a go-between who can repair and mediate the broken conversation between them, and Hathach, who has been appointed as Esther's servant, is perfect in the role of mediator. As a high-ranking servant, he is connected to the court, including the queen but without his own authority, and thus a trustworthy messenger. Furthermore, as a eunuch he can be close to both men and women.

The failed clothed communication in Est. 4:4 opens and adds emphasis to the critical scene, the beginning of the turn of events in Esther. Esther 4 marks the first transition of authority from Mordecai, who triggered the crisis, to Esther, who is preordained to solve it. Clines offers a fine analysis of the scene. "The passing of responsibility must not be narrated briefly," he writes, "for it is a crucial moment in the total narrative. And the narrative must not simply *replace* Mordecai by the figure of Esther, since Mordecai must retain a significant role in the story as a whole."[29] He detects the transition from Mordecai to Esther in three subsequent scenes of communication:

1. V. 4: the tacit, rejected "gift of clothes."
2. Vv. 5-9: the communication mediated by Hathach, the message being both oral and written, but with no words reported.
3. Vv. 10-17: "a three-speech dialogue of Esther, Mordecai, and Esther economically moves the action forward by argument, counter-argument and resolution."

Clines concludes: "In the three scenes there is a movement from ignorance to understanding and from understanding to decision."[30] Interestingly, the ignorance is symbolized in the failed interpretation of Mordecai's symbolic

---

28. Clines comments on the clothes as a means of communication that the written copy of the edict (4:8) "is a physical counterpart of the clothes that Esther has sent out in the previous communication scene (v. 4), but unlike the clothes, the edict is a token that cannot be refused. This is because with clothes Mordecai has a choice, but with the edict there is no choice" (Clines, *Esther Scroll*, 35). However, it is not the edict as such that persuades Esther to intervene; rather, it is, Mordecai's combined threat and flattery (4:12-14) that persuades Esther to change her decision.
29. Clines, *Esther Scroll*, 33 (original emphasis).
30. Ibid., 34.

clothing by the ignorant Esther. Here, as opposed to the little child in *The Emperor's New Clothes*, the ignorant, naïve youth is incapable of reading the tacit, symbolic communication.

Let us have a closer look at the second and third scenes of communication, Est. 4:5-16. They consist of five sub-scenes of mediated communication:

1. Vv. 5-6: Esther → Hathach → Mordecai: "Why do you not change your clothes?"
2. Vv. 7-9: Mordecai's first message → Hathach (→ Esther): "We have been sold to annihilation; see Haman's written edict; go and entreat the king."
3. Vv. 10-12: Esther → Hathach → Mordecai/anonymous messengers: "I will not follow your command since I shall surely die if I do so."
4. Vv. 13-14: Mordecai's second message → anonymous messengers → Esther: "All Judeans will die, even you, but maybe you have been chosen as the savior."
5. Vv. 15-16: Esther's second message → anonymous messengers → Mordecai: "I will entreat the king if all Judeans are behind me."

The exchange of information between the interlocutors is carried by mediators, but the better the understanding between Mordecai and Esther, the less indicated are the mediators. In (2) the messenger is one, identified person, Hathach the servant; in (3) Esther calls Hathach to convey the message to Mordecai, but Mordecai gets the message from anonymous messengers (*wayyāgîdû*). In (4) and (5) the messengers are totally anonymous. After the dialogue, the chapter closes with Mordecai doing "everything as Esther had ordered him" (4:17); there is no more mediated speech and the delegation of power and authority has happened. Esther is transformed from being an associate of Ahasuerus to being closely related to the Judeans. She can go to the king as the mediator between him and her people, while Mordecai for a time is relegated to stay in the background. The play can go on.

2.4. *Esther Meets the King, Esther 5:1*

> On the third day *Esther put on her royal robes* and stood in the inner court of the king's palace, opposite the king's hall. The king was sitting on his royal throne inside the palace opposite the entrance to the palace.

Esther has been converted from being the sleeping agent, left in the king's harem, becoming the active protector of the Judeans. Still, her identity is hidden as she dresses up as the queen to go and intercede with her almighty and terrifying husband who whimsically might easily kill her for disturbing his majestic calm (cf. Est. 4:11). From the outset, she does not know if she is in the king's good graces or not, since she has not been called to be his sexual partner for a month—she might believe that she isn't. So, she dresses up in her royal robes before approaching the king. This means that she is especially beautiful in the eyes of the king, as she was when she was chosen as the favored queen; it also means that she reminds him of her position as queen. And finally, it marks her as the opposite of the former queen Vashti who refused to wear the royal crown at the king's party and thus embarrassed not only the king but all men in Persia. Dressed (up) as a queen, Esther is ready to impress and influence the sovereign who is portrayed in all his royal splendor, sitting on his royal throne inside the palace opposite the entrance to the palace.

Esther MT does not tell how Esther was dressed before her change of clothes in 5:1. The Greek versions do the gap-filling, though, emphasizing the change from her "garments of service" into her "garments of glory" (Add Est. D:1, AT), thus pointing to her change of social context from a religious and virtuous Judean to the beautiful queen, from Mordecai's ward to Ahasuerus' wife. Before that, in Add Est. C:12-13 her resolution to go to the king is accompanied by a change of clothes in preparation for her petitionary prayer to God for help in her fearful situation:

> Then Esther the queen fled to the Lord, seized with the agony of death. Taking off the garments of her glory, she put on the garments of distress and mourning, and instead of costly perfumes she covered her head with ashes and dung, and she utterly humbled her body; every part that she loved to adorn she covered with her tangled hair.

After having changed from her royal garments, she prays for three days, but there is no further mention of a fast; for the Greek interpreters, the spoken words of the individual prayer are far more important than the tacit communal act of fasting. The reference to "garments of distress and mourning" highlights that the prayer comes from a person who knows that she is in grave danger, totally dependent on divine intervention, and thus full of penitence.[31]

---

31. Add Est. C:12-13 LXX. There are no important differences between LXX and AT. For a further analysis of the meeting between Esther and the king, see Chapter 3 above.

The emperor's clothes are also described in the Greek versions: "He was seated on the throne of his kingdom, clothed in the full array of his splendor, all covered with gold and precious stones." The following words interpret the effect of the clothes: "And he was most terrifying." (Add Est. D:6, LXX). In Chapter 2, above, we saw how this scene, together with the description of Esther's entrance accompanied by her two maids, added to the Greek novella's romantic ambiance. But even if we do not get the full description of this conversion in Esther MT, we as readers understand the importance of the change of clothes, since it introduces the entire, very important scene, marking Esther's transition from one sphere of influence (Mordecai's) to another (the king's).

Another piece of royal equipment plays an important informative part in the introduction to the dialogue between Esther and Ahasuerus, the royal scepter:

> As soon as the king saw Queen Esther standing in the court, she won his favor and he held out to her the golden scepter that was in his hand. Then Esther approached and touched the top of the scepter. (5:2)

A short visualization of the scene may open the reader's eyes to the phallic features of the scepter which Ahasuerus holds out to Esther as a sign of his benevolence. His sexual interest in the luxuriously dressed queen is intimated by the first words in the sentence: "As soon as the king saw Queen Esther standing in the court she won his favor." As in Esther 2, the king sees (*kir'ôt hammelek*) Esther and likes her (*naśe'āh ḥen be'ênāyw*). In Esther 2 this means that he chooses her for sexual activity.[32] Here, the sexual choice is indicated by the king holding his golden scepter out to her, an attitude that is particularly interesting, since she had not been called to him for thirty days before (Est. 4:11). Esther's acceptance of her role is indicated by her touching the top of the scepter, another semi-sexual act.

Thus, the clothing plays a communicative role in the sexual play between the two; Esther uses her female attributes to entice the thick-headed king, who believes that he is in command of the situation, only to be lured and put off by her coy request of first one, then a second private party. And thus alerted, the reader can continue his/her reading in fearful expectation.

---

32. On the function of the male gaze in Esther, see Chapter 4, section 4.1. above.

2.5. Dressing Up Mordecai, Esther 6:6-11

> So Haman said to the king, "For the man whom the king wishes to honor, *let royal robes be brought, which the king has worn*, and a horse that the king has ridden, with a royal crown on its head. *Let the robes and the horse be handed over to one of the king's most noble officials; let him robe the man whom the king wishes to honor*, and let him conduct the man on horseback through the open square of the city, proclaiming before him: 'Thus shall it be done for the man whom the king wishes to honor.'"
>
> Then the king said to Haman, "Quickly, take the robes and the horse, as you have said, and do so to the Jew Mordecai…" (Est. 6:7-10)

All the malice between Haman and Mordecai, all the peripetic reversal of fate for them is inherent in the dialogue between Ahasuerus and Haman in the king's bedchamber one early morning after a sleepless night for the king. Haman vaingloriously believes that he is the king's favorite, but as fate has it, he has been surpassed by his archenemy, Mordecai. As emphasized by many commentators, Haman's request is to be equal to the king; he wants the royal clothing to be his, just like the signet ring, so that he will appear royal to spectators. As phrased by Berlin:

> He has already been designated as a person, to whom everyone must bow, making him a kind of surrogate king, and now he wants to masquerade as the king, wearing the king's own robe and sitting on the king's own horse. *All that is missing is his taking the king's wife, and that is what it looks to Ahasuerus that he is doing in 7:8.*[33]

It is no coincidence that the reversal of fate between Haman and Mordecai is expressed in terms taken from the vestimentary code. As we have seen above, clothes are a strong semantic marker of change, and here it is even strengthened by contextual cultural information. Berlin points to the many incidents in the Hebrew Bible where symbolic value is added to royal and other "professional" clothing. Further, she refers to the Greek author Plutarch (*Artaxerxes* 3) according to whom one of the ceremonies when a new Persian king was initiated was "the laying aside of his own personal robe and the putting on of the robe of Cyrus the Elder," and also, that in Persia nobody but the king is allowed to wear the royal robe.[34] The author of Esther might have known this—we cannot know—but under all circumstances Haman's request suggests that he aspires to a position

---

33. Berlin, *Esther*, 61 (my emphasis).
34. Ibid., 59–60.

in the Persian society even higher than the one he already possesses as second-in-command. A public parading of the honored man, dressed as a king and mounted on the king's own horse, is basically a demonstration of usurpation of the royal power. One can only wonder why Ahasuerus consents to the proposal—the only explanation, it seems to me, is the king's naïve stupidity. Ahasuerus has seemingly never taken Haman's aspirations seriously; this is indicated by the carelessness he demonstrates when he gives the signet ring and the authority to exterminate all Judeans in his empire to Haman (Est. 3:10-11). Now, he does not even consider that Haman thinks of himself when he proposes to dress the honoree in royal garb. He simply and happily orders Haman to show this honor to Mordecai, and even tells him to lead the parade through the city himself.

The narrative interprets the course of events itself: after the embarrassing public parading of his defeat to Mordecai and his own loss of eminence and glory, Haman "hurried to his house, mourning and with his head covered" (6:11-12). He covers his head in shame, since he understands the message that he has lost the fight with Mordecai. The covering also presages the final covering of Haman's head, just before he is taken away from Esther's quarters to his execution on his own gallows (7:8-10). The interpretation is confirmed by Haman's wise wife, Zeresh, who interprets the incidents for him: "If Mordecai, before whom your downfall has begun, is of the Jewish people, you will not prevail against him, but will surely fall before him" (6:13). Ominously, the story continues: "While they were still talking with him, the king's eunuchs arrived and hurried Haman off to the banquet that Esther had prepared" (6:14). Haman's feelings must be at least mixed at the incident, and it would not have helped that the king's eunuchs *hurry* (*bāhal*, hiph'il) him away. As readers, we are prepared for the final showdown.

The dressing of Mordecai in royal garments, on the other hand, foreshadows his rise to power in Esther 9–10. What Haman wants, namely, to be equal to the king, is what Mordecai will be. The description of the incident is uncharacteristically brief (Est. 6:11), and there is no mention of Mordecai's feelings in the text. It is as if there is no need to mention them. In a flash we understand the meaning of the vestimentary code, the defeat of Haman and rise of Mordecai to royalty. Yet, the Greek translations grasped the hint of the underlying significance. Their rendition of the closing remarks in Esther 10 reads: "And Mardochaios took over[35] from King Artaxerxes, and he was great in the kingdom and extolled by the Judeans. And being loved, he spent his life for his whole nation" (10:3

---

35. According to the note given in NETS, the verb *diedékheto* possibly means "succeeded."

LXX).[36] In the Greek versions, Mordecai fulfills the rise to royalty which is only indicated as a possibility in Esther MT, where he ends up as next in rank to King Ahasuerus. This notwithstanding, even the Hebrew Esther proudly highlights his power and glory through a rhetorical question: "All the acts of his power and might, and the full account of the high honor of Mordecai, to which the king advanced him, are they not written in the annals of the kings of Media and Persia?" (10:2). But the most important account of Mordecai's accomplishment in Esther MT is related in the closing remark: "…he was powerful among the Jews and popular with his many kindred, for he sought the good of his people and interceded for the welfare of all his descendants" (10:3).

3. Conclusion and Outlook

In this chapter we have identified the vestimentary code as an important semantic marker in the book of Esther. Our readings have categorized clothes as "tacit" communication of importance, highlighting characters and preceding central narrative incidents. References to clothing add yet another layer of meaning to the characterization of the persons and connect narrative scenes as intertexts. The question remains: Is the book of Esther especially focused on clothing? This question cannot be fully clarified here, but a preliminary look at narrative texts[37] suggests that it is characteristic of the Diaspora novellas Esther, Joseph, and Judith. Lawrence M. Wills understands the changing of clothes to be a common stage in the rites-of-passage before the heroines' prayers in the Diaspora novellas, including the pseudepigraphic tale of Joseph and Aseneth. This is especially evident in Judith,[38] but as indicated above just as important

---

36. AT: "…and loved by all the Judeans. He led them and bestowed glory on his whole nation."

37. The meaning and function of cultic dress in the Hebrew Bible, especially in the Priestly writings will not be treated in these short remarks. On clothing in the Hebrew Bible as material objects and social constructs and extensions of people, see Bethany Joy Wagstaff, "Redressing Clothing in the Hebrew Bible: Material-Cultural Approaches" (PhD diss., University of Exeter, 2017).

38. "In Judith each part is marked by clear outward indicators of role or status: The woman begins in the clothing of wealth and position; takes off these clothes (separation); clothes herself in the garments of mourning, which eliminate the indicators of social or gender roles; and begins to pray; then she bathes and reclothes herself in new garments similar to the old, but even more splendid (incorporation)" (Lawrence M. Wills, *The Book of Judith: Introduction, Commentary, and Reflections*, NIB 3 [Nashville: Abingdon, 1999], 1075–183 [1142]).

in Esther where the Greek versions pay even more attention to Esther's change of clothes than the Hebrew.

Above, we have analyzed the function of clothes in Esther. In the Joseph-novella, which for the past almost 150 years has been considered a parallel to Esther, clothes are important as a signal, too. When the ageing Jacob gives Joseph a long robe with sleeves—in LXX an even more costly variegated "coat of many colors"—it is a sign of the father's special love for Joseph, a sign which is immediately understood by his brothers (Gen. 37:3-4). When the brothers want to intimate to the father that Joseph has been killed, the means is his bloodstained robe (Gen. 37:31-33). Wanting to seduce Joseph, the wife of Potiphar "caught hold of his garment, saying, "Lie with me!" But he left his garment in her hand and fled and ran outside." Afterwards, she uses the garment as (fake) proof of attempted rape which launches Joseph's demise and following rise to power (Gen. 39:11-18). This rise is also accompanied by a change of clothes. When Joseph has interpreted Pharaoh's dreams and is released from the dungeon, he shaves and changes his clothes, before he goes to Pharaoh (Gen. 41:14), a scene which is often considered by scholars to be reminiscent of Esther's visit to Ahasuerus. When Pharaoh subsequently appoints him as second in command, a position identical to Mordecai's in the book of Esther, it is signified by yet another change of clothes:

> And Pharaoh said to Joseph, "See, I have set you over all the land of Egypt." Removing his signet ring from his hand, Pharaoh put it on Joseph's hand; he arrayed him in garments of fine linen, and put a gold chain around his neck. (Gen. 41:41-42)[39]

Finally, after his reconciliation with his brothers, when they are setting out for their return to Canaan, Joseph gives all of them a set of garments, "but to Benjamin he gave three hundred pieces of silver and five sets of garments" (Gen. 45:22).

In the book of Judith, clothing is of importance as well, especially in connection with the presentation of its main character, the courageous widow Judith. The fearful Israelites in Bethulia prepare to fight the approaching Assyrian army with acts of penitence and prayer. They humble their spirits through fasting, and all of them (including their foreign slaves and their cattle!) wrap sackcloth about their waists; even the

---

39. The text continues: "He had him ride in the chariot of his second-in-command; and they cried out in front of him, 'Bow the knee!' Thus he set him over all the land of Egypt" (Gen. 41:43). This scene is reminiscent of Mordecai's ride on Ahasuerus' horse in Est. 4.

altar is wrapped in sackcloth. More importantly though, the introduction of Judith in ch. 8 is accompanied by detailed descriptions of her clothes. Mourning her late husband, she lives in a tent on the roof-top, dressed in sackcloth and garments of widowhood. When she decides to take action against the Assyrian field marshal Holofernes, she strips herself naked,[40] and cries out to the Lord for help (Jdt. 9). After finishing her prayer, she enters the house, removes the sackcloth, strips off the clothing of her widowhood, takes a bath and perfumes herself, fixes her hair and puts on turban before putting on party clothes, makeup and jewelry (Jdt. 10:1-5). This lengthy description surpasses even the description of Esther dressing up for her visit to Ahasuerus in the Greek versions, and her efforts bear fruit—Holofernes is awestruck, and his fate is sealed.

This short review of the two closest parallels to the book of Esther intimates that a full study of clothes as a semantic code in Diaspora novellas would be relevant and productive. This is not the place for such an investigation. However, the exegesis and discussion of clothes in Esther above might pave the way to and inspire further studies of this intriguing field.

---

40. Judith refers to "my father Simeon, to whom you gave the sword in hand for vengeance on aliens, the ones who ravaged the virgin's vulva for defilement and stripped naked the thigh for shame and polluted the vulva for disgrace" (Jdt. 9:2). The reference is to Simeon and the other sons of Jacob taking a gruesome revenge for the Shechemites' rape of their sister Dinah, Gen. 34.

Chapter 6

HAMAN, THE SCAPEGOAT

In his epoch-making monograph *Character and Ideology in the Book of Esther*, Michael V. Fox put an epigraph over each chapter that characterized one of the literary personae in the book of Esther. The epigraphs quoted earlier scholarly assessments of the characters, all expressing an attitude that Fox repudiated. The only exception was the chapter on Haman, the villain of the narrative, since "Haman alone," in Fox's words, "has evoked no contrary view and so gets no epigraph."[1] For Fox, as for many others, Haman is devious, driven by pride, he needs to confirm his power at every step, he is a control freak, and worst of all, Haman is the proverbial anti-Semite.[2]

More than 20 years after the first edition of Fox's book, however, Haman finally had his say in a unique and imaginative essay by Philip R. Davies, "Haman the Victim."[3] The article is set as an autobiographic monologue by Haman. Sitting on death row, listening to the Jews celebrating the death of the man they thought plotted to exterminate them, a man they clearly viewed as simply evil,[4] Haman tells the story of the conflict at the Persian court from his point of view. Well—he wasn't too happy about Mordecai's attitude in the first place. But all the fuss about Haman being an Agagite and an Amalekite and Mordecai being

---

1. Fox, *Character and Ideology*, 3. The exception is even more interesting since Fox's intention explicitly is to deepen our understanding of the characters. According to Fox, a literary portrayal has an "unlimited potential" (ibid., 3). Apart from Haman's, though.
2. Ibid., 178–82.
3. Philip R. Davies, "Haman the Victim," in *First Person: Essays in Biblical Autobiography*, ed. Philip R. Davies (Sheffield: Sheffield Academic, 2002), 137–54.
4. Ibid., 138.

a descendent of Saul[5] was sheer tactics from the part of Mordecai, and brilliant at that. What Mordecai wanted to achieve was, of course, the high position at court that Haman held and the means he used was to plot against Haman. "He managed to explain his aversion against me in a way that could arouse sympathy," as Haman puts it.[6] The story from 1 Samuel 15 of Saul sparing the Amalekites, which Haman himself had never heard about, was the reason for Mordecai's hatred of all Amalekites[7] and for his shame of Saul's disgrace when he lost the favor of his god and was killed in battle, "his body exposed on the walls of a Philistine city." Now Mordecai was "determined to avenge the reputation of that line."[8] The personal was intermingled with the political; Mordecai's ambition of climbing the ladder at the Persian court was concealed behind the race-card: Haman is an anti-Semite.[9] In passing, Haman almost names himself a scapegoat, but what interests him—and obviously also his ghostwriter Philip Davies—is the effect of playing the race-card. "I am the so-called 'enemy of the Jews' now," Haman writes. "But some time, it might turn on the Jews themselves. For there will always be people looking for a scapegoat."[10]

But can we believe Davies' Haman? Isn't it an easy and all-too-well known and much-used defense strategy to declare oneself the misunderstood scapegoat? Haman's story with its references to Hebrew Bible/Old Testament narratives in need of deconstruction leaves its reader in a kind of confusion. Is Haman trustworthy or is his tale just another clever plot? And is this the only answer to the challenges posed to the reader by the story of Esther and Mordecai and the 75,311 dead Persians? This chapter seeks to dismantle the relationship between Haman and Mordecai as a path to understanding the structure of underlying conflict in the book of Esther.

1. *Rivals and Brothers, Scapegoats and Violence*

From the outset, Fox's monolithic attitude towards Haman has provoked me, and in what follows I will propose a counter reading of the portrait

---

5. On the conflict between King Agag of Amalek and Saul of Israel, see below.
6. Davies, "Haman the Victim," 143.
7. The story in 1 Sam. 15 is also the "the story behind the story": from the outset it was the Israelites who were the aggressors against the Amalekites; Davies refers to Exod. 7:9-14 (ibid., 145).
8. Ibid., 146.
9. See the discussion ibid., 142 n. 8.
10. Ibid., 147.

of Haman in conversation with the Haman/Davies portrait. It is also a counter-reading of the book of Esther in its *Wirkungsgeschichte*. I cannot help but wonder if the effect of the Esther narrative in the carnival of the Purim festival[11] is not in part due to the scapegoating of Haman. In what follows, we shall search for narrative traces of this scapegoating of Haman.

The methodological point of departure is René Girard's presentation of mimesis and mimetic desire, that is, the desire for something—the object or ultimately the being—possessed by somebody, the person whom Girard names "the rival" and "the mediator." According to Girard, desire is never neutral, but the desired object is not necessarily of any value *per se*; ultimately, the desired object has the function of symbolizing the (material, social, intellectual, personal) being possessed by the rival:[12]

> ...*the subject desires the object because the rival desires it.* In desiring an object the rival alerts the subject to the desirability of the object. The rival, then, serves as a model for the subject...in regard to desires.[13]

Thus, desire is always mediated to the desiring subject by somebody else, whom the subject wants to imitate, the rival and mediator. The desiring subject wants to possess the same object, the same being or, as in our case, the same power as possessed by the rival. As a consequence, because the two share their desire, mimetic desire inevitably leads to conflicting desire, to violence.[14] However, at the same time the rival functions as a mimetic model for the desiring subject. Girard refers to the well-known cry of the model: "Imitate me!"[15]—but also to the equally well-known "Don't imitate me!" meaning: "Do not appropriate *my* object." This is what Girard names "the double bind," a "contradictory double imperative, or rather a whole network of contradictory imperatives."[16] Moreover, through their shared desire for the same object and in their struggle for the object, the differences between the two lose their stability and they become "brothers" or "doubles."

---

11. Cf. Berlin, *Esther*; LaCocque, *Esther Regina*.
12. René Girard, *Violence and the Sacred* (Baltimore: The Johns Hopkins University Press, 1977), 148.
13. Ibid., 145 (original emphasis).
14. Ibid., 148.
15. Ibid., 146.
16. Ibid., 147.

2. *The Shared Object—Power in Persia*

It is as brothers or doubles in their desire for power in Persia that Haman the Agagite and Mordecai the Jew present themselves in the book of Esther. In their fight for power, their success—or in Greek *kúdos*—is constantly inverted.[17] The change of *kúdos* thus signifies the reversal of fortune, also demonstrated in the concept of peripety. As discussed in Chapter 2, ironic peripety is one of the governing literary vehicles in Esther.[18] Peripety, however, demands balance to be effective. Only if there is balance between two halves of a narrative, two incidents, the fate of two persons, or within the turn of one person's fate, there is peripety. Accordingly, narrative peripety will point to mimesis and to the phenomenon of "doubles" or "brothers" in Girard's universe. And balance there is in the Esther narrative, indeed:

Two men, Haman and Mordecai, fight for power, and due to peripety one falls from the power he had gained at the beginning of the narrative[19] while in the end the other rises to the same empowerment. Their struggle is literally for the power over the Persian Empire through the power personified in King Ahasuerus, for the king is portrayed as a weak man who can be influenced by anybody, and whose power is only apparent.[20] The one who has the largest influence on the king is the *de facto* owner of the power.

Possession of power in Esther is demonstrated by possession of the power over the Judeans (cf. Est. 10:3). He who can determine the fate of the Judeans is the winner of the battle for power. Either the Judeans will be slain, or they will survive and gain the upper hand. The rest of the Persian population are only walk-on players in the game, destined to be killed by numbers (8:11; 9:2) or to desert/convert to Judaism. To put the argument differently: One man, Haman, plots against the other, Mordecai, using hyper-dimensioned violence, not only homicide on his opponent,

---

17. Cf. Girard, *Violence and the Sacred*, 158. Girard defines *kúdos* in the Greek literature in terms of "semidivine prestige, or mystical election attained by military victory"; or with Emile Benveniste, "a talisman of supremacy" (ibid., 152).

18. On peripety in Esther, see Goldman, "Narrative and Ethical Ironies."

19. With reference to Mordecai's services for Ahasuerus in Est. 1–2, Beal concludes: "It appears almost as if Haman is getting Mordecai's reward" (Beal, *Book of Hiding*, 53).

20. On the one hand he cannot withdraw his decrees (cf. Est. 1:19; 8:8); on the other they can be overruled if needed (Est. 8:8). On the character of Ahasuerus, see Levenson, *Esther*, 13–14; Fox, *Character and Ideology*, 171–7; on Ahasuerus as ridiculous and a buffoon, see Goldman, "Narrative and Ethical Ironies."

but genocide on his opponent's people. The other averts the attack in a no less hyper-dimensioned retaliation on all Persians. Peripety and equilibrium points to mimetic doubling; the mimetic struggle for absolute power labels Haman and Mordecai as mimetic doubles or brothers, enemy brothers.[21]

This can be further substantiated. As noted already by Ben-Chorin in his *Kritik des Esther-Buches* from 1938, Haman and Mordecai are each other's doubles: Mordecai "is Haman with a reversed label."[22] First, Haman and Mordecai are both presented as foreigners in the Persian society, the one being an Agagite, the other a Benjaminite. When the narrator of Esther (MT) calls Haman ben Hammedata an Agagite (Est. 3:1),[23] he hints at Agag, king of the Amalekites (1 Sam. 15:8). Mordecai, on his side, is presented as a Benjaminite with an ancestor of the name Kish, who was among the exiles of 597 BCE (Est. 2:5-7).[24] This does not make Mordecai an immediate offspring of King Saul's father Kish; but in the narrative economy the mention of the name Kish collapses the time gap. Of both Haman and Mordecai, then, it is true that their line of "royal" descent is rather dubious. This, however, does not affect their textual status of mimetic doubles; quite the contrary.[25]

Secondly, as seen by both antique and modern commentators, Haman's and Mordecai's pedigrees activate the old story of enmity between Amalek and Israel as told in 1 Samuel 15, where Saul spares Agag, the King of Amalek (together with the fattest part of his livestock) despite Yahweh's clear command (1 Sam. 15:1-9). Behind this narrative lies an intertextual web, *via* Deut. 25:17-19 ("Remember what Amalek did

---

21. Girard, *Violence and the Sacred*, 77.

22. "Er ist der Haman mit umgekehrtem Vorzeichen" (Ben-Chorin, *Kritik des Estherbuches*, 9). Ben-Chorin refers to D. Eduard Reuss: "so erklären wir kurz und gut, dass es uns unmöglich ist, zwischen Haman und Mordechai einen Unterschied zu finden" (D. Eduard Reuss, *Das alte Testament*, vol. 7 [Braunschweig, 1894], 200; cf. Ben-Chorin, *Kritik des Estherbuches*, 15). With reference to Ben-Chorin, Bernhard W. Anderson states: "Mordecai, on his rise to power, proves to be the worthy successor of Haman; in fact, even a Jewish theologian fails to find any essential difference between the two men" (Anderson, "The Place of The Book of Esther in the Christian Bible," 39); Fox uses the quote from Ben-Chorin as his ironic epigraph for his discussion of Mordecai (Fox, *Character and Ideology*, 185).

23. The Greek versions did not catch the importance of the Agagite lineage. Both LXX and AT calls him "a Bougean."

24. These two lines of descent are never openly displayed; they are merely hinted at in the presentation of the two protagonists.

25. For a different evaluation, see Fox, *Character and Ideology*, 180–1.

to you on your journey out of Egypt...") to Exod. 17:8-14, the story of how "Amalek came in the desert and fought with Israel at Rephidim."[26] The intertextuality is theologically authenticated by the closing of Exod. 17:8-14, which reads: "Then the Lord said to Moses, 'Write this as a reminder in a book and recite it...'" (Exod. 17:14). Thus, God's command to remembrance through writing and reading is fulfilled (also) by the book of Esther. Through the activation of the narrative web the informed reader/audience is invited to see the reciprocity of Haman and Mordecai, that they are each other's mimetic doubles.

Through the narrative economy and by means of the intertextual links, it is intimated—but only intimated—to the informed reader that Haman initiates retaliation for his ancestors' defeat: the genocide on the Persian Judeans is revenge for the slaying of Amalek and his people in Exodus 17.[27] This is the only serious reason given by the text for his "overkill" reaction to Mordecai's lack of subservience. At the narrative surface level, though, his wish for expanding the retaliation from the offending person, Mordecai, to all Judeans remains as unexplained as Mordecai's refusal to bow to Haman. There seems to be a blurring of the personal and the political domains, here. According to Fox, Haman's basic fault is his personal pride (not his political ambitions); his is a "vast and tender ego" in need of constant confirmation, thus his rage over Mordecai's defiance. Accordingly, "the conflict between Haman and the Jews is...essentially personal, to be explained primarily as a defect of Haman's psyche rather than as a clash between two races." Haman "makes antisemitism an *instrument* for achieving perfect personal revenge. The tribal conflict

---

26. Cf. Berlin, *Esther*, 24–5, 33–4. From Haman's point of view (in Davies' representation), the old enmity has its point of departure in Exod. 17:9-14, as mentioned above. What Haman "forgets" to tell, however, is that the story begins in Exod. 17:8 (not 17:9): "Then Amalek came and fought with Israel at Rephidim." At least in the Hebrew Bible/Jewish context Amalek is the aggressor (*pace* Haman's ghostwriter Davies, "Haman the Victim," 144–5).

27. The meaning of the tacit reference to 1 Sam. 15 in Esther is traditionally viewed as a justification of the Judeans' slaying of the Persians. When they kill their "Amalekite" enemies under Mordecai's (Saulide) command, they retrieve the failure of Saul who did not and therefore was abandoned by God and replaced by David. The sin of Saul, that he took the livestock which should have been "utterly destroyed," i.e. which was set aside as God's part of the spoil, is a rectification of Saul's failing. When the Judeans refuse to take spoil (Est. 9:10, 16), they "go beyond [Mordecai's] requirements and spontaneously show a better way to conduct a war" (Fox, *Character and Ideology*, 216). Fox understands this as "an assertion of dignity and self-sufficiency" (ibid.).

is the context for the personal one."²⁸ As commented by Levenson (in another connection, though) and discussed by Davies, "the personal has become the political."²⁹ But in a Girardian reading of Haman's character, his personal desire is not just a matter of objectless personal pride but of being and remaining in political power. His "Don't imitate me"—or: "Do not appropriate *my* object"—is hidden behind a political agenda, the cleansing of the King's land of supposedly disloyal citizens (Est. 3:8).³⁰ To Haman, Mordecai's refusal of making homage to him becomes the *týpos* of the Judeans estrangement from the Persian *communitas*.

3. *Violence and Society*

Let us turn to a brief presentation of Girard's understanding of the dynamics of violence and society. The ultimate threat to society is the chaos of mimetic rivalry, since rivalry inevitably leads to violence. If overpowered by mimetic violence, by a chain reaction of revenge and retaliation, society dissolves. "If left unappeased, violence will accumulate until it overflows its confines and floods the surrounding area. The role of sacrifice is to stem this rising tide of indiscriminate substitutions and redirect violence into 'proper' channels," as Girard puts it.³¹

Now, what is the connection between violence and dissolution on the one hand, enemy brothers and scapegoats on the other? In Girard's thinking these things belong together, since societal dissolution is the result of undammed mimetic violence. If the fight between enemy brothers escalates then violence will be communicated through imitation to the rest of the society. What is needed is a means of subduing mimetic violence; and this means is to collectivize the violence on the one hand and to aim the collective violence toward one person, a scapegoat or substitute victim, on the other. In other words, killing the substitute victim—the scapegoat—is society's cure against a growing, internal disease that threatens to destroy society. If society succeeds in aiming the violence toward one person who is deemed responsible for the threat,

---

28. Ibid., 179–81.
29. Davies, however, contests this understanding, since "racial hatred is a syny drome in which the two are not so easily disentangled, since it overwrites the personal with a stereotype and needs to invoke political…reasons for behaviour that exhibits traits of *personal* dislike" (Davies, "Haman the Victim," 142 n. 8, original emphasis). From a general, moral perspective, Davies might be right on this; but from the perspective of a "mimetic" reading, Levenson is right.
30. Cf. Girard, *Violence and the Sacred*, 11.
31. Ibid., 10.

then the killing/sacrifice of this person, the substitute victim, will cure the impending societal collapse:

> The sacrifice serves to protect the entire community from *its own* violence; it prompts the entire community to choose victims outside itself. The elements of dissension scattered throughout the community are drawn to the person of the sacrificial victim and eliminated, at least temporarily, by its sacrifice.[32]

The killing of the scapegoat, then, works as an effective antidote against the pollution of society; this leads to the ritualizing of the killing, and eventually the sacrifice, the ritual, will become preventive.[33]

If collectivizing violence into ritualizing and sacrifice of the scapegoat as the substitute victim helps to heal a society of its own violence, then it can also be used as a way of uniting a group in need of assemblage. In the words of Girard: "The purpose of the sacrifice is to restore harmony to the community, to reinforce the social fabric. Everything else derives from that."[34] If individuals are to be persuaded to be part of a crowd or made to feel at home in a certain guild, the singling out and presentation of a mutual potential enemy, a scapegoat, is extremely effective. This technique is well known by any populist politician, the scapegoat being African Americans, Jews, Romanies, or just ordinary immigrants and asylum seekers. In his book *The Scapegoat*,[35] Girard identifies a possible solution to a collective crisis through *collective persecution*. The persecutors, that is those who see themselves as threatened by collective crisis, "look everywhere for other likely indications—other stereotypes of persecution—to confirm their suspicion."[36] They accuse the intended scapegoat(s) of fundamental crimes. It might be

> those people whom it is most criminal to attack, either in the absolute sense or in reference to the individual committing the act [i.e. the persecution]: a king, a father, the symbol of the supreme authority, and in biblical and modern societies the weakest and most defenseless, especially young children. Then there are the sexual crimes: rape, incest, bestiality...[37]

---

32. Ibid., 8.
33. Ibid., 102.
34. Ibid., 8 (original emphasis).
35. René Girard, *The Scapegoat*, trans. Yvonne Freccero (Baltimore: The Johns Hopkins University Press, 1986).
36. Ibid., 15.
37. Ibid.

Are there traces of this kind of collective violence in Esther? The answer is in the affirmative. When Haman asks the king for authorization to persecute the Jews, his reason is that they disturb public order and attack the king's authority: "There is a certain people," he says to the king, "scattered and separated among the peoples in all the provinces of your kingdom; their laws are different from those of every other people, and they do not keep the king's laws, so that it is not appropriate for the king to tolerate them. If it pleases the king, let a decree be issued for their destruction" (Est. 3:8-9). This is an example of the concept of collective persecution.

As a mimetic parallel indicated by the book's peripety, we find traces of collective violence or persecution in the description of the Judeans' fight against their enemies on the thirteenth of Adar in Esther 9. They "gathered in the cities throughout all the provinces of King Ahasuerus to lay hands on those who had sought their ruin" (9:2), and they "struck down all their enemies with the sword, slaughtering, and destroying them" (9:5). The semantic structure of the last sentence speaks for itself; the emphasis on the gathering of the Judeans in the first is a reminder of the underlying purpose and dynamism of collective violence, the gathering of individuals into a body of people. This aspect is upfront already in Est. 8:11:

> By these letters the king allowed the Jews who were in every city to assemble and defend their lives, to destroy, to kill, and to annihilate any armed force of any people or province that might attack them, with their children and women...

4. *The Individual and the Collective Scapegoat*

The only problem left is that in Esther we do not have *one* victim, *one* scapegoat, as required by Girard in *Violence and the Sacred*. Haman's originally intended victims who in the end turn the situation upside-down are a collective, "all the Judeans"; the actual final victims of the communal violence when the Judeans strike back are legion, too: 75,311 Persians. If we look for a single scapegoat, how does Haman qualify for the role? What is the connection in the book of Esther between collective violence and the scapegoating of Haman?

Here, we must take a detour *via* the relation between King Ahasuerus and Haman. The narrative about Haman's fall discloses an ostensible mimetic conflict between Ahasuerus and Haman over Esther and strengthens Haman's effect as a scapegoat. When Haman throws himself "on the couch where Esther was reclining" (Est. 7:8) to pray for dear life, the king, returning from an "accidental" walk in the park, accuses him of assaulting the queen, and thus assaulting the king's sovereignty[38]. The incident reflects that the surrogate victim, like the collectively persecuted (cf. above), must commit a crime, in his case the crime against the king's property, by—allegedly—trying to rape the queen.[39]

One might think, then, that in the narrative economy the king's execution of Haman in Esther 7 would have been the logical remedy against the decree against the Judeans. The killing of the Persians could have been avoided by sacrificing Haman, and the story could have ended happily in Esther 7 with Haman hanging on the gallows he had built for Mordecai. The implied narrator, however, insists on bringing the story to a more violent culmination through the insistence on the irrevocability of Haman's and the king's decree against the Judeans. Why is that?

In the narrative logic, Haman's death is not allowed to work as sufficient satisfaction because Haman himself has mobilized a myriad of enemies, thus destabilizing the balance between the antagonists. Within the narrative logic the Judeans simply had to "destroy, to kill, and to annihilate any armed force of any people or province" (Est. 8:11) in order not to be sacrificed on Haman's altar of arrogance and anti-Semitism. Within this logic Haman, not the Judeans, is to blame for the slaughtering of Persian children, women, and men because of the irrevocability of the decrees. It was Haman who put the Persians on the altar.

Thus, the book of Esther is a narrative about collective violence; but it is also a narrative in need of redemption from the blood guilt of the slaughtering. One might think that the slaughter of the Persians *would be* the sacrifice that would gather the dispersed Judeans of Persia. But in a larger social context in which the narrative functions as a foundational myth, that is, in antique Judaism, the blunt killing is not acceptable anymore, and the accusation of bloodshed might be a factor that would lead this vulnerable community into a new, internal moral crisis.[40] In a world on the verge of anti-semitism, the early Jewish community cannot afford to lean on a foundational myth that paints them as aggressors committing genocide in

---

38. Ibid. Cf., e.g., the story of Absalom who, by "going in" to "his father's concubines in the sight of all Israel," assaults the sovereignty of his father, King David's (2 Sam. 16:20-23).

39. Girard (*Scapegoat*, p. 15) mentions rape as one of the "reasons" for making an individual a scapegoat.

40. Cf. the ritualizing of the original sacrifice and the substitution of a human victim by a sacrificial animal, see below.

their adopted homeland. If the myth is to be effective, the cruelty of the collective violence must be hidden as "choses cachées depuis la fondation du monde," as *Things Hidden since the Foundation of the World*, to quote another of Girard's famous titles.[41] The collective brutality needs another name, "self-defense" caused by the deeds of Haman, the villain. In the end the collective crisis is not the dispersion of the Judeans all over the provinces of Persia; the crisis is the outburst of violence that threatens to dissolve the corporate respectability.[42]

Secondly, from the perspective of mimetic desire within the Esther narrative, Haman also serves as a scapegoat for the apparent hero who saved the community from the jeopardy he himself seemingly had led them into; the person who was (or seemed to be?) in need of an enemy as a remedy for the scattered and separated situation of the Judean people in all the provinces of Persia (Est. 3:8). This person is Mordecai, Haman's double, "Haman mit umgekehrtem Vorzeichen."[43] It is Mordecai who from the beginning puts his people at risk of annihilation. Mordecai causes the threat to the Jews when he refuses to bow down and do obeisance to Haman, his mimetic enemy brother (3:2)—even the narrator cannot offer any legitimate reason for that.[44] His symbolic obstinance presages his craving to acquire the object of his mimetic desire, the power in Persia, symbolized by the power over the Jews. This is what the quest for the scapegoat has shown. If anyone had seen through Mordecai's shrewd plot, they would have realized that the proper felon of the book of Esther is Mordecai, the Judean—Mordecai, the hero.[45]

Here, we must add yet another aspect of Girard's cultural theory, the concept of substitution:

> Ritual sacrifice is founded on a double substitution. The first, which passes unperceived is the substitution of one member of the community for all, brought about through the operation of the surrogate victim. The second, the only truly 'ritualistic' substitution, is superimposed on the first. It is the

---

41. René Girard et al., *Things Hidden since the Foundation of the World*, trans. Stephen Bann and Michael Metteer (London: Athlone, 1987).

42. Cf. also Ben-Chorin's problems with the book as described above.

43. Ben-Chorin, *Kritik des Estherbuches*, 9.

44. This enigma has caused a lot of speculation throughout the history of exposition of Esther.

45. The fictive Haman does: "Mardukai was too good a schemer for me. I tried my hand at the game, but he was a master. Of course, he didn't react as I had hoped. Far from trying to stop my little ploy, he did just the opposite. He immediately dramatized the whole thing, put on mourning clothes, paraded up and down" (Davies, "Haman the Victim," 149).

substitution of a victim belonging to a predetermined sacrificial category for the original victim. The surrogate victim comes from inside the community, and the ritual victim must come from outside.[46]

If my analysis is correct, Haman the Amalekite is the victim who substitutes Mordecai as the sacrifice that would unite the scattered Judeans. Mordecai would be the perfect sacrifice, since during the narrative he shows himself to be the born leader. He is (allegedly) of royal descent (Est. 2:5-6), he is dressed up as a king (Esth 6) and he conquers the role as vizier for the almighty Persian king whose protector he has been from the beginning of the narrative (Est. 2:21-23). This qualifies him as the person, most suited to substitute the collective in need of redemption from the collective crisis of institutional collapse and cultural eclipse.[47] As a leader, he represents and incorporates the people.[48] But he is also a king in need of a surrogate victim, who mirrors him enough to serve the role. Thus, Haman, Mordecai's mimetic twin, ends in the gallows, and therefore the 75,311 Persians die with him.

To sum up: Esther is a book about mimesis on more than one level. What we have is a story of two enemy brothers, Haman the Amalekite and Mordecai the Judean, and a story about how the dispersed Judeans gathered and became one festival-celebrating national congregation. The act of killing united them in the celebration of Purim and made them speak unanimously. In the circle beyond that story we find the people that needed this story to revitalize their *commmunitas* through corporate memory and ritual—the Judeans of the Diaspora.

5. Conclusion: Of Scapegoats and Carnivals

This brings me to my closing remarks on scapegoats and carnival.[49] Our reading of Esther has pointed to the function of the story as a community-creating narrative, the community in question being the Judean

---

46. Girard, *Violence and the Sacred*, 102.
47. Cf. Girard, *Scapegoat*, 14.
48. In *Violence and the Sacred*, 104–18, Girard discusses ceremonies in monarchies of continental Africa in which the king, on special days such as his enthronement, is required to commit all imaginable forbidden acts, especially incest and eating of unclean and tabooed food.
49. "Almost every society has festivals that have retained a ritualistic character over the centuries. Of particular interest to the modern inquirer are observances involving the deliberate violation of established laws… Such violations must be viewed in their broadest context: that of the overall elimination of differences" (ibid., 119).

community in the Diaspora.⁵⁰ The narrative serves as a foundational myth for the festival of Purim, the festival that more than any other celebrates Jewish self-confidence.⁵¹ What Haman said about the Jews is only half a lie. What the Jews wanted to achieve was to be "a people" and to "follow their own law."⁵² In the book of Esther, this is what happens when they gather around Esther and Mordecai and follow their call to fight the Persians (9:1-18) and later to celebrate Purim (9:19-32). The descriptions of these two unifying affairs are characterized by their almost tedious, scrupulous repetitiveness and their focus on Esther's and Mordecai's authority over the, up till then, scattered Judeans of Persia:

> Thus because of all that was written in this letter, and of what they had faced in this matter, and of what had happened to them, the Jews established and accepted as a custom for themselves and their descendants and all who joined them, that without fail they would continue to observe these two days every year, as it was written and at the time appointed. (9:26-27)

Even Haman's role as a scapegoat is repeated in detail as the reason for the very celebration:

> So the Jews adopted as a custom what they had begun to do, as Mordecai had written to them. Haman son of Hammedatha the Agagite, the enemy of all the Jews, had plotted against the Jews to destroy them, and had cast Pur—that is "the lot"—to crush and destroy them; but when Esther came before the king, he gave orders in writing that the wicked plot that he had devised against the Jews should come upon his own head, and that he and his sons should be hanged on the gallows. Therefore these days are called Purim, from the word Pur. (9:23-26).

Purim is defined by, among others, Adele Berlin and André LaCocque as a carnivalesque holiday, at day where almost anything goes.⁵³ It is interesting in this connection to note Berlin's description of Purim as a

---

50. About the date and place of the "biblical" books of Esther, MT, LXX, and AT, see Chapter 2, above.

51. Cf. Berlin, *Esther*, xlv. Fox also points to the reenactment of the ancestor's experience as the focus of Purim (Fox, *Character and Ideology*, 152). A reversed testimony of this understanding is the repeated accusations of Jewish nationalism from especially Christian commentators; but also, the critique of Esther and Purim from reformed Jews like Ben-Chorin, cf. above.

52. Cf. Est. 2:8.

53. According to Berlin, "there is no complete breakdown or reversal of norms (as many discussions of carnival would have it), but a symbolic or partial reversal of norms" (Berlin, *Esther*, xlviii, cf. xlix).

"*miming* of a reversal, imitating or pretending to turn society's norm on their head." She continues: "Costumes and masks, excessive drink, noise, rowdiness, and even (mock) violence are some of the common manifestations that symbolize both the make-believe and the permissible reversing of the rules of society."[54] One of the victims of this "mock violence" at Purim is Haman, whose name is to be blotted out through excessive noise-making, in order to follow the command of Deut. 25:19: "Thou shalt blot out the remembrance of Amalek."[55]

But moreover, the carnivalesque feast of Purim, with its excessive drink and noise, mirrors Ahasuerus' abundant—in a Hellenistic context, over-abundant—party in Esther 1. In both instances the wine flows until, ideally, every man is drunk beyond normalcy.[56] In Esther 1 the party continues for six months, only to be followed by yet another party "for all the people present in the citadel of Susa, both great and small, a banquet lasting for seven days, in the court of the garden of the king's palace" (1:5), that is, in Susa. At the closing of Esther, these same inhabitants of Susa are killed on a second day on the request of Esther; this can be viewed as yet another case of very ironic peripety (9:11-15). At Purim, the festival only takes one day, but in the cities this day is followed by a second day of Purim, remembering the second day of killing in Susa (9:18-19). Thus, peripetic imitation continues past the limits of the book and brings the foundational myth of Purim out into world materiality.

---

54. Berlin, *Esther*, xlviii (original emphasis). For Esther as a book of disguise and hiding, see Beal, *Book of Hiding*.

55. When Haman's name is read out during the public chanting of the Megillah Esther in the synagogue, which occurs 54 times, the children of the congregation engage in noisemaking to blot out his name. It can be traced back to the thirteenth century CE and is in accordance with a passage in the Midrash, where the verse "Thou shalt blot out the remembrance of Amalek" (Deut. 25:19) is explained to mean "even from wood and stones." So, people wrote the name of Haman on two smooth stones, which were knocked together until the name was blotted out, or on the soles of their shoes, and at the mention of the name stamped with their feet as a sign of contempt. Another method was to use a noisy rattle, in Yiddish a *grager*, cf. http://en.wikipedia.org/wiki/Purim, accessed 17 August 2018.

56. "There has been much discussion around the saying of the Babylonia teacher Rava (*Meg.* 7b) that a man is obliged to drink so much wine on Purim that he becomes incapable of knowing whether he is cursing Haman or blessing Mordecai. The more puritanical teachers tried to explain this away, but the imbibing of alcohol was generally encouraged on Purim and not a few otherwise sober teachers still take Rava's saying literally" (Louis Jacobs, "Purim," *EncJud* 16, ed. Fred Skolnik et al., 2nd edn [Detroit: Thomson Gale, 2007], 740–1 [41]).

What are the results of our counter-reading, then? Is Haman a scapegoat? Yes. Is he to be believed in his prison cell on death row as portrayed by Philip Davies, claiming that he was a totally innocent scapegoat? No! Haman is not "not-guilty." That would have disqualified him as a scapegoat. But Haman is not the only guilty person in the book of Esther. When a scapegoat is identified, the person—or persons—in need of a scapegoat are inevitably uncovered.

Part III

Ideologies

Chapter 7

There Is a Certain People—
Or: How the Judeans Became the Jews

> Haman said to King Ahasuerus, "There is a certain people scattered and separated among the peoples in all the provinces of your kingdom; their laws are different from those of every other people, and they do not keep the king's laws, so that it is not appropriate for the king to tolerate them." (Est. 3:8)

The words of the archvillain in the book of Esther, Haman the Agagite, ignite the main conflict in the book by pointing to the question of ethnic uniqueness among the Judean exiles in Persia. Although the words are meant to be slandering—and obviously serve as desired in the mind of the king—like all good slandering they are only a half-lie. The Judeans, presumably like any other people in the Persian Empire, did adhere to their own laws; the lie is that they did not keep the king's laws. Haman also remarks that "certain people" are "scattered and separated" in all the provinces and thus points to one of the problems solved at the end of the narrative. By ch. 9, the Judeans have become one people with a community-creating religious holiday of their own and with their leader(s) in a second to non-political position in their adopted country. This happens through two basic actions, the slaughtering of the Judean's Persian enemies and the instigation and celebration of the first feast of Purim, as discussed in Chapter 6, above.

Through the centuries of tradition, exposition, exegesis, and reception, the book of Esther has been criticized for being overtly nationalistic, especially from the perspective of Christian writers as against the claim by other, mostly Jewish, scholars that the killing of the Persian enemies in the end of the book of Esther has nothing to do with nationalism but is (1) compulsory self-defense against attackers or (2) a carnivalesque hyperbole or plain humor. As mentioned in Chapter 1, "nationalism" is part of the background for the general criticism of the book, and we shall return to the question in Chapter 8, below. In this chapter, however, we shall not discuss the book from the point of view of nationalism, but as a question of ethnicity. Similarly, we shall not deal with questions of theology or ethics, but of sociology and religion.[1]

A Judean nation state or nationalism *per se* are not the focus of the book of Esther. Actually, the question is whether the concept of nationalism makes sense at all in the Persian and Hellenistic periods. The issue in the book of Esther is that of ethnicity. The original homeland of the exiled Judeans in Persia or the carrying off from Judah is only mentioned once in the Hebrew book of Esther (Est. 2:5-6), and the quintessential symbol of a nation state, the king, is never mentioned. There is no longing for Jerusalem or for the Temple as in the Zion theology of Second Isaiah; there is no interest in rebuilding the temple and the Davidic monarchy as in Chronicles, Ezra–Nehemiah, Zechariah, and Haggai; there is no covenant or Law as in the Deuteronomistic writings. There are no plans of returning whatsoever.[2] What the Judeans in Persia want in Esther is to be a people (*'ām*), not a nation or a state.[3] And on the road to this, they become the archetypical and model Judean Diaspora community who survive the enmity of their surroundings, prosper, and acquire enough influence in their adopted country to be able to take care of their own.

The question to be discussed in the following is how the Judeans became the Jews, or rather, *if* and/or *how* the Judeans became the Jews in the book of Esther.

1. *The Use of* yᵉhûdîm *in Esther*

From the outset, the Judeans in Esther are described as one group with a certain ethnicity and their own language, scattered among other ethnic groups with their own languages in the vast empire of King

---

1. On the question of nationalism in Esther, see Levenson, "The Scroll of Esther in Ecumenical Perspective."

2. "From a theological point of view, however, we can see in Esther an alternative to the lack of political realism in Second Isaiah and his successors… What Esther lacks in poetic power it gains in a realistic assessment of the options open to Israel in the radically new situation of Diaspora, in which shrewd statespersons were at least as essential to survival as were prophets." (Levenson, "The Scroll of Esther in Ecumenical Perspective," 449).

3. Cf. also Timothy Laniak, "Esther's *Volkcentrism* and the Reframing of Post-Exilic Judaism," in Greenspoon and Crawford, eds, *The Book of Esther in Modern Research*, 77–90; Levenson, *Esther*, 14–15.

Ahasuerus (Est. 1:22). The multitude of ethnicities is emphasized: Ahasuerus "ruled over one hundred twenty-seven provinces from India to Ethiopia" (1:1), and the letters with the decree about Vashti's expulsion from court and the compulsory male mastering of all households in Persia was sent "to all royal provinces, to every province in its own script and to every people in its own language" (1:22). Ethnic diversity is a major theme in this chapter, and the Judeans are just one people out of many.

At the end of the book, the implied reader's interest is focused on only one people, labeled by four different nouns: $y^e h\hat{u}d\hat{\imath}m$ ('Judeans'), *'aḥaw* ('his brothers'), *'am* ('people') and *zera'* ('descendants'); the rest of the peoples have vanished from the text:

> For Mordecai the Judean (*ha-y^{e}hûdî*) was next in rank to King Ahasuerus, and he was powerful among the Judeans (*la-y^{e}hûdîm*) and popular with his many kindred (*lerob '^{e}ḥāw*) for he sought the good of his people (*l^e 'ammô*) and interceded for the welfare of all his descendants (*l^{e}kol zar'ô*). (Est. 10:3, NRSV modified)

Here, the Judeans act as one people, united by military victory over their (alleged) enemies, with one leader, and the *y^{e}hûdîm* instigating a religious festival that emphasizes intra-ethnic solidarity. This assemblage of the *y^{e}hûdîm* is shown almost graphically in the book; the designation *y^{e}hûdîm* is clustered in Esther 8–9, the story of the planned pogrom, where the security situation comes to a head for the *y^{e}hûdîm* and they are forced to act in community against a communal enemy.

In other words, the question of ethnicity becomes important only at the end of the book. What will be of interest in this chapter, then, is *why* and *how* the *y^{e}hûdîm* become a people in the Esther narrative, which leads to a question of how to *understand* and *appraise* the ethnogeny in Esther. These questions are closely linked to the festival of Purim, which therefore must be treated in this connection as well.

2. *Are the Judeans in Esther Jewish?*
Or: How to Define Ethnicity?

In most translations of the book of Esther, the term *y^{e}hudî* is translated "Jew, Jude, Juif, Jøde, etc." cf. Greek *Ioudaios*, Latin *Iudacus*. This translation has led to severe misunderstandings, as discussed in Chapter 1; religious anti-Semitism ("the Jews killed Jesus") was transferred into cultural ethnic anti-Semitism. Just one example suffices:

Yes, God has marked them in their very natures. Clearly, a Jew has something about him that makes him immediately recognizable and distinguishable from other people, they rouse disgust and horror.[4]

An important question to be discussed, then, is how to translate the Hebrew word *y^{e}hûdî*. What does the concept of ethnicity connote in Esther and contemporary literature? From the outset, most of us have a commonplace understanding of ethnicity as a unity of a certain group of men, women, and children who live together and share the same geographical space, language, history, and values—and, when it comes to the people of the *y^{e}hûdîm*, also the same religion, Judaism or Jewishness. This commonsense understanding ("a Jew is a Jew is a Jew…") is not adequate from an academic position, and it has been challenged over the past ca. 100 years, most radically from scholars who argue for a constructivist understanding of ethnicity ("a Jew is something you become…") but also from sociologists that argue for a view between the two extremes.[5] Also, it has been discussed whether ethnicity should be defined from endemic criteria, that is, if they belong to a group because they match certain criteria within this group, or by demarcation between ethnic groups.[6] In other words the question is: are you a *y^{e}hûdî* because you belong to the group of *y^{e}hûdîm*, or are you a *y^{e}hûdî* because you are not something different, for example, a Median or a Persian?

The extant theoretical discussion is not of immediate importance in the present context.[7] It is not the intent to describe the historical facts of the segregation of the group of *y^{e}hûdîm* or how they segregated themselves from the ethnic majority/majorities in the Persian Empire in the sixth century BCE and later. The intent is to follow the literary construction of the people of *y^{e}hûdîm* in the book of Esther. Here, there is no discussion of the criteria for being a *y^{e}hûdî*; the persons involved know their ethnicity very well right from the outset, and so does apparently the author, too.

---

4. *Grosses Vollständiges Universal Lexicon* (Leipzig/Halle, 1775), cited in Shaye J. D. Cohen, *The Beginnings of Jewishness: Boundaries, Varieties, Uncertainties* (Berkeley: University of California Press, 1999), 25.

5. For an overview of the discussion, see Stewart A. Moore, *Jewish Ethnic Identity and Relations in Hellenistic Egypt: With Walls of Iron?* (Leiden: Brill, 2014).

6. Fredrik Barth, "Introduction," in *Ethnic Groups and Boundaries: The Social Organization of Culture Difference*, ed. Fredrik Barth (Oslo: Universitetsforlaget, 1969), 9–38.

7. For an overview and introduction to the vast discussion of the definition of ethnicity, I refer to the compiled articles in John Hutchinson and Anthony D. Smith, eds, *Ethnicity* (Oxford: Oxford University Press 1996).

From this "emic,"[8] point of view, the criteria for belonging to the *y^ehûdîm* are found in the description of Mordecai *ha-y^ehûdî* in Est. 2:5-6:

> Now there was an *'îš y^ehûdî* in the citadel of Susa whose name was Mordecai son of Jair son of Shimei son of Kish, a Benjaminite. He[9] had been carried away from Jerusalem among the captives carried away with King Jeconiah of Judah, whom King Nebuchadnezzar of Babylon had carried away.

Nevertheless, it is necessary to step back to ask the "etic" question what the concept of ethnicity means in an ancient context. Shaye J. D. Cohen discusses the question thoroughly in his monograph *The Beginnings of Jewishness*.[10] He agrees with Fredrik Barth (and many others) that *ethnos* is a social-cultural construction and that groups define themselves as an "us" over against "others." But he disputes that "the culture of a group (customs, values, habits, language, etc.)" can be separated from its identity.[11] He quotes affirmatively A. D. Smith's definition:

> For short we must define the *"ethnie"* or ethnic community as a social group whose members share a sense of common origins, claim a common and distinctive history and destiny, possess one or more distinctive characteristics, and feel a sense of collective uniqueness and solidarity… It is the myth of a common and unique origin in time and place that is essential for the sense of ethnic community.[12]

---

8. The terms emic/etic were coined in 1967 within the field of linguistics by Kenneth L. Pike, who writes: "The etic viewpoint studies behavior as from outside of a particular, and as an essential initial approach to an alien system. The emic viewpoint results from studying behavior as from inside the system" (Kenneth L. Pike, "Etic and Emic Standpoints for the Description of Behavior," in *The Insider / Outsider Problem in the Study of Religion*, repr., ed. Russell T. McCutcheon [London: Cassell Academic, 1999), 28–36). For a short introduction to the emic/etic discussion, see McCutcheon's introduction to the first part of this volume, ibid., 15–22.

9. Modified from the NRSV. The NRSV and several other English translations emend the Hebrew text of v. 6 and read "Kish had been carried away…" in order to hide the time gap between the fall of Jerusalem and the Persian period. This *pius fraus* disturbs the message of Mordecai's family tree, that he was one of the original exiles; see Chapter 6 above.

10. Cohen, *Beginnings of Jewishness*. The main focus of the book is not on the early Second Temple period, i.e. the presumed date of the book of Esther, but from the Maccabean period and beyond.

11. Ibid., 5–6.

12. Anthony D. Smith, *The Ethnic Revival* (Cambridge: Cambridge University Press, 1981), 66; cf. Cohen, *Beginnings of Jewishness*, 6 n. 9.

Against this background, he concludes, "The Jews (Judeans) of antiquity constituted an *ethnos*, an ethnic group."[13]

According to Cohen, "all occurrences of the [Greek] term *Ioudaios* before the middle or end of the second century B.C.E. should be translated not as 'Jew,' a religious term, but as 'Judean,' an ethnic-geographic term…'a member of the tribe of Judah'."[14] Here, he is followed by Steve Mason, who argues that it makes no sense to talk about religion as a specific concept in antiquity until after the Maccabean Wars.[15] In Cohen's perception, however, this does not mean that religion is not a part of Judean ethnicity, only that it is not the primary or only signifier.[16] Anne-Mareike Wetter[17] adheres to a parallel definition by A. D. Smith and John Hutchinson, and demonstrates that several characteristics of an *ethnie* in the above definition appear in Mordecai's genealogy: "A name (*yᵉhûdî*), references to more or less mythical ancestors, shared historical memories, and a link with a homeland."[18] She, however, insists on also

---

13. Cohen, *Beginnings of Jewishness*, 7.

14. In the Hellenistic period, the meaning of *Ioudaios*, the translation of the Hebrew *yᵉhûdî* holds three basic meanings, as a function (1) of birth and/or geography, (2) of religion and culture, or (3) of politics. However, "before 100 B.C.E. *Ioudaios* always and only meant 'Judean' in sense I." Ibid., 70–1.

15. Steve Mason, "Jews, Judeans, Judaizing, Judaism: Problems of Categorization in Ancient History," *JSJ* 38 (2007): 457–512. Mason, however, understands ethnicity from the perspective of demarcation (cf. Barth, "Introduction"). He focuses on the understanding of the Greek term *Ioudaismos*, which according to him erroneously has been translated in scholarly literature as a religious term, Jewish, rather than an ethnic term, Judaic/Judean. The Greek word *Ioudaismos* is used in only one Jewish text, 2 Maccabees (2 Macc. 2:21; 8:1; 14:38*2; cf. *4 Macc.* 4:26) where "Ἰουδαϊσμος appears to have been coined in reaction to cultural Ἑλληνισμος" (ibid., 464). For Mason, the dichotomy between *Hellenismos* and *Ioudaismos* in 2 Maccabees indicates that for Judas Maccabeus Judaism is not "a system of life, but a newly coined countermeasure against Ἑλληνισμος" (ibid., 480).

16. See also the discussion in John J. Collins, *The Invention of Judaism: Torah and Jewish Identity from Deuteronomy to Paul* (Oakland: University of California Press, 2017), 2–4. Collins comments on Mason's position: "His [Mason's] objection to the word 'Jew' in the context of antiquity is that he takes it to refer to a religion in the modern sense of the term, as a privatized area of life that can be bracketed off from the rest of society" (ibid., 4).

17. Anne-Mareike Wetter, "How Jewish is Esther? Or: How is Esther Jewish?— Tracing Ethnic and Religious Identity in a Diaspora Narrative," *ZAW* 123 (2011): 596–603; cf. Anne-Mareike Wetter, *"On Her Account": Reconfiguring Israel in Ruth, Esther, and Judith*, LHBOTS 623 (London: Bloomsbury T&T Clark, 2015).

18. Wetter, "How Jewish is Esther?" 598.

paying attention to the religious content of the term *yᵉhûdîm* in Esther, despite the absence of explicitly religious language throughout the book.[19] To be a *yᵉhûdî* includes religion, she argues, and she concludes:

> No translation of *yᵉhûdîm* seems satisfactory, and yet translate we must. Taking everything into account, I tend towards rendering *yᵉhûdî(m)* as Jews—not because the *yᵉhûdîm* in Esther conform to the image of Jewishness found in other biblical writings, or to our own ideas of what Jewishness is all about, but because I believe the book is an attempt to fill an ambiguous term with distinct meaning. The "Jews" in Esther may not fulfil our expectations, but they clearly think of themselves as the rightful heirs of the "Jewish" literary tradition, a tradition they appropriate on the one hand, and from which they emancipate themselves on the other.[20]

Wetter is right that it makes no sense to separate religion from the rest of the cultural specifics of the *yᵉhûdîm* in Esther. On the other hand, I find Cohen's (and Mason's) arguments persuasive that the best translation before 2 Maccabees is "Judean." The importance of religion and the understanding of ethnicity in Esther in not a matter of "either–or," it is "both–and." In Esther, as in the Hebrew Bible as such, there is no concept of *Ioudaismos* or "*yahădut*," only individuals who are *yᵉhûdîm*, that is, people who share "a sense of common origins, claim a common and distinctive history and destiny, possess one or more distinctive characteristics, and feel a sense of collective uniqueness and solidarity"[21]—including religion. But Esther is not a book about antique or modern "Jewishness" or "Judaism" as such, and in my view Wetter mis-names the cultural and literary heritage appropriated by the Judeans when she writes about "Jewish" tradition. The Judeans in the Diaspora, as well as other groups of Judeans in the fourth–second centuries BCE, did not have a *Jewish* tradition and heritage but a heritage from the Hebrew Bible, the accumulating collection of works in progress. I read Esther as one of the steps on the road to the "invention of Judaism." The narrative and ideological interest lies with the group of *yᵉhûdîm*, not with the other ethnic groups. Seen from this perspective, the "enemies" in Esther serve as the means of conceptualizing "otherness." A group that must redefine itself as a community—from being separated exiles and individuals to being a people, an *ethnie*, with all that it entails—needs a group of "others," or maybe even better an amorphous crowd of "others"

---

19. Ibid., 596–7.
20. Ibid., 603.
21. Cf. the quote from Smith, *The Ethnic Revival*, p. 111 above.

as their absolute antithesis.[22] We shall return to this discussion below, but before that we shall see how the ethnic conflict is presented in the book of Esther.

3. *There Is a Certain People*

At the beginning of the book of Esther all is well and peaceful in the vast realm of King Ahasuerus. The multitude of peoples and their good relationship to the king and each other is emphasized in the first chapter which tells the long and elaborate story of the king's banquet for all his officials and ministers (Est. 1:3-4). Here, the *y^ehûdîm* are not even mentioned, though we must suppose that their leaders were included among the many invitees from the 127 provinces. The crisis in the introductory chapter is not ethnic but defined by gender. The conflict is not between peoples but between men and women, husbands and wives. The consequences of Queen Vashti's insubordination, that all women will be insubordinate to their husbands, will strike the world order of all the peoples in Persia—including, we must assume, the Judeans, although it might be considered whether the implied narrator would want to exclude the Judean men from the irony. The conflict, in other words, is general and humane, not specifically ethnic.[23] Judean ethnicity is an issue for the first time in Est. 2:5-6, the presentation of Mordecai, quoted above. He is an *'îš y^ehûdî*, a Judean with a pedigree ("son of Jair son of Shimei son of Kish, a Benjaminite") that brings him in close connection not only with the original exiles[24] but also with the kingdom of Saul. Apart from a few instances in lists in Chronicles and Est. 2:5, the name Kish refers to Saul's father, and Mordecai is a Benjaminite like Saul.[25] "By virtue of Mordecai's being a *yehudi* and a Benjaminite he is a symbol of the authentic exilic Jew," Berlin states.[26] This is the first preclusion of the conflict between Haman and Mordecai. Esther 2:6 is also the first mention of Esther, Mordecai's cousin and ward, daughter of his fathers'

---

22. Cf. Barth, "Introduction."
23. On the importance of gender in Est. 1, see Beal, *Book of Hiding*, and Chapter 3, above.
24. "He had been carried away from Jerusalem among the captives carried away with King Jeconiah of Judah, whom King Nebuchadnezzar of Babylon had carried away" (Est. 2:6).
25. In Ezra 1:5 and 4:1 the descendants of the tribes of Judah and Benjamin constitute the rightful heirs to the land of Judah and thus the authentic Judaic community.
26. Berlin, *Esther*, 25 (original emphasis).

late brother. The two of them hide their Judaic descent in the rest of the chapter (cf. Est. 2:10) and the question of ethnicity is concealed; Judaism becomes part of Esther's hidden identity as discussed in Chapter 2 above. Still, there is peace and happiness in the royal court.

However, there is no narrative Paradise without a serpent, the mandatory villain who initiates the crisis that fuels the story. Haman, the arch villain in the book of Esther, puts the question of ethnicity on the agenda, as we saw earlier. After the showdown with Mordecai who refuses to bow down to him, Haman, the non-Persian, demands the king that all the Judeans in Persia be nihilated, without presenting the apparent reason. Instead, he pulls "the race card" saying:

> There is a certain people scattered and separated among the peoples in all the provinces of your kingdom; their laws are different from those of every other people, and they do not keep the king's laws, so that it is not appropriate for the king to tolerate them. If it pleases the king, let a decree be issued for their destruction, and I will pay ten thousand talents of silver into the hands of those who have charge of the king's business, so that they may put it into the king's treasuries. (Est. 3:8-9)

Without even accepting the bribe, the king approves of the plan and issues a decree, and Haman initiates the ethnic cleansing. In the following chapters, Mordecai and Esther cunningly thwart the plans and reverse the irreversible royal decree by a second decree, written by Mordecai:

> He wrote letters in the name of King Ahasuerus, sealed them with the king's ring, and sent them by mounted couriers riding on fast steeds bred from the royal herd. By these letters the king allowed the Jews who were in every city to assemble and defend their lives, to destroy, to kill, and to annihilate any armed force of any people or province that might attack them, with their children and women, and to plunder their goods on a single day throughout all the provinces of King Ahasuerus, on the thirteenth day of the twelfth month, which is the month of Adar. A copy of the writ was to be issued as a decree in every province and published to all peoples, and the Jews were to be ready on that day to take revenge on their enemies. (Est. 8:10-13)

Since both of the decrees are issued with plenty of time before the planned pogrom and the anti-pogrom, there is also plenty of time to take precautions, which is exactly what is done by some Persians: "Many of the peoples of the country professed to be Jews, because the fear of the Jews had fallen upon them" (Est. 8:17, NRSV). The verb "professed" is a translation of the Hebrew *mity^{e}hûdîm*, a *hapax* which is difficult to translate. Did they convert to Judaism? Were they circumcised? Or did they merely pretend to be Judeans? The Septuagint translates: "And many of the nations were circumcised and became Judeans out of fear for the Judeans" (Est. 8:17 LXX).²⁷ This rendition seems to be an exposition rather than a translation, bearing on the Hellenistic context of the Septuagint.²⁸ Nevertheless, the Greek term *ioudaïzein* might lead us on the right track for understanding the Hebrew. Cohen discusses *ioudaïzein* based on the use of similar verbs in classical Greek, that is, verbs with the name of a region or an *ethnos* as the noun stem plus the verb stem *-izein*. These verbs have three basic meaning: (1) to give political support (a political meaning); (2) to adopt customs or manners (a cultural meaning); (c) to speak a language (a linguistic meaning). When used in the political and cultural meaning, the subjects are generally people "from whom such behavior would not be expected… The verbs refer not to a change of essence but to a change of behavior, not 'to be' but 'to be like'."²⁹ Discussing *ioudaïzein* in Esther, Cohen refers to the translation of *mityᵉhûdîm* in the NRSV and NJPS translations: "And many of the people of the land professed to be Jews…" the meaning of which "is not that many non-Jews converted to Judaism but that they pretended to be Jews; they professed themselves to be something they were not."³⁰ As Cohen dryly comments: "the Jews had just been given carte blanche by the king to kill their enemies, and therefore many gentiles pretended to be Jews in order to protect themselves." Cohen continues by discussing three further instances of *ioudaïzein* in Jewish Greek texts, one in Paul's letter to the Galatians (Gal. 2:14), where it unambiguously means "to live Jewishly," and two passages in Josephus' *Jewish War* where the meaning is more ambiguous: it might be cultural or political—or both. Interestingly, the first passage from Josephus likens the narrative in the Greek Esther, telling about gentiles circumcising and Judaizing in order to save themselves from the hands of the Jews; the second also holds the theme of enmity between the Jews and their neighbors.³¹ On this basis, the simplest understanding of *mityᵉhûdîm* seems to be that out of fear for the Judeans lots of Persians pretended to be Judeans (the cultural meaning of *ioudaïzein*) or at least to be their supporters (the political meaning). How they were supposed to do that is not discussed

---

27. AT reads differently—and remarkably: "And many of the *Judeans* were circumcised, and no one rose up against them for they feared them." (NETS translation); see the discussion in de Troyer, *End of the Alpha Text*, 337–8.

28. Mason discusses the meaning of *ioudaïzō* and *ioudaïsmos* in 2 Maccabees (Mason, "Jews, Judeans, Judaizing, Judaism," 460–8).

29. Cohen, *Beginnings of Jewishness*, 178.

30. Ibid., 181.

31. Ibid., 182–5.

in the text. Either it was deemed superfluous, because the implied reader was supposed to understand immediately; or it was superfluous, because it was without significance for the narrative. The important message was that the Persians "Judaized," not how they did it. There is no need or reason to infer an anachronistic religious meaning of *mity^ehûdîm* as done by, for example, Fox: "…many of the peoples of the land became Jewish," meaning "the action of the gentiles is to be understood as joining the Jewish people."[32]

However, the (pretended) Judaism among the Persian leadership does not help the rest of the Persians. On the thirteenth day of the month of Adar, "the Judeans got their enemies in their power and no one could withstand them, for the fear of them had fallen upon all the peoples. Indeed, all the officials of the provinces—the satraps, the governors, and the king's stewards—showed deference (*m^enaśś^e'îm*) to the Jews, because the fear of Mordecai had fallen upon them" (Est. 9:2-3, NJPS).[33] After yet another day of recommenced killing in Susa, this time prompted by Esther and with special emphasis on the hanging of Haman's ten sons (9:11-15), everything ends in bliss among the Judeans when Purim is instigated. The regulations for Purim are written down by Mordecai and sent in exactly the same way as the royal decrees in Esther 3 by Royal Persian Mail (Est. 9:21-24):

> In view, then, of all the instructions in the said letter and of what they had experienced in that matter and what had befallen them, the Jews undertook and irrevocably obligated themselves and their descendants, and all who might join them, to observe these two days in the manner prescribed and at the proper time each year. Consequently, these days are recalled and observed in every generation: by every family, every province, and every city. And these days of Purim shall never cease among the Jews, and the memory of them shall never perish among their descendants. (Est. 9:26-28, NJPS)

It is my contention that the instigation of Purim as a Judaic, meaning pre-Jewish, festival is the objective of the book of Esther. This holiday helps the scattered Judeans, plagued by the lack of common objectives within and without the Persian Empire, to become an *ethnie*, the Judean— or Jewish—community. I do not pretend that this is a new or original

---

32. Fox, *Character and Ideology*, 103. 105. Cf. also Laniak: "As a byproduct of saving her people in Persia, their community swells with converts from the Persian Empire" (Laniak, "Esther's *Volkscentrism*," 81).

33. I use the NJPS translation here since it is closer to the original Hebrew. Many modern translations translate *m^enaśś^e'îm* "helped, supported, unterstützten, etc."

understanding of the book of Esther; but I would propose another path to this interpretation which also might address and resolve the question of how we can relate to the—at least from a narrative perspective—apparently superfluous genocide of the Persians.

To come that far, we must take a couple of detours.

4. *Purim and Tradition*

When studying the Hebrew book of Esther, the reader might get the idea that the final two chapters (Est. 9:9–10:3), about the instigation of Purim, are secondary additions to one—or maybe more—narratives about intrigues at the Persian court. As mentioned in Chapters 1 and 2, Clines in 1984 published a monograph that became a classic in modern Esther scholarship, in which he presented this idea as his main result.[34] Based on scrupulous literary analyses, Clines proposed that "MT represents a deliberate excision of *all* religious language"; that is, that it had been removed from Esther MT which he considered to be a later version of the book than the Alpha-text.[35] I for my part find it hard to understand the rationale behind the book of Esther without Purim, and in the following I shall try to present my case.[36] If there were no Purim it is my contention that we would not have the book of Esther today, at least not as a Biblical book. Purim and Esther create a reciprocal rationale, and understanding Purim is a prerequisite for understanding Esther. This only seems to present a problem for historical-critical scholars.

Before Clines' monograph, Gillis Gerleman proposed that the book of Esther and Purim were created as a counterpart to the exodus and *pesach* narratives in the Torah.[37] According to Gerleman, the doubling of the main protagonist, Esther *and* Mordecai, is striking and points to the doubling of Moses and Aaron in the Exodus narrative. There is a distribution of roles among the two of them where Mordecai tacitly pulls

---

34. "…I believe that we find that, far from presenting a vivid, subtle and dramatic story such as chs. 1–8 contained, 9.1-19 is striking for its poor construction, its inferior narrative development, and its logical weaknesses" (Clines, *Esther Scroll*, 39).

35. For the textual history of the "biblical" books of Esther, see Chapter 2 above.

36. In retaining the "originality" of the Purim in the Masoretic Esther novella, I concur with a long line of scholars whom I shall not evoke in the following. Most of the earlier scholars understood the book as a historical representation of the background of Purim. I do not.

37. Gillis Gerleman, *Esther*, BKAT 21 (Neukirchen-Vluyn: Neukirchener Verlag, 1973), 13.

the strings while Esther does the public work; this distribution of roles compares to Moses (the tacit leader) and Aaron (the public speaker). The intertextuality (Gerleman does not use this word) is supported by other factual and formal similarities, or rather loans, from Exodus, first and foremost Esther's and Mordecai's kinship. Esther's status as Mordecai's adopted daughter is reminiscent of Moses' status as adopted into the Egyptian royal family.[38] Other indications are the secrecy of Esther's nationality and her anonymity, which parallels Moses' in the house of Pharaoh[39] and which seems superfluous in the narrative economy; this indicates that the narrator has taken in external material which does not compare well to the rest of the narrative. Gerleman finds echoes even on the semantic level; according to him, the phrase *hā'îš mordŏkay* ("the man Mordecai," Est. 9:4) mirrors Moses, especially in Exod. 11:3, where *hā'îš mošeh* ("the man Moses") is described as "a man of great importance in the land of Egypt, in the sight of Pharaoh's officials and in the sight of the people." This, according to Gerleman, substantiates that Esther picks up elements of style from Exodus. In other words, the connection sheds light on peculiarities about Esther and Mordecai.[40]

Gerleman also finds parallels at the narrative level, for instance, Moses' visit to Pharaoh as a parallel to Esther's visit to Ahasuerus when they both hesitate because their visit is life threatening. The enigmatic reference to a place (*māqôm*) in Est. 4:14 must, according to Gerleman, be a reference to a supernatural power, one that is plausibly dependent on the narrative of Moses' encounter with the divine in Exod 3:5. Both Moses and Esther save their people, and in that case Esther one-ups Moses (and accordingly Purim bests Pesach) since Esther saves them from death, Moses only from slavery.[41] The killing of the Persians compares to the killing of Egyptians, "when the Israelites fled as hunted slaves before the superior force";[42] likewise the Persian's fear for the Jews which makes them

---

38. "There is no doubt that it is a direct loan from...the account of Moses' childhood" (ibid., 15, my translation from German).

39. "[T]he narrative in Exod. 2 must take for granted that Moses in the house of Pharaoh was considered an Egyptian and that his affiliation to the Jewish people was only made known when he 'went out to his kin'... (Exod 2:11ff.)" (ibid., 17, my translation from German).

40. "It is hard to defy the corollary that the Esther narrative has created its characters in accordance with the pattern of the account of Moses" (ibid., my translation from German).

41. Ibid., 20.

42. Ibid., 21.

mityᵉhûdîm compares to and even "outmatches the events at the night of Pesach."[43] When the Israelites leave Egypt, they are allowed to plunder the Egyptians (Exod. 12:33-35), which they do; the Jews in Esther, on the other hand, do not take spoil (this is emphasized three times), an attitude that is very positively portrayed in the book.[44] In conclusion, Gerleman finds in Esther a "deliberate and consistent desecration and de-theologization [*Entsachralisierung und Enttheologisierung*] of a central tradition of the salvation-history."[45]

These and further observations, especially concerning the philology of the term Purim, leads Gerleman to the conclusion that Purim was a totally profane festival, celebrated by the Jews in the Persian Diaspora; this festival was given a historical justification and binding authority through the book of Esther. Moreover, as indicated by the polemic and besting in Esther, it should be considered whether the book represents an attempt at having Purim replace the old Pesach as the central cultic holiday in the Diaspora for the community of well-integrated Jews in Persia.[46]

Gerleman's theory has not attracted many followers and his detailed observations are not very convincing from a current scholarly point of view; there are too many "loose ends" and overtly optimistic interpretations of connections. Many of his literary observations, the doubling of the protagonist, for example, are better explained through narrative theory and folk-lore studies. Furthermore, some of the connections seem rather contrived, not least the proposal of a connection between the plundering in Exodus and the Jews not taking spoil in Esther. There is neither a semantic nor a thematic connection between the two pericopes; that the Jews do not take spoil in Esther has a much closer explanation in the book's overt intertextuality to the Amalekite and Saul traditions.[47] In fact, Gerleman's proposal of Purim as a replacement of Pesach has clearly proven not to be successful. Pesach is still the most important Jewish holiday, even in the widespread Diaspora of today's world, as opposed to Purim, whose legality has been discussed in rabbinic literature.

This notwithstanding, Gerleman's arguments serve as an inspiration for further thoughts about the "invention" of Purim. Laniak finds Gerleman's observations "compelling." Referring to Levenson,[48] Laniak adds that the

---

43. Ibid., 22 (my translation from German).
44. Ibid., 21.
45. Ibid. (my translation from German).
46. Ibid., 27–8.
47. See n. 27 in Chapter 6.
48. Levenson, *Esther*, 73.

7. There Is a Certain People

most subtle intertextuality might be that "the month of 'fate' in Esther 3 (Nisan) was the very month God had originally chosen for Jewish triumph in the first chapter of their history."[49] In contrast to Gerleman, however, Laniak does not see Esther as a replacement of the Moses tradition, but as a continuation:

> Like the early chapters of Exodus, Esther is a narrative of deliverance followed by a law that requires its annual re-dramatization. Esther, in the end, affirms Israel's traditions by creating new Torah. It demonstrates that such a dramatic deliverance of God's chosen people ought to be institutionalized any time it occurs.[50]

Abraham D. Cohen also points to the coincidence between the dating of the *pur* and Passover, also shedding light on the connection between Exodus and Esther. He writes:

> In casting the lots in Nissan, and then announcing the results of the lottery on the 13th of the month, Haman sought to demonstrate to the Jews, *immediately before* their celebration of Passover, his denial of God's providential relationship towards them… But as it turned out, the Jews battled with their adversaries on the 13th and 14th days of the month, and celebrated their victory on the subsequent 14th and 15th days. Purim, preceding Passover by exactly a month, came to parallel and affirm Passover's meaning of Divine providence towards the Jewish people.[51]

The observations by Gerleman, Levenson, Laniak, and Cohen corroborate the impression that the book of Esther is a community-building book. More observations can be added. In my opinion, the most important might be that just as the exodus narrative in its final form leads to the writing of the covenant that affirms the relationship between God and his people, so Esther leads to no fewer than two written decrees, confirmed by all the Judeans, that they must celebrate Purim as a communal holiday with fasting, happiness, mutual giving of gifts (portions), and donations to the poor (Est. 9:20-23). The writing process is obviously very important and should not be overlooked. Just as the Decalogue is written and rewritten in Exodus 24 and 34 (after the Israelites have rejected its most important commands), so the decree of Purim is written and rewritten "for the

---

49. Laniak, "Esther's *Volkcentrism*," 86. Surprisingly, Gerleman does not note this convergence.
50. Ibid.
51. Cohen, "'*Hu Ha-goral*,'" 91.

purpose of confirming with full authority the aforementioned one of Mordecai the Jew" (Est. 9:29, NJPS).[52]

The book of Esther is a novel about how to live and survive in the Diaspora. It is not a book or a report about the actual living conditions or the history of the Judeans in Persia;[53] Esther is a book about how solidarity with and within the Judahite community can support the lives of the Judeans in a potentially hostile environment, and how Judean cunning outsmarts foreign stupidity.

5. *Purim and Genocide*

It is as if the whole narrative composition of Esther points towards the unavoidable confrontation between Haman and Mordecai, between the Persian "strawman" and the Judeans. The motif runs like a *basso ostinato* through the book. This theme was discussed in Chapter 6; here it must suffice to call attention to the fact that at the end of the book we reach the dramatic culmination, where all the peripeties, all the collocations of previous conditions found in the book, are wrapped up. The book ends with the detailed description of how the Judeans "struck down all their enemies with the sword, slaughtering, and destroying them, and did as they pleased to those who hated them" (Est. 9:5). As discussed before, this part of Esther has provoked a discussion of the ethics of the book, ranging from dismissive abhorrence to the explanation that the book is a farce, a carnivalesque narrative in which everything is turned upside down and nothing should be taken at face value. The later position is argued very convincingly by, among others, Adele Berlin and André LaCocque.[54] In my opinion, though, there seems to be more at play than carnival.

Two French thinkers can help us in the search for the function of Purim in Esther, Emile Durkheim and René Girard. For Durkheim, religion and society—or culture—are two sides of the same coin. Religion, conceived as a set of normative agreements or morality, is the sum of forces that integrate a society—here, understood as a cultural rather than a political,

---

52. On writing in the book of Esther, see Clines, *Esther Scroll*, 22–4.

53. The historical picture of life among the exiled Judeans in Babylon and Persia is getting ever clearer, but we still need a thorough treatment of the latest archives from the period; see Oded Lipschits and Manfred Oeming, eds, *Judah and the Judeans in the Persian Period* (Winona Lake: Eisenbrauns, 2006); Reinhard Gregor Kratz, *Historical & Biblical Israel: The History, Tradition, and Archives of Israel and Judah*, trans. Paul Michael Kurtz (Oxford: Oxford University Press, 2015).

54. Berlin, *Esther*; LaCocque, *Esther Regina*.

national, or ethnic concept. Community is created through each private individual's participation in a common cultural matrix of immaterial concepts such as common language, norms, narratives, traditions, experiences, and ideals. Community depends on a common culture (*moralité*). Without this common moral consciousness societies would fall apart, and each person would be left as a kind of animal, defenseless against all kinds of powers. Left to him/herself, the individual is in danger of losing his/her humanity: "man is man only because he is civilized."[55] Durkheim's perception of religion and society/culture/community does not necessarily imply theistic conceptions; but his idea of the development of communities correspond to religious celebrations, at least in what Durkheim names "primitive societies." In this room of otherness, holiness, the participants experience a common power which sets them apart from everyday normalcy, individuality, and separateness and unites them in the social community. The force that emerges in this community is what Durkheim calls "effervescence." He writes about the rising of effervescence in primitive, Australian societies:

> The very fact of assembling is an exceptionally powerful stimulant. Once the individuals are assembled, their proximity generates a kind of electricity that quickly exports them to an extraordinary degree of exaltation. Every emotion expressed is retained without resistance in all those minds so open to external impressions, each one echoing the others. The initial impulse thus becomes amplified as it reverberates, like an avalanche gathering force as it goes... Probably because a collective feeling cannot be expressed collectively unless a certain order is observed that permits the group's harmonious movements, these gestures and cries are inclined to be rhythmic and regulated, and become chants and dances.[56]

According to Durkheim, then, the force that emerges in the collective life of the community generates effervescence, the dynamic ("kind of electricity") that creates and sustains the community as such. In our case, this community-building force would be the feasting and gladness, and the sending of gifts of food to one another and of presents to the poor (cf. Est. 9:22).

---

55. Émile Durkheim, *The Elementary Forms of Religious Life*, abridged with an Introduction and Notes by Mark S. Cladis, trans. Carol Cosman, Oxford World's Classics (Oxford: Oxford University Press, 2001), 159.
56. Ibid., 162–3.

It is tempting to label the thinking of René Girard[57] "the dark side of the (same) force." In Girard's thought world violence and disintegration, brotherly hatred and scapegoats belong together, because the disintegration of society is the result of unrestrained mimetic violence, caused by mimetic, "brotherly" envy. If the fight between brothers escalates—as is the case in the book of Esther, where Mordecai and Haman are painted as enemy brothers and mimetic twins—then the violence is passed on to the rest of the society. What is needed is suppression of mimetic violence, in other words, to collectivize the violence and aim it against one person, the scapegoat. In the thought world of Girard, then, the killing of the substitute sacrifice, the scapegoat, becomes society's cure against societal disintegration. This is the reason for the highly profiled, public murder of Haman, who is hanged on his own stake, fifty cubits high, which he originally had put up for Mordecai (Est. 5:14; 9:10). The mimetic relationship between Mordecai and Haman, Judeans and Persians, and the complicated psycho-social background for Purim was discussed in Chapter 6, above. Here it suffices to say that the collective violence of the killing is hidden in the carnival of Purim, even better and more effectively, I believe, than in the book of Esther itself. Therefore, the book of Esther needs Purim.

James W. Watts has pointed to the interrelatedness of text and ritual. He argues that "old texts were used in antiquity to validate the forms of important rituals. The rituals in turn lent their cultural influence to the texts that prescribed them."[58] Watts, however, is more interested in the authoritative function of text, especially Torah, on ritual than *vice versa*. Therefore, Watt's examples, first and foremost Nehemiah's reading of the Torah in Neh. 8:1-12 and the reports on Josiah's reformation in 2 Kings 23 and 2 Chron. 35:1–19, do not compare to the situation in the book of Esther. Nevertheless, Watts' article inspires further thinking about the connectedness between text and festival. In the case of Esther we do not find an "old" text authorizing a new or reformed ritual, as in Watts' examples. Rather, what we find in Esther is a *new* festival authorized by a *new* text. Moreover, Purim is not a religious festival or ritual *per se*; the giving of presents and sharing of food is not connected to any religious space (a temple or an altar) and does not demand the presence of religious personnel such as priests or Levites. On the contrary, in the book of Esther Purim is set in the private space. No prayers are authorized, no readings

---

57. Girard, *Violence and the Sacred*. For a further presentation of Girard, see Chapter 6, above.

58. James W. Watts, "Ritual Legitimacy and Scriptural Authority," *JBL* 124 (2005): 401–17 (402).

are prescribed; Purim in Esther is as secular (or non-secular) at the book itself.[59] This notwithstanding, Esther *and* Purim draw on the intertextual connection to Exodus and Pesach, and to the narratives from the intertextual web of 1 Sam. 15:1-9 (Saul spares the Amalekites): "Remember what Amalek did to you on your journey out of Egypt..." (Deut. 25:17-19); the story of how "Amalek came in the desert and fought with Israel at Rephidim" (Exod. 17:8-14); and "Then the Lord said to Moses, 'Write this as a reminder in a book and recite it...'" (Exod. 17:14).[60] The merry feast of Purim is authorized through the reference to the bloody clashes between the forefathers of Mordecai and Haman. At the same time, it is "domesticated" into a nice get-together for family and friends sharing presents and meals, just like the *pesach* once instigated by God but renewed by Ezra the Scribe in Nehemiah 8 in the guise of *sukkoth*.

In the book, the carnivalesque chaos of Purim is buried in the tedious decrees of Mordecai and Esther, carefully written down and posted to everybody by imperial mail. Yet, the almost ritualized writing of the decrees serves as a framework for the carnival that unifies the $y^e h\hat{u}d\hat{i}m$ in a close-knit community, governed by one man, Mordecai ha-$y^e h\hat{u}d\hat{i}$. From being exiles, scattered among many other peoples and in the pursuit of identity,[61] they have become a people, an *ethnie* with a cultural community, created partly through violence, partly through decree, including a religious communality. The implied reader knows very well that Purim is a religious holiday, and this knowledge is redundantly present within the literary presentation. This is the religion which, together with other strands of Judean religious strands, would later develop into what we now refer to as full-scale antique and rabbinic Judaism.

---

59. Cf. the discussion in Chapter 1, above.
60. On this connection, see the commentaries and Chapter 6, above.
61. The religious collectivization is already present in Esther 4 where Esther demands that all Judeans in Susa participate in her fast. There, however, the act is somber and non-violent.

Chapter 8

THE SMALL SPRING AND THE DRAGONS:
READING THE BOOK OF ESTHER
AS CHOSEN TRAUMA

1. Chosen Trauma

The Cypriot-American psychiatrist Vamik D. Volkan describes the identity of larger groups (ethnic, national or religious) in the image of a tent, and the personal core identity of an individual as a garment.[1] The personal garment "fits the person snugly" and is the basis of the individual's inner sense of sustained sameness, the individual's working model which he or she, not an outsider, senses and experiences—in other words, his or her own perception of his or her personality.[2] On top of this garment there is a second layer, the large-group identity, "a loose covering made of the canvas of the large group's tent (the large-group identity) through which the person shares a persistent sense of sameness with others in the large group. Both garments provide security and protection." When there is a storm, that is, in a period of collective crisis, "the garment made of the tent canvas takes on greater importance, and individuals may collectively seek the protection of, and also help defend, their large-group tent." As a psychoanalyst, Volkan is interested in the psychological dynamics that create the large-group tent, and one of these is the shared memory of trauma, "what 'others' did to 'us' and additional aspects of large-group conflicts and large-group identity difficulties."[3] These shared memories can be transmitted over generations (transgenerational transmissions) and

---

1. Vamik D. Volkan, "Transgenerational Transmissions and Chosen Traumas: An Aspect of Large-Group Identity," *Group Analysis* 34 (2001): 79–97.
2. Ibid., 81.
3. Ibid., 83–4.

can develop into a "shared mental representation of a traumatic past event during which the large group suffered loss and/or experienced helplessness, shame and humiliation in a conflict with another large group."[4] For this phenomenon Volkan has framed the term "chosen trauma." Sharing the chosen trauma links the members of the group together, even if a traumatic memory can lie dormant over generations—"the chosen trauma becomes woven into the canvas of the ethnic or large-group tent."[5] And most importantly:

> Leaders intuitively seem to know how to reactivate a chosen trauma, especially when their large group is in conflict or has gone through a drastic change and needs to reconfirm or enhance its identity.[6]

2. *Trauma and Collective Memory*

In the previous chapter we discussed the narrative violence in the book of Esther and its backdrop in the need for identity making in the Diasporic Judean community in the Persian and later periods. There we used Durkheim's theory of the effect of effervescence and Girard's theory of mimetic violence as a heuristic tool to understand the meaning-making of

---

4. Ibid., 87.

5. Ibid., 88. He continues: "Since a large group does not choose to be victimized or suffer humiliation, some take exception to the term 'chosen' trauma. I believe that it reflects a large group's unconscious 'choice' to add a past generation's mental representation of an event to its own identity, and the fact that, while groups may have experienced any number of traumas in their history, only certain ones remain alive over centuries."

6. Ibid., 88. As an advisor of and participant in political negotiations of reconeciliation—e.g. as a member of the International Negotiation Network under the directorship of the former American President Jimmy Carter (1989–2000)—Volkan has discussed chosen traumas since the early 1990s; cf. the extant bibliography in "Transgenerational Transmissions and Chosen Traumas." One of Volkan's prime examples of the effect of transgenerationally transmitted chosen trauma is the Serbian "myth" of the battle at the Kosovo Polje (the Field of the Black Birds) in 1389 which was transmitted and transformed over centuries and resulted not only in the fatal shots that started World War I but also was a major game changer for Slobodan Milošević during his fight for ethnic cleansing of Kosovo in the 1990s (ibid., 89–95). On the battle at Kosovo Polje as collective trauma, see Ivana Spasić, "The Trauma of Kosovo in Serbian National Narratives," in *Narrating Trauma: On the Impact of Collective Suffering*, ed. Ron Eyerman et al., The Yale Cultural Sociology Series (Boulder: Paradigm, 2013), 81–105.

the narrated collective violence in Esther. We concluded that the implication of the book of Esther and the holiday of Purim was to help the scattered Judeans in the Diaspora, plagued by the lack of common objectives, to become an *ethnie*, the Judean—or Jewish—community. In the book, the conflict between Mordecai and Haman was doubled or mirrored by the conflict between the Judeans and the Persians, and through their defeat of their enemies the Judeans were united as a *communitas*. For the readers of the book, this conflict became a part of their shared communal memory, a traumatic experience the memory of which served very well as a chosen trauma, even if it was never a real but a fictive, narrated experience. It confirmed the self-image of the Diasporic Judeans as victims of anti-Semitism. There was an "us" and a "them."

The term "communal memory" is used by Jeffrey C. Alexander and others to describe the phenomenon of chosen trauma from a sociological perspective. According to Alexander, communal memory of collective trauma is a cultural construction propagated by carrier groups such as political or religious leaders. In a recent publication, Alexander and his co-editor Elizabeth Butler Breese write:

> Collective traumas are reflections neither of individual suffering nor actual events, but symbolic renderings that reconstruct and imagine them in a relatively independent way. This spiral of signification is the work of culture creators, who create scripts that answer the four "w" questions: What happened? Who were its victims? Who were its perpetrators? And what can be done? These scripts are not descriptions of what is; they are arguments for what must have been and, at least implicitly, of what should be.[7]

These four "w" questions can be identified in the book of Esther. Q: What happened? A: A pogrom was instigated in Persia. Q: Who were its victims? A: Judeans in Persia. Q: Who were its perpetrators? A: Haman and the powers he commanded. Q: And what can be done? A: The Judeans unite against their enemies.

But does it really make sense to perceive the book of Esther as trauma literature?[8] Does Esther bear the marks of trauma, dissociation and

---

7. Jeffrey C. Alexander and Elizabeth Butler Breese, "Introduction: On Social Suffering and Its Cultural Construction," in Eyerman et al., eds, *Narrating Trauma*, xi–xxxv (xxvii). Cf. Alexander's influential Introduction, "Toward a Theory of Cultural Trauma," in *Cultural Trauma and Collective Identity*, ed. Jeffrey C. Alexander et al. (Berkeley: University of California Press, 2004), 1–30.

8. Since the turn of the century, trauma hermeneutics have played an increasingly important role in Biblical exegesis. For an introduction to exegesis of Biblical texts as trauma literature, see Eve-Marie Becker, "'Trauma Studies' and Exegesis: Challenges,

confusion, chaos, numbness resulting in loss of language, and loss of faith in core beliefs? Unlike other books in the Hebrew Bible, for example, 1–2 Kings, Esther is not a book about the people's sinfulness and not a theodicy. Unlike Lamentations, the most important example of survival literature in the Hebrew Bible in which the traumatized survivors of the fall of Jerusalem openly accuse God of over-punishment, Esther does not engage in God-talk. Unlike the book of Jeremiah, the book of Esther does not engage in self-blaming and affirmation of the divine world-order. Unlike Genesis and Exodus, the book of Esther shows no interest in Abraham's covenant with God, that will guarantee the exiles that they shall return to the land of the fathers.[9]

Esther is another kind of trauma literature, a means of repair, a postulate of order and strength, a narrative of an evaded trauma meant to create and uphold meaning and courage in a foreign society.

3. *We Shall Overcome*

The book of Esther tells the story of a disaster that never happened. At the brink of the annihilation of the Judean people, a cunning woman led by a wise man saved their people from the hands of a powerful, though stupid king and a shrewd slanderer. The powerless were empowered in a foreign world so that they could set a new world order. Mordecai the Judean became vizier—in the Greek Alpha-text even king—of the extant Persian Empire. As discussed in the previous chapters, this goal was more

---

Limits and Prospects," in *Trauma and Traumatization in Individual and Collective Dimensions: Insights from Biblical Studies and Beyond*, ed. Eve-Marie Becker et al., SANt 2 (Göttingen: Vandenhoeck & Ruprecht, 2014), 15–29; this volume contains studies that were presented as papers at an international conference on the subject in 2012. Boase and Frechette, eds, *Bible through the Lens of Trauma*, offers essays by leading scholars of the field, especially Hebrew Bible; the introduction to this volume gives a useful overview over biblical interpretation employing trauma hermeneutics. For a reading of the Hebrew Bible as literature of trauma and resilience, see David M. Carr, *Holy Resilience: The Bible's Traumatic Origins* (New Haven: Yale University Press, 2014).

9. On Lamentations as survival literature, see Tod Linafelt, *Surviving Lamentations: Catastrophe, Lament, and the Protest in the Afterlife of a Biblical Book* (Chicago: University of Chicago Press, 2000); on the book of Jeremiah, see Else K. Holt, "Daughter Zion: Trauma, Cultural Memory and Gender in OT Poetics," in Becker et al., eds, *Trauma and Traumatization*, 162–76; on Genesis, see Kathleen M. O'Connor, *Genesis 1–25A*, Smyth and Helwys Bible Commentary (Macon: Smyth & Helwys, 2018).

or less reached already when Haman was executed, his house given to Esther, and the kings signet-ring to Mordecai, thereby signifying the total take-over of power. But as discussed above, the book could not end there; the extinction of 75,311 Persians was an essential and indispensable part of the narrative. With its reference to the fights with the Amalekites in Exod. 17:8–14, the story of how "Amalek came in the desert and fought with Israel at Rephidim," it parallels and completes stories in the narrative complex of the conquest of Israel which are no less bloodthirsty, violent, or appalling, especially in the book of Joshua. Moreover, it concludes and rights King Saul's sins in 1 Sam. 15:1-9, where he neglects the divine command of a band against the Amalekite king Agag and his possessions.[10] As such, the book of Esther helps shape the collective memory and brings the story of old victories over the transgenerational gap. Where the conquest narratives tell the story about how the Israelites gained control over their own land, the book of Esther illustrates that the Judeans can win control over the Persian Empire, if needed by way of violence, and thereby over their own lives as a people, an *ethnie*. It is possible to live in the Diaspora and live well.

The book of Esther, though, does not talk about assimilation in the foreign country. On the contrary, it illustrates the importance of belonging to the Judean people. Esther, on the one hand, assimilates to the Persian court and gets access to the king's attention. On the other hand, she thereby loses contact with the pain over the threat against her people, illustrated by the sight of Mordecai in sackcloth and ashes (Est. 4). She misinterprets his change of clothes into garments of mourning and offers him clothes, suitable for a Persian citizen. The whole conversation between them takes place trough middlemen, another illustration of the distance between them. Only when Mordecai forces Esther to remember where she belongs does she understand his message and decide to take on responsibility in a way that is only possible for her, the Judean mole at the Persian court (as discussed in Chapter 3, above). It is by way of her action, amply emphasized by the tripling of the king's invitation to ask for whatever she wants, up to the half of the kingdom (Est. 5:3, 6; 7:2) and the doubling of her parties with Haman and the king (Est. 5:5-6; 7:1-10), that the Judeans get the upper hand in a world filled with enemies.

But how does this "getting the upper hand" work in the book and in the community? Jonathan Grossman understands Esther as a carnivalesque presentation.[11] He takes his point of departure in Mikhail Bakhtin's

---

10. On this complex of texts, see Chapter 6 above.
11. Grossman, *Esther*, 235–9.

definition of carnival as "an eruption of ever-present but suppressed popular sentiments" that "found expression in several 'reversals' manifested during public carnival celebrations."[12] Grossmann mentions four of Bakhtin's characteristics of the carnival: (1) the marginal becomes the central, (2) the lowly becomes elevated, (3) the internal and concealed become external and public, and (4) the weak grow strong, while the strong grow weak. All these motifs manifest themselves in Esther.[13] This, however, is a matter of the "theological carnivalesque," not of "a literary license for the carnivalesque celebration erupting in the streets," as proposed by Kenneth Craig:

> Contra the prevalent academic view, it seems more likely that the connection between the carnivalesque elements of the narrative and the festival was a development, with the festival gradually taking shape around comic, antiestablishment elements of the narrative.[14]

Grossman concludes:

> Esther's anarchism does not seek to destabilize society's foundations for its own sake but as a psychological and theological argument… The motif of reversal, which is so prevalent in carnival celebrations, in Esther is evidence of the instability of life in general, of the temporariness of roles, and the tenuousness of one's situation.[15]

Amy Kalmanofsky suggests understanding the oracles against the foreign nations[16] in the prophetic books as "revenge fantasies."[17] Revenge fantasy is a well-known genre from the modern world of movies, with Ridley

---

12. Ibid., 235.
13. Ibid., 236. In his discussion, Grossmann refers to Mikhail Bakhtin, *The Dialectic Imagination*, trans. C. Emerson and M. T. Holquist (Austin: University of Texas Press, 1981); Kenneth Craig, *Reading Esther: A Case for the Literary Carnivalesque*, Literary Currents in Biblical Interpretation (Louisville: Westminster John Knox, 1995); Yona Shapira, "A Postmodernist Reading of the Biblical Book of Esther: From Cultural Disintegration to Carnivalesque Text" (PhD diss., State University of New York, 1996).
14. Grossman, *Esther*, 238.
15. Ibid., 239.
16. E.g. Isa. 13–23; Jer. 46–51; Amos 1–2; Obadiah.
17. Amy Kalmanofsky, "'As she did, do to her!': Jeremiah's OAN as Revenge Fantasies," in *Concerning the Nations: Essays on the Oracles against the Nations in Isaiah, Jeremiah and Ezekiel*, ed. Else K. Holt, Hyun Chul Paul Kim, and Andrew Mein, LHBOTS 612 (London: Bloomsbury T&T Clark, 2015), 109–27.

Scott's *Thelma and Louise* (1991) and Quentin Tarantino's *Inglourious Basterds* (2009) and *Django Unchained* (2013) as instructive examples. In revenge fantasies,

> victims transform into avengers, and acts of violence are avenged… [T]he victims of violence are recast as victors. The transformation of the victims, whether directly or indirectly, into the avenger is the narrative focus and defining characteristic of revenge fantasies.[18]

In a footnote, Kalmanofsky mentions the Esther narrative as another possible example of revenge fantasy in the Hebrew Bible. In my opinion, this suggestion makes sense. The prophetic oracles against the nations tell the story of a victim turned avenger, of the violated becoming the violator, and of violence avenged.[19] That is also the case in the book of Esther—only, that in Esther the violence against the prospective victim is never acted out. It never passes the phase of planning because of Esther's obstruction of it, the constructed trauma remains a construction, and so the revenge stands alone in the narrative. However, the revenge fantasy at the conclusion of the Esther story retains its force of empowerment for the minority population of the Judeans in the Persian Empire and later the Jews in the Hellenistic and Roman eras.

The same proposal is made by Sarah Emanuel in her article "Trauma and Counter-Trauma in the Book of Esther."[20] With reference to Judith Herman, a leading voice in the psychoanalytic discourse of trauma, she states:

> Because the mourning stage of recovery is so difficult, many survivors of trauma experience moments of resistance to it. During this time, survivors can create revenge fantasies as a form of counter-trauma and post-traumatic wish fulfillment.[21]

This post-traumatic wish fulfillment can help to bring order amid chaos and thus, as discussed in Chapters 6 and 7, create a "new" Judean *ethnie* in the Diaspora on the ruins of the lost homeland in Judah. Large parts of

---

18. Ibid., 111.
19. Ibid., 126–7 n. 6.
20. Sarah Emanuel, "Trauma and Counter-Trauma in the Book of Esther: Reading the Megillah in the Face of the Post-Shoah Sabra," *The Bible & Critical Theory* 13 (2017): 23–42.
21. Ibid., 37.

the Hebrew Bible served this goal; the book of Esther did it in a peculiar way, through the use of hyperbole, carnival, and humor. Esther is, as posed by Emanuel, "a text that offers comic relief in the face of communal rupture."[22]

Interestingly, Emanuel combines her trauma-oriented reading of Esther with a discussion of the reception of the book in the twentieth century. It is no surprise that the book of Esther and the celebration of Purim played an important role in the survival strategy of the Jews in and outside the Nazi concentration camps, during the so-called Shoah. For many Jewish communities, Hitler became known as the modern Haman. This reference to Hitler as another Amalek, however, "does not mean to associate him solely with Haman as a fellow Jew hater, but also with one who—from an implied audience perspective—deserves to be defeated violently, year after year."[23] Even more interesting, though, the acknowledgement of the empowering force of Purim to the suppressed Jews was shared by the Nazi regime and Adolf Hitler himself:

> In fact, the notion that the Jews loved to celebrate in the face of gentile destruction led Hitler to enact his own Purim pranks throughout the Shoah. Echoing anti-Jewish interpretations of Esther, such as those made by Martin Luther, Heinrich Ewald, and Lewis Bayles Paton…as well as those instigated in the film *Jud Süss*…Hitler situated himself as the gentile victim of Jewish violence. In order to avenge Haman, his sons, and the 75,000, Hitler sought to outwit the Jews on their own holiday, and, to a certain extent, even appropriated the holiday as his own. On Purim in 1942, the Nazis hanged ten Jews in Poland to punish them for hanging Haman's ten sons… Likewise, on the following Purim, the Nazis told Jews in the ghetto of Piotrkow that they would exchange ten Jews for ten Germans in Palestine… Hitler's vengeance against the Jews for their actions in Esther continued for years, and in 1944, he argued that 'unless Germany is victorious…Jewry could then celebrate the destruction of Europe by a second triumphant Purim festival' ….[24]

Now, the question can be raised whether the Judeans in Persia and the Jews of the Hellenistic period were as immersed in a sea of enemies as is often taken for granted? Were the Judeans/Jews really in need of protection against their surroundings? In his provocative study of the living conditions for the Jews in the Second Temple period, Erich S.

22. Ibid., 27.
23. Ibid., 32.
24. Ibid., 32–3.

Gruen argues for a more nuanced image.[25] Gruen questions "the drastic alternatives" often posited in scholarly and popular literature, "that the diaspora Jews either assimilated to classical culture by diluting their own traditions, or separated themselves from the larger world to maintain the purity of their faith and heritage." Rather, "for most Jews, the rendition of a Jewish identity and accommodation to the circumstances of diaspora were joint goals—and often successfully achieved."[26] In the Hellenistic metropolis Alexandria, for example, the Jews were part of society and allowed to live among other ethnic and religious groups but had a tendency to keep to themselves in what was known as the Jewish quarters.[27] "Nothing compelled the Jews to develop a theory of diaspora," Gruen claims, "Jews of the Second Temple period did not perceive themselves as victims of a diaspora."[28] He reads the book of Esther as an example of Diaspora humor[29] and tries to find his way through the diverse understandings of the book. In the end, he criticizes the "standard explications" for having "a serious drawback: they pay inadequate attention to the comic features that permeate the narrative."[30] And if taken into consideration, the humorous aspects are too often explained as smiling through one's tears. "Nothing in the text implies that Jews in the Persian domains lived in dread of disaster." Rather, the conflict in Esther is painted as a personal rivalry between Haman and Mordecai, and the enemies were not "inveterate anti-semites" but "directed by Haman's edict to conduct genocidal sweeps."[31] All in all, in Gruen's perception, the book is filled with humor, not realism:

> Would Gentiles target themselves for eradication by behaving wickedly to Jews in the interim? And then present themselves conveniently for the slaughter on the designated day? Evidently so. When the time came, five hundred Persians were available in the citadel of Susa itself (presumably with the gate swung invitingly open) to be cut down by Jews. And no fewer than seventy-five thousand victims made themselves available to be butchered by Jews in the provinces on the same day, all done in "self-defense"—without a single Jewish casualty! That scene contains more slapstick than solemnity.[32]

25. Erich S. Gruen, *Diaspora: Jews amid Greeks and Romans* (Cambridge, MA: Harvard University Press, 2002).
26. Ibid., vii.
27. Ibid., 5.
28. Ibid., 135.
29. Ibid., 137–58.
30. Ibid., 146.
31. Ibid., 147.
32. Ibid.

So, at the end of the day, the humor in Esther carries its own impact, Gruen concludes:

> This is not consolation for anxiety-ridden diaspora Jews, nor is it mere vicarious wish-fulfillment against their foes… Life in the Persian empire (or its representation in the subsequent diaspora) was comfortable enough to generate witty parody and healthy hilarity. Not a bad recommendation.[33]

A few comments on Gruen's reading are in order. First of all, it seems a bit peculiar to describe the report of the Persian genocide as "slapstick." The orderliness in the execution of the slaughter on a fixed date, the Judaization of a lot of Persians, and the emphasis on the Judeans abstaining from taking spoil points in another direction. As discussed above, there are indeed many humorous features in the book of Esther, and Gruen's presentation of the laughable foolishness of especially the Persian characters is insightful and convincing. But when it comes to the killing of the Persians, the fun comes to an end; the Judeans in the Diaspora needed an excuse for the atrocities (as we have seen in Chapters 6 and 7), an excuse that a slapstick comedy would never need.

This critique, however, does not necessarily mean that life in the Persian Diaspora was a life marked by perpetual threat, and Gruen might very well be right that for the common Judean exiled in Persia life was not totally unpleasant. This might even be the reason for the call out for awareness of Judean ethnicity propagated in the book of Esther. Among other things, the book is also an effective warning against too-ready assimilation into the Persian society. Thus the need for a chosen trauma; thus the over-kill reaction to Haman's decree ("over-kill" since a lot of Persians decided to show themselves as Judeans, and who says that the rest of them could not have been persuaded to leave their neighbors in peace out of mere convenience?); and thus the emphasis on the uniting of the Judean community under one, beloved leader and the celebration of their brotherliness in the joyous feast of Purim.

4. *The Final Battle*

The translators of the Greek versions of Esther apparently added to and repaired what religiosity and emotionality they thought necessary within the Hebrew book of Esther (see Chapters 2 and 3, above). From an ideological perspective, the apocalyptic Additions A and F at the beginning and closing of the Greek Esthers point to the stirring qualities

---

33. Ibid., 147–8.

of the Hebrew story, however "mock–apocalyptic"[34] they might seem to a modern reader. The Hebrew Esther, with its message of the necessity and possibility of living as an ethnic group among other groups in the Diaspora in awareness of the conceivable machinations of the surrounding society, was an apt inspiration for the message of apocalyptic fantasies of universal fights and triumphs in the additions. Added as a framework for the original book with its mundane carnivalesque humor and grotesque violence, Additions A and F lift the book into higher spheres, and thereby add to their interest and importance for the generations in the Hellenistic period. According to Wills, in the Greek novels of the Hellenistic era such apocalypses, often in the shape of dreams and oracles, served to give notice to the rousing adventures to come.[35] The apocalyptic introduction to Esther, Mordecai's dream in Add Est. A:5–10, globalizes the struggle between two persons (Haman and Mordecai) and nations (Amalekites-turned-Persians and Judeans) already present in Esther MT:

> Look! Two great dragons came forward, both ready to fight, and a great noise arose from them! And at their sound every nation prepared for war, to fight against a nation of righteous people. Look! A day of darkness and gloom! Affliction and anguish! Oppression and great chaos upon the earth! And the whole righteous nation was in chaos, fearing the evils that threatened themselves, and they were ready to perish. Then they cried out to God, and from their cry, as though from a small spring, there came a great river, abundant water; light, and the sun rose, and the lowly were exalted and devoured those held in esteem.[36]

The Greek versions enroll God, who was only indirectly present in the Hebrew Esther, in the fight between the Jews and their enemies, between the righteous nation and the rest of the world. At the cry from the righteous, the salving river rises, and chaos turns into light and sunshine. One might wonder, however, who the two great dragons mentioned are, but this is explained in Mordecai's exposition of his dream in Add Est. F:3–9:

> There was the little spring that became a river, and there was light and sun and abundant water; Esther is the river, whom the king married and made queen. The two dragons are myself and Haman. The nations are those that

---

34. Wills, *The Jewish Novel*, 166.
35. Ibid., 116.
36. Add A:5–9, LXX. There are only minor differences between the LXX and AT, apart from the interesting change of subject in v. 9, where AT reads: "And *we* cried out…"

gathered to destroy the name of the Judeans. And my nation, this is Israel, who cried out to God and were saved. The Lord has saved his people, and the Lord has rescued us from all these evils, and God has done signs and great wonders that have not happened among the nations. For this purpose he made two lots, one for the people of God and one for all the nations, and these two lots came to the hour and the right time and to the day of decision before God, and for all the nations. And God remembered his people and vindicated his own inheritance.

Mordecai's exposition explains everything: Esther is the source of rescue and salvation from the battle between the two dragons, Haman and Mordecai. On top of this battle comes the universal battle between the nations and Israel where God intervenes with signs and wonders. The text is reminiscent of discourse known from Exodus and Deuteronomy: When the people *cry out to God* he saves them through *signs and wonders*, and he *remembers his people*. In this way, the Greek book of Esther is inscribed in the over-all Salvation History, and thus appeals to its Jewish audience with an offer of resilience for the anxiety ridden. Moreover, through the apocalyptic discourse the battle between Israel and the nations is described as a chaos-battle, reminiscent of creation theology and *Völkerkampf*, the universal battle that involves heaven and earth.[37] At the end of the day, the Esther narrative has been moved from its (mock-) historical setting to mythology, and thus entered the path of chosen trauma defeated, the chaos of trauma overcome. Esther is marked as a story of indubitable trust and resilience.

5. *Concluding Outlook*

As we saw above, the book of Esther gained a long history of reception. In her magisterial article, Sarah Emanuel not only treats the reception in the time of Holocaust but also presents the aftermath in the Sabra culture in Israel after World War II. Sabra is a term coined in the 1930s for a Jew born in Israel. Emanuel writes:

> Not only was the Sabra raised on Zionist myths commemorating Jewish victories over enemies of the people/place of Israel (e.g., Exodus, Esther, Judith, Maccabean martyr texts), but was taught that the New Jew fulfilled the promise of Esther by constructing "Jewish political power resulting

---

37. This latter theme is most prevalent in the dream report in Addition A and is downplayed in the exposition (Add Est. F), but it is indirectly mentioned in Add Est. F:8, where the "the hour and the right time and to the day of decision before God" are mentioned.

in Jewish safety—all without the benefit of any divine intervention." The idea…was for the New Jew to internalize a Jewish "myth of deliverance"—to recognize that Israel's victories are not only replays of Jewish victories past, but victories won by "the few in face of the many." The Esther narrative thus worked on the Sabra in profound ways, telling them that the Jewish people can—and will—rise.[38]

The Sabra ideology emphasized the strength and ability of the New Jew in contradistinction to the stereotypical physiognomic image of Jews having a "big nose, big lips, and protruding mouth," and also as "black, ugly, and physically inept." Early Zionist textbooks scorned Diaspora Jews for being "passive victims," Emanuel writes, while they "referred to Sabra leaders as the resurrected Maccabees, Mordecais, and Masada martyrs who defend themselves, fight for their land, and die as heroes."[39] Put shortly, the Sabra "were trained to see themselves as always 'better than' their persecuted predecessors—the '(despised) *Diaspora Jew[s].*'"[40] In the post-Holocaust Sabra, we find a fine example of the power of chosen trauma. "Even though the archetypal Sabra was not a direct victim of anti-Jewish violence, he was nevertheless part of a culture that carried with it generations of anti-Semitism and anti-Judaism."[41]

Having come this far, the question returns, then: What to do with the book of Esther? Can we read it and teach it—maybe even preach it—today for its indisputable literary and entertaining qualities, or is it so stained by its inherent call for violence and revenge that we should take leave of it? Are we amused or offended? These are the questions treated in the concluding chapter.

---

38. Emanuel, "Trauma and Counter-Trauma," 34, with reference to her anonymous reviewer for the first quotation, and for the latter to Oz Almog, *The Sabra: The Creation of the New Jew*, trans. Haim Watzman (Berkeley: University of California Press, 2000), 35, 37.

39. Emanuel, "Trauma and Counter-Trauma," 34, with reference to Almog, *The Sabra*, 37–8.

40. Emanuel, "Trauma and Counter-Trauma," 36, with reference to Natan P. F. Kellermann, *Holocaust Trauma: Psychological Effects and Treatment* (New York and Bloomington: iUniverse, 2009), 111 (original emphasis).

41. Emanuel, "Trauma and Counter-Trauma," 35.

Chapter 9

GENOCIDE IN ESTHER?
A CONCLUDING DISCUSSION

In 2010 I started my studies in the book of Esther at the library of Columbia Theological Seminary, Decatur, GA. Almost every day, my husband and I had lunch in the impressive Oxford-like refectory where important professors of the institution, past and present, were looking down from their picture frames on the walls. We had the pleasure of eating together with the students and discussing important or everyday matters with them over burgers, chicken, and fried okra. One particular day, I raised an academic question inspired by Adele Berlin's perception, that the book of Esther is a carnivalesque farce: "Can slaughtering 75,311 Persians be fun?" The question was tentatively answered by a few of the students, but the discussion was ended by one of them, Wylie Hughes, who said: "No Ma'am, killing is never fun. I've been there and killing is never fun." This M.Div. student who was in his late twenties (and apart from everything else a wonderful blues bass player) continued by telling me that he had been in the American Marine Corps and served in Iraq. He knew what he was talking about. He did not go into details, but his words of experience left an indelible mark on me.

The more I study Esther as a biblical book, the more pressing to me becomes the question of violence in Esther, the slaughter of the 75,311 Persians, including women and children. Therefore, here at the conclusion of our readings in Esther, let us return to the theological and ethical questions raised in Chapter 1, for since Esther is part of the canonical Bible, both for Jews and Christians, the question in the end is—also—a matter of theology.

1. *Violence in the Hebrew Bible: The Example of 1 Samuel 15*

There is no need to discuss the presence of violence, physical and psychological, in the Hebrew Bible that eventually also became the Christian Old

Testament. Neither is it possible to deny the presence of divinely ordained violence in almost all parts of its books. The prophetic books are full of proclamation of Yahweh's wrath against his people, fulfilled violently through his worldly emissaries, Israel's neighbors Babylon and Assyria. The narratives in the Pentateuch about the conquering of the promised land and the ensuing settlement in Joshua and Judges, on the other hand, tell time and again how God commands the Israelites to annihilate the people that stand in their way both outside and inside the land. One of these narratives about how the Israelites consolidate their power in the land, the narrative in 1 Samuel 15 of Saul's victory over the Amalekites, became of great importance for the book of Esther, as we have considered above. Up till now, we have not discussed the ideology of the 1 Samuel 15 but since it works as an intertext in Esther, and thus influences the message of this book, however tacitly, it deserves a thorough reading.

Referring to events before the conquest when the Amalekites opposed the Israelites (Exod. 17:8-16), God through his spokesman Samuel orders Saul to "go and attack Amalek, and utterly destroy all that they have;[1] do not spare them, but kill both man and woman, child and infant, ox and sheep, camel and donkey" (1 Sam. 15:1-3). Saul attacks and defeats the Amalekites, takes their king, Agag, alive, "but utterly destroyed all the people with the edge of the sword" (vv. 7-8).[2] Against God's command to lay a ban (*ḥerem*) on the spoils, "Saul and the people spared Agag, and the best of the sheep and of the cattle and of the fatlings, and the lambs, and all that was valuable, and would not utterly destroy them; all that was despised and worthless they utterly destroyed" (v. 9). This is seen by God and Samuel (and the text) as a severe disobedience, even if Saul reassures Samuel that he intends to sacrifice to God the best of the sheep and the cattle, which he and the people spared exactly for that reason (vv. 15, 21). However, Saul's good intentions do not make it up for his noncompliance:

> And Samuel said, "Has the LORD as great delight in burnt offerings and sacrifices, as in obeying the voice of the LORD? Surely, to obey is better than sacrifice, and to heed than the fat of rams. For rebellion is no less a sin than divination, and stubbornness is like iniquity and idolatry. Because you have rejected the word of the LORD, he has also rejected you from being king." (vv. 22-23)

---

1. *'attā lek wᵉhikkîtā 'et-'amāleq wᵉhaḥăramtem 'et-kol-'ăšer-lô wᵉlô taḥmol 'ālajw.*
2. *wᵉ 'et-kol-hā'ām heḥĕrîm lᵉpî-ḥāreb.*

9. Genocide in Esther? A Concluding Discussion

A couple of details in the narrative call for comment. First: *ḥerem* ("the ban") is often understood as a ritualistic practice, whereby the enemy is sacrificed to the deity, either as thanksgiving for victory or as fulfilment of a promise to the God before a battle.[3] The practice was known in the entire ancient Near East, and is described, for example, at the stela, erected by the Moabite king Mesha in the ninth century BCE, where the victims of *ḥerem* are the Israelites.[4] According to John J. Collins,[5] most of the passages in the Hebrew Bible that deal with *ḥerem* are found in the Deuteronomistic corpus—as is 1 Samuel 15. In Deuteronomy, however, *ḥerem* is presented as a necessary means against religious pollution of the Israelites when they meet the foreign tribes on their way and during the conquest. According to Collins, "Deuteronomy does not eradicate the sacrificial aspect of the ban, but it seeks to rationalize the practice by justifying it... Ethnic cleansing is the way to ensure cultic purity."[6] In 1 Samuel 15, however, the reason for the command to "utterly destroy" the Amalekites is neither cultic nor a prevention of religious impurity, but pure revenge (or justice) from the side of God for the Amalekites' opposition to the Israelite conquest, as reported in Exodus: "Thus says the LORD of Hosts, 'I will punish the Amalekites for what they did in opposing the Israelites when they came up out of Egypt'" (v. 2).[7] In 1 Samuel 15, then, ethno-religious purity does not seem to be of importance, and God outright dismisses Saul's proposal of giving the best part of the conquered livestock as sacrifice.

At this point, the narrative indirectly imparts the impression that Saul's offer of a sacrifice is a second thought, and that he and the people from the outset had planned to eat the better parts of the spoil themselves.

---

3. For a thorough introduction to *ḥerem* in the ancient Near East and the Hebrew Bible, see Susan Niditch, *War in the Hebrew Bible: A Study in the Ethics of Violence* (New York: Oxford University Press, 1993), esp. Chapter 1, "The Ban as God's Portion" (pp. 28–55).

4. "The Moabite Stone," trans. W. F. Albright (*ANET*, 320–1).

5. John J. Collins, "The Zeal of Phinehas: The Bible and the Legitimation of Violence," *JBL* 122 (2003): 3–21 (7).

6. Ibid. Michael V. Fox comments on the conquest narratives: "In actuality, the inhabitants of Canaan were almost certainly not slaughtered by the Israelites, who themselves descended in large part from the indigenous population. Like the schematic notion of the Israelite invasion of Canaan, the ban is a literary 'ideal,' an expression of the belief that the people of Israel had to make a fresh start, to live free of all ties with the Canaanite culture. *But it is a reprehensible way of expressing that ideal*" (Fox, *Character and Ideology*, 225 n. 21, my emphasis).

7. See the discussion in Niditch, *War in the Hebrew Bible*, 61–2.

Why else would they spare "the best of the sheep and of the cattle and of the fatlings, and the lambs, and all that was valuable, and would not utterly destroy them; all that was despised and worthless they utterly destroyed" (1 Sam. 15:9)? In other words, what Saul and the people did was to take spoil (*šālāl*), and this is exactly what Samuel concludes in v. 19, when he asks accusingly: "Why did you swoop down on the spoil (*ta'aṭ 'el-haššālāl*) and do what was evil in the sight of the LORD?" This formulation would later be of immense importance for the outcome of the Esther narrative.

Secondly: from the outset the sparing of the best of the livestock against God's demand for a total *ḥerem* is described as a joint venture of Saul and the people (1 Sam. 15:15), but Samuel's scolding starts a veritable blame game. When Samuel blames Saul for this noncompliance, Saul first tries to make the people the scapegoat[8] ("But *from the spoil the people took sheep and cattle*, the best of the things devoted to destruction, to sacrifice to the LORD your God in Gilgal," v. 21), and when this explanation is not accepted by Samuel, Saul attempts to soften him and God, claiming that he was more or less forced to take the spoil by the people: "I have sinned; for I have transgressed the commandment of the LORD and your words, *because I feared the people and obeyed their voice*" (v. 24). This excuse, however, does not help either, for already in v. 17 Samuel has foreseen Saul's bleak justifications when he emphasizes his role as head of the tribes of Israel and Yahweh's anointed king of Israel. In the end, Saul is the only one responsible for doing what was evil in the eyes of Yahweh (v. 19).

Saul's failure to make *ḥerem* on the enemies and their property, marks the end of his kingship and the beginning of his struggle with David over the Israelite monarchy. The result of the struggle is sealed from the beginning, for Saul's failure is not so much a failure of warfare or religious practice as of disobedience of the divine command. Here we are at an important theme in Deuteronomistic theology, obedience to God. In the later parts of Deuteronomistic thinking not sacrifice but obedience is the ultimate concern—a thought that returns in, for example, the late Psalm 50 and in Jeremiah's temple sermon in Jeremiah 7, which in my opinion points to a rather late dating of 1 Samuel 15. God does not want anything but adherence to his word, however pious the intention. In other words—what is important is not the fate of the Amalekites but theology. But does this explanation redeem the narrative from a broader theological point of view?

---

8. On the concept of scapegoating, see pp. 91–92, 96–97, in Chapter 6 above.

2. *The Problem of Violence in Esther*

Violence, and divinely justified violence at that, is upfront in 1 Samuel 15, and the narrative and its ideology live on and impact its intertexts as a legitimization of annihilation of enemies, for example, in the book of Esther.[9] Scholars perceive of the problem rather differently.

As discussed in Chapter 1, Berlin, LaCoque, and others understand the violence in Esther as part of the carnivalesque nature of the story. Berlin considers the problem in her commentary[10] and—from a modern Jewish position—in an exposition from 2016, "Amalek and Esther: Vanquishing the Eternal Enemy."[11] Here, she especially treats the relation of Esther to 1 Samuel 15 and Deut. 25:17-19 and discusses how a modern reader may react to the violence in the Hebrew Bible as a prerequisite to evaluate the violence in Esther. Her point of departure is that some modern readers find the violence in the Bible "embarrassing and wish it away by skipping those sections in public readings of the Bible. Others explain it in various ways," she continues, and then lists and comments four of these explanations (pp. 6–8):[12]

(1) "We should accept that ancient values were different from our own and try to understand ancient stories in their own social and moral context. Revenge was an accepted practice in the ancient world, including in Israel." In general, Berlin is persuaded by this argument: "That's how I deal with the fact that, for example, the Bible accepts slavery, and it views women quite differently from the way we do today. I am old enough to

---

9. On the alleged peculiarity of the violence against innocent women and children in Esther, Fox dryly comments: "It is strange that Christian theologians, starting with Luther, have been more disturbed by the defensive action of the Jews in Ester's time than by the aggressive and more destructive conquest by the Israelites in Joshua's" (Fox, *Character and Ideology*, 225 n. 20).

10. Berlin, *Esther*, xvi–xxii. She sums up her opinion: "Scenes of tumultuous riots and violent mock-destruction are completely at home in farcical and carnivalesque works; in fact, they are their hallmarks. Chapter 9 is the climax of the carnivalesque, the peak of disorder. Exaggeration and irrationality reach new heights, even for this book. *But it is all in fun; nothing here is real. It is emotional release at its wildest*" (81, my emphasis).

11. Adele Berlin, "Amalek and Esther: Vanquishing the Eternal Enemy." Manuscript March 19, 2016. Germantown Jewish Centre, Philadelphia, published at Academia.edu by the author. The essay is an exposition for the day of *shabbat zakor* "so named because of the special maftir from Deuteronomy 25:17-19 telling us to remember the memory of Amalek" (1). *Shabbat Zakor* comes just before Purim, so that the memory of Haman being an Amalekite is kept alive (2).

12. Ibid., 6–8.

know that values change rather quickly, within one lifetime, let alone over thousands of years." This, however, is "not the best explanation for the massacre in Esther."

(2) "It is right to use power against an evil force when you have it." This argument is rarely made to explain Esther, and "whether or not you agree with this premise" Berlin does not find it "a convincing explanation of the massacre in Esther."

(3) The violence in Esther is a "matter of justified self-defense"—an approach that "fits better because the original decree against the Jews was never rescinded."

(4) Jon Levenson's argument that revenge in the Hebrew Bible, as exemplified in the closing verse of Psalm 137,[13] should not be understood "from an ethical point of view but from the viewpoint of biblical theology. According to that viewpoint, this is not revenge against Edom for the destruction of Jerusalem. Rather, the theological position is that the punishment is inherent in the sin."[14] Berlin comments: "I see the destruction of the enemy as a return to the world order as it should be, before the destruction... In other words, the hope is for a world without evil. This explanation works well for much of the Bible's violence, especially for what looks like revenge. It may undergird the killing of non-Jews in Esther but there is something more going on in Esther."[15]

(5) Finally, Berlin returns to her view that Esther is a carnivalesque comedy, a genre in which "riots and mock battles are completely at home" together with "the grotesque and the violent in general." She explains that "[t]his is the same type of action found in uncensored fairy tales and in James Bond movies, with the pyrotechnic orgy of violence that kills off all the baddies at the end." This ending, she continues, "releases pent up pressure, as the carnivalesque is designed to do. Doing violence in

---

13. "Remember, O LORD, against the Edomites / the day of Jerusalem's fall, / how they said, / 'Tear it down! Tear it down! Down to its foundations!' // O daughter Babylon, you devastator! / Happy shall they be who pay you back / what you have done to us! // Happy shall they be who take your little ones / and dash them against the rock!" (Ps. 137:7-9 NRSV).

14. Berlin, "Amalek and Esther: Vanquishing the Eternal Enemy," 8. Berlin refers to Jon D. Levenson, "The Horrifying Closing of Psalm 137, or, The Limitations of Ethical Reading," in *Biblical Essays in Honor of Daniel J. Harrington, SJ, and Richard J. Clifford, SJ. Opportunity for No Little Instruction*, ed. Christopher G. Frechette [*sic*], Christopher R. Matthews, and Thomas D. Stegman, SJ (New York/Mahwah, NJ: Paulist, 2014), 18–40.

15. Berlin, "Amalek and Esther: Vanquishing the Eternal Enemy," 8.

carnivalesque fiction is supposed to reduce the urge to do it in real life." Moreover: "To the extent that diaspora Jews are always a bit nervous about their safety, this story assures them of their power to protect themselves. Or at least it lets them imagine they can."[16] Berlin concludes:

> At last, the story of Saul receives the proper ending. In the do-over, Saul's descendant and all Israel get it right. The enemy is totally dispatched, including their possessions, and the Jews live happily ever after. In the mock battles of the carnivalesque world of the book of Esther, the eternal enemy of Israel is vanquished once and for all.[17]

According to Berlin, then, it is a mistake to perceive of the violence in the book of Esther at face value. That is a failure of understanding its genre and through its hyperbolic style the story itself warns its reader against this mistake. Esther is not history writing; it is pure fiction, and thus should be read as such. But still the question remains: Is this also a way of doing away—or skipping over—the brutality of the closing of Esther? How do we, as modern readers, react to the open approval of violence in the Hebrew Bible?

Jonathan Grossman criticizes the approach of Berlin and others; even if there are strong comic elements of the story, "we must take care not to confuse the *style* of writing with the *purpose*."[18] Grossman himself, however, does not discuss the book's attitude to violence at length but seems to dismiss it:

> The fundamental assumption underlying the modern moralizing at the text's expense never appears in the text. A close reading of the narrative shows that the narrator hints, in different ways, that the war of the 13th and 14th of Adar should not be viewed as indiscriminate mass murder.[19]

Grossman then continues to sum up the results of his reading of Esther as a "book of hiding." He urges that all the characters in the book and also its messages are concealed by the author for two reasons: (1) It "allows the reader to become a partner in the process of decoding the narrative and exposing its meaning," and thereby "enhances his identification with the narrative."[20] (2) The message of the book is a message of concealment

---

16. Ibid., 9.
17. Ibid., 11.
18. Grossman, *Esther*, 235.
19. Ibid., 191.
20. Ibid., 1.

itself: "a concealing style reflects and dovetails with the morals of the narrative. Thus, esoteric writing not only is a literary device but can help focus the reader on the narrative's theme."[21] Grossman then continues to show how the book has two different layers of meaning, an open surface meaning and a subsurface, almost hermetic, meaning. However, as Grossman warns in his conclusion:

> Secret writing entails risk; many readers are bound to fall into the trap and be led astray by the plain message… Esther stands out as unique among the biblical books in that its composition is not foolproof. The reader who fails to sense the hidden level of the story will miss its main messages and morals.[22]

I shall not go into detail with Grossman's readings here; I do not find them persuasive, even if I must admit that it might be due to my lack of education in the Talmud and its hermeneutics. Thus, I might be one of the readers who "fails to sense the hidden level" and thus misses "its main messages and morals." For me, at the end of the day the question returns: Is Grossman's reading also a way of skipping over the brutality of the closing of Esther?

Another approach to ironies and hidden messages in the book of Esther is offered by Carolyn J. Sharp, who understands the plot of Esther as "the pinnacle of dramatic irony within the literature of the Hebrew Bible."[23] She discusses in detail the closing of Esther, taking her point of department in the existence of a number of "happy endings" in the Hebrew Bible (e.g. the ending of the Joseph story in Genesis) that alerts the reader to irony.[24] How is this irony presented? First, can we as readers trust the narrator's presentation of the Jewish slaughter "to defend their lives" as justifiable? In retrospect, the question is whether that phrase has been used ironically, since the narrative elements underline the slaughter as atrocity.[25] This atrocity is not "to be approved of by the implied audience" but as "ironizing" the holy-war mentality.[26] Esther, however, is a book of paradoxes, Sharp infers. Thus, "it may be advisable to construct a reading that neither indulges in an earnest 'straight' reading of the ending nor completely rejects the ending as not being consonant with the cues of

---

21. Ibid., 2.
22. Ibid., 244–5.
23. Carolyn J. Sharp, *Irony and Meaning in the Hebrew Bible*, Indiana Studies in Biblical Literature (Bloomington: Indiana University Press, 2009), 65.
24. Ibid., 67.
25. Ibid., 68.
26. Ibid., 69–70.

9. Genocide in Esther? A Concluding Discussion

the ironic narrative as a whole."[27] The slaughter of the Persians is neither wholly appropriate and justifiable, nor "an ethically repugnant sign that the Jews had become no better than their bloodthirsty, xenophobic enemies."[28] The Jewish action against the Persians must be seen as excessive, and excessiveness in the book of Esther—Sharp discusses a number of examples—is not "just a droll texture to an amusing tale" but "a serious matter of profligacy, overzealousness, and misuse of power." Excess in the book of Esther should not be valorized, nor be taken lightly by the implied audience.[29] Sharp also considers the legislation of Purim and the empowerment of Mordecai as "a little too elaborate,"[30] and she reaches the conclusion that

> the story narrates a fullness of action that is far more than the implied audience has been led to expect. The comeuppance of the Persians is comic in the classical sense: the ending arrives at a satisfying closure that, on the face of it, seems appropriate to the crime committed by the highest Persian officials. The implied audience is invited to laugh in triumph.[31]

However, "the celebratory laughter of Esther" is a laughter of ironic mockery that aims in a number of different directions, against the powerless Persians, against the Jews who launch "a merciless killing spree," and against the implied audience "whose expectations have been reversed again and again by the plot turns of this book."[32]

Sharp concludes that "The implied audience that has perceived the irony understands that much has been left unspoken."[33] Unfortunately, it seems that neither the implied audience nor later generations of audiences did perceive the irony of Esther too well. This appears blatantly from the book's reception history and its effect through history, and one cannot but ponder whether the literary strategy of irony demonstrated by Sharp, as admirable as it might be, has failed in its goal. For this reason, when all is said and done, I do not find Sharp's ingenious reading helpful in our theological quest.[34]

27. Ibid., 70.
28. Ibid., 71.
29. Ibid., 74.
30. Ibid., 75.
31. Ibid., 79.
32. Ibid.
33. Ibid., 80.
34. Neither do I share Sharp's final evaluation of the Esther character: "Just as Joseph was no Moses, so Esther is no Daniel. Rather, she may be read as a fully assimilated, sexually compromised female ruler whose foreignness is inscribed insistently

From quite another methodological point of view Michael V. Fox discusses the ethical problems at length in his characterization of the Jewish people and with quite another result. Although he has a lot of sympathy (and excuses) for the violence, everything is not well with the narrative. Fox understands the Jews' fight against the Persians in ch. 9 as "necessary, defensive, and justified."[35] He admits that "Mordecai's decree instructs the Jews 'to take vengeance on their enemies' (8:13)," but sees their vengeance as "directed against actively hostile, armed enemies. It is not a vendetta..."[36] This notwithstanding, "the Jews' struggle is not...without moral blemish. Mordecai's edict is tainted by the permission to kill the enemies' children," an undertaking that Fox deems "unnecessary and excessive," like the "saturation bombing of Nuremburg and Dresden."[37] When it come to the second fight on the 14th of Adar, where Esther asks for additional killings in the citadel of Susa (Est. 9:11-15), the "moral ground" is even "shakier," because the danger no longer exists.[38] In conclusion, Fox finds the power fantasy present in the report of the battles and the schematic character of the war "disturbing." He writes:

> It is doubtful that the conduct of war, even on the part of the defender, is (if the power balance allows) ever free of vengeance, brutality, and overkill. The battles of Adar certainly were not.

In a footnote, Fox adds:

> The book's moral faults are not ameliorated by the fact that the book is deliberately hyperbolic or humorous, as B. Jones (1977) thinks: "Surely, the author did not expect his readers to keep a straight face while hearing the great king rejoice that so many of his subjects have been killed... The repetition of the ten long names of Haman's ten sons must have added to the pleasure of the listeners" (p. 180). A humorous tone would not justify a

in the powerful silences between the lines of this overwritten book" (Sharp, *Irony and Meaning*, 81). In my opinion, here Sharp in her search for hidden meaning goes far beyond what can be exegetically deduced from the text.

35. Fox, *Character and Ideology*, 221.
36. Ibid., 221–2. According to Fox, the Jews "are not even attempting to 'blot out the memory of Amalek'" (223).
37. Ibid., 224. He comments: "The inclusion of women and children in the scope of the authorization respects literary values—the neatness of the tit-for-tat schema—at the expense of ethical value: the exclusion of noncombatants from hostilities" (ibid.).
38. Ibid., 225.

repugnant attitude. A story that treated, say, wife-beating with good humor would not be more acceptable just because the author expected the audience to laugh at it. However, the book does not view the battles and the slaughter as in any way funny.[39]

At this point of the discussion, Fox's attitude seems to be the more fruitful and empathic answer to the problem raised by Wylie Hughes' remark.

3. *Violence and Old Testament Theology*

Now, let us broaden the considerations again and return to the question of how to cope with the presentation of violence in the Hebrew Bible. This is not a new question in biblical theology, but the scholarly approach has changed strikingly during the later decades.

Terence E. Fretheim, who passed away in 2020, was one of the leading voices in the current discourse on violence and the image—or presentation—of God.[40] That the Old Testament is a book full of violence is beyond discussion, also to Fretheim. In post-9/11 theology there is a call for "'self-reflection by the religious traditions on their role in generating, sponsoring, promoting, supporting, and maintaining such violence.' That would include the role that the Bible has played in the perpetration of violence across the globe over the centuries."[41] In his analysis, Fretheim distinguishes between human and divine violence,[42] and he regards divine violence as a response to unjust human violence: "If there were no human violence, there would be no divine violence."[43] Fretheim continues:

---

39. Fox, *Character and Ideology*, 226 with reference to Bruce Jones, "Two Misconceptions about the Book of Esther," *CBQ* 39 (1977): 171–81.

40. Terence E. Fretheim, "Is the Biblical Portrayal of God Always Trustworthy?," in Terence E. Fretheim and Karlfried Froelich, *The Bible as Word of God in Postmodern Age* (Minneapolis: Fortress, 1998), 97–111; idem, "God and Violence in the Old Testament," *WW* 24 (2004): 18–28; idem, "'I was only a little angry': Divine Violence in the Prophets," *Interpretation* 58 (2004): 365–75.

41. Fretheim, "God and Violence," 19. Fretheim quotes Stephen J. Stein, "The Web of Religion and Violence," *RSR* 28 (2002): 103–8.

42. Fretheim recommends a broad understanding of violence as "any action, verbal or nonverbal, oral or written, physical or psychical, active or passive, public or private, individual or institutional/societal, human or divine, in whatever degree of intensity, that abuses, violates, injures, or kills" (Fretheim, "God and Violence," 19).

43. Ibid., 21.

> If human violence were the only story about violence in the Bible, this could be a briefer, if bloody, discussion. But that is not the case. *The most basic theological problem with the Bible's violence is that it is often associated with the activity of God; with remarkable frequency, God is the subject of violent verbs.* From the flood, to Sodom and Gomorrah, to the command to sacrifice Isaac, to the plagues, to all the children killed on Passover night— and we are not yet through the book of Exodus! What will we make of this divine violence?[44]

Divine violence in the Old Testament often entails divine anger and judgment, and thus is justified—as mentioned above—as a response to human violence.[45] However, "some of the ways in which God's violence is depicted in the Bible should not stand unchallenged."[46] Some of the violence against the peoples that the Israelites meet during the conquest—1 Samuel 15 serves as Fretheim's example—have often been

> spiritualized ("put on the whole armor of God"), historically adjusted (turn the conquest into a land settlement or a primitive view that Israel outgrew), idealized (taking a Utopian stand against idolatry), viewed as a metaphor for the religious life, or reduced to God's mysterious ways.[47]

Fretheim rejects these explanations, and yet he tries to understand such violence, "if not to excuse in every respect the God who is portrayed here (nor those who carried out the divine commands)."[48] He lists four points of considerations: (1) God works through imperfect human beings and does not perfect them before working with them; (2) human beings will never have a perfect perception of God's will; (3) God chooses to involve himself in violence to make an end to evil, for thereby he "may prevent an even greater evil.[49]

Point (1) is the central theme of Fretheim's follow-up article about divine violence in the Prophets.[50] Here, God is portrayed as a relational God in a relational world:

---

44. Ibid. (my emphasis).
45. In a footnote (ibid., 22 n. 15), Fretheim emphasizes that "Wrath and violence are not divine attributes, but responses to creaturely sin, indeed the sins of violence." For further discussion, he refers to Terence E. Fretheim, "Theological Reflections on the Wrath of God in the Old Testament," *Horizons in Biblical Theology* 24 (2002): 14–17.
46. Fretheim, "God and Violence," 22.
47. Ibid., 27.
48. Ibid.
49. Ibid., 27–8.
50. Fretheim, "I was only a little angry."

> To live in a relational world inevitably means that every creature will be affected by every other; each individual is involved in the plight of all. Violence perpetrated anywhere reverberates everywhere through this relational structure of life, leading to even further violence. Because Israel understood that God is related to, and indeed deeply engaged in the affairs of this world, even the Creator will be affected by and caught up in every act of violence. Though there may be non-violent breakthroughs, an avoidance of interrelational violence is simply not possible for either Israel or God. The Bible tells it like it is.[51]

In the prophetic books God's violence is mediated through human agents, often foreign military powers like Assyrians and Babylonians, and serves as a correctional punishment of his people. But since God is not a God that micromanages his creation (another theme, characteristic of Fretheim's thinking), he limits himself in the exercise of divine power. "This divine self-limitation, necessary for the genuine freedom of creatures within the relationship, is a key factor in understanding violence."[52] This means that the agents, used by God, may exceed their mandate and overdo the violence against God's people. Such texts (e.g. Zech. 1:7-17) reveal "a divine vulnerability, for God opens the divine self up to hurt should things go wrong."[53] Therefore, God can also be described as regretting his anger.[54] Here, we reach an important aspect of Fretheim's theology:

> If there were no divine *anger* at sin/evil, then *human* anger toward that which is oppressive and abusive would not carry the same weight. At the same time, if there were no sorrow associated with divine anger, then human anger would be given a freer range regarding harshness.[55]

This is "not a matter of despair, but of hope. God does not simply give people up to violence." Fretheim concludes:

> By so participating in their messy stories, God's own self thereby takes the road of suffering and death. Through such involvement, God takes into the divine self the violent effects of sinful human activities and thereby makes possible a non-violent future for God's people.[56]

---

51. Fretheim, "I was only a little angry," 367. God as a relational God is the guiding principle of Fretheim's Old Testament theology; see Terence E. Fretheim, *God and the World in the Old Testament: A Relational Theology of Creation* (Nashville: Abingdon, 2005).
52. Fretheim, "I was only a little angry," 368.
53. Ibid., 373.
54. Ibid., 373–5.
55. Ibid., 374–5.
56. Ibid., 375.

I have spent quite some effort on Fretheim's position because he goes carefully and with an open mind into the question of the presentation of violence in the Old Testament and its ethical implications. The trouble with his approach, however honorable be the intentions, is, however, that the latter article only takes into account the cases where the divine violence is directed toward God's own people. This, of course, is due to the subject—violence in the prophetic literature. But it seems to cover Fretheim's position more generally. In his first article, Fretheim does not spend much effort on the problems of violence against the foreign peoples, like Amalekites or Persians, as discussed above. In the end, his thoughts orbit around two centers, like in an ellipsis, God as a relational God and God as "a God merciful and gracious, slow to anger, and abounding in steadfast love and faithfulness" (Exod. 34:6).[57] But what, then, about the divinely sanctioned violence against Israel's powerless enemies? What about the women and children of Amalek and Persia?

It might be claimed that since God is only present as a hidden force in Esther, the violence in Esther 8–9 is not divinely sanctioned and that, thus, God cannot be held responsible for it. But through the intertextual connection between 1 Samuel 15 and Esther, the slaughtering of the Persians is indeed presented as a fulfillment of a divine command. This is also how most of the commentators understand the reference. The information in Est. 8:11 that the Judeans are allowed to take spoil and to plunder[58] is an open reference to 1 Samuel 15; what God did not allow Saul to do is permitted (by God?) to the Judeans in Persia. When we are informed no fewer than three times in Esther 9 that they did not touch the plunder,[59] this adds to the intertextuality and puts the Judeans in a positive and respectable light, as a "narratorial sign of their noble restraint," to borrow a phrase from Sharp.[60] Even if permitted, they, in contrast to the deplorable Saul, did not take advantage of their enemies; they just defended themselves. So, the problem remains: Is the book of Esther a book that sanctions and justifies, maybe even encourages violence? At the

---

57. Fretheim mentions Exod. 34:6-7 as "a biblical center in terms of which all other texts are to be interpreted… That center provides a kind of canon within the canon that means that not everything in the Bible is to be placed on the same level of importance and may provide a place on which we can stand to bring a critical word to bear regarding some portrayals of God (Fretheim, "God and Violence," 26).

58. $š^e lālām\ lābôz$. Cf. the permit to the Persians in Est. 3:13 to do the same.

59. $babbizzâ\ lô'\ šāl^eḥû\ 'et-yādām$, Est. 9:10, 15, 16.

60. Sharp, *Irony and Meaning*, 69. Sharp does not share this understanding of the remark.

end of the day, is there really merit to the argument of those theologians who claim that the book is a fiercely nationalistic book of Jewish hatred toward their gentile surroundings? Recalling my discussion in Chapters 6–8 above, I would state that I have serious misgivings about readings that take the violence in the book of Esther at face value. In the hope of clarifying the issue, I shall now return to John J. Collins' discussion of violence in the Hebrew Bible.

Biblical violence was the subject of Collins' Presidential Address at the Annual Meeting of the Society of Biblical Literature in Toronto, Ontario, Canada (November 23, 2002).[61] Here, he took his point of departure in the ideology of the *ḥerem* (as discussed above). He quotes Susan Niditch for the position that the ban as a sacrifice adds more value to human life of the enemy than ideologies that allow for arbitrary killing in war. Collins comments dryly: "One hopes that the Canaanites appreciated the honor."[62] Putting the ban into its proper context in the ancient world increases rather than lessens it problematic nature from an ethical point of view, he maintains,[63] and this leads him to discuss the relation between history and ideology. No matter if scholars present the Israelites' opponents as "people of markedly inferior type" (William Foxwell Albright) and the Canaanite civilization and religion as "one of the weakest, most decadent, and most immoral cultures of the civilized world at that time" (George Earnest Wright), or—as in more recent scholarship—the Israelites are understood not as marauding gangs but as "peasants in revolt" (George E. Mendenhall) or "quiet hard-working settlers in the hill country" (Israel Finkelstein and Neil Asher Silberman), the moral problem remains. It is relevant no matter that the texts are not historical accounts from the Bronze Age, for the texts represent "programmatic ideological statements from the late seventh century B.C.E. or later." And it is relevant no matter that the theology of Deuteronomy and Joshua (and 1 Sam. 15, I would add) were directed toward insiders who posed a threat to the hierarchy rather than against ethnic outsiders. As ideological statements they are still problematic, for texts have a life of their own.[64]

---

61. Collins, "The Zeal of Phinehas." Collins is the author of several publications discussing violence and ethics in the Old Testament and the Bible, including: *Does the Bible Justify Violence?* (Minneapolis: Fortress, 2004); "Biblical Theology Between Apologetics and Criticism," in *Beyond Biblical Theologies*, ed. H. Assel, S. Beyerle and C. Böttrich, WUNT 295 (Tübingen: Mohr Siebeck, 2012), 223–41.
62. Collins, "The Zeal of Phinehas," 6.
63. Ibid., 7.
64. Ibid., 10–12; see the references in nn. 31–5.

Collins then discusses examples of divinely sanctioned violence that in their turn have sanctioned further violence: (1) the story of Phineas (Num. 25:10-15) that serves as an example for the zealot Mattathias in 1 Maccabees 1, and (2) the biblical analogies drawn in the English Puritan revolution from, for example, Exodus and the book of Daniel. A generation later, the Puritan immigrants in New England applied the biblical texts of conquest to their own situation, "casting the Native American tribes in the role of the Canaanites and Amalekites." Even later, the very same texts have been used by the Boers in South Africa, Zionists in Israel, and even "provide the underpinnings for support of Israel among conservative Christians."[65]

In his conclusion, Collins asks the decisive question: What are we, as biblical scholars at the beginning of the twenty-first century, to say about the history and impact of the biblical texts of violence?[66] It does not help to do away with or skip over the problem by applying, for example, allegorical methods to the texts in order to save them. Such methods are "hardly viable in the modern world", and no matter what we "still have texts that speak rather clearly of slaughtering human beings."[67] A more promising strategy is to discriminate between the texts and privilege texts that emphasize the Deuteronomistic concern for slaves or the suffering servant, maybe even as a model for Christian belief. However, Collins claims: "Such a selective reading, privileging the death of Jesus, or the model of the suffering servant, is certainly possible, and even commendable, but it does not negate the force of the biblical endorsements of violence that we have been considering."[68]

Collins recommends another path, namely to acknowledge that the Bible—including the New Testament—"not only witnesses to the innocent victim and to the God of victims, but also to the hungry God who devours victims and to the zeal of his human agents. And therein precisely lies its power."[69] The Bible gives an unvarnished portrayal of human life and thought; it does not demystify or demythologize itself, and it does not claim that its stories are "paradigms for human action in all times and places."[70]

---

65. Ibid., 12–14. Cf. also the discussion of the *Wirkungsgeschichte* of the war narratives in esp. Christian tradition in Niditch, *War in the Hebrew Bible*, 1–5, 24–7.
66. Ibid., 18–21.
67. Ibid., 19.
68. Ibid.
69. Ibid., 19–20 with reference to David Shulman, *The Hungry God* (Chicago: University of Chicago Press, 1993).
70. Ibid., 20.

4. *The Authority of the Bible*

This leads Collins to consider the authority of the Bible. Historically, people have appealed to the Bible's authority as a God-given investment. This may be even more pertinent among Protestants, especially Lutherans, than among Catholics, and it has become a hallmark among conservative evangelical communities. But the many different voices in the Bible that discuss and contradict each other point in another direction:

> The Bible has contributed to violence in the world precisely because it has been taken to confer a degree of certitude that transcends human discussion and argumentation. Perhaps the most constructive thing a biblical critic can do toward lessening the contribution of the Bible to violence in the world, is to show that that certitude is an illusion.[71]

Three decades ago, Robert P. Carroll took the discussion even further. He wrote:

> The Bible is a profoundly problematical collection of books in many senses—religious, cultural, political, intellectual, moral, ethical and aesthetic—as well as posing problems for modern strategies of reading (Marxian, feminist, philosophical, postmodernist, etc.).[72]

All the books in the Hebrew Bible/Old Testament (as well as the books of the New Testament) present us with narratives, ethics, poetry, theologies that are far from our age in message and form. Biblical books need careful exposition and a critical mind from their readers. Blind belief in the authority of the Bible for people of faith, be it Christians or Jews, must not stand in the way for the appropriation of the message for its modern readers. Writing about the New Testament (but the assertion also applies to the Old), Carroll insists:

> It requires little criticality to read about slavery, cruelty in the name of God, antisemitism and prejudice in the scriptures and not be made aware of gaps between the text and modern values. In such ways the Bible deconstructs itself for the modern reader.[73]

---

71. Ibid., 21.
72. Robert P. Carroll, *The Bible as a Problem for Christianity* (Philadelphia: Trinity Press International, 1991). Interestingly, the original British edition was published as *Wolf in the Sheepfold* (London: SPCK, 1991).
73. Carroll, *The Bible as a Problem for Christianity*, 86.

Serious attempts have been made by good people to save the authority of the Bible, for if we do not have the Bible as an authority, how would we find our ethical compass?[74] Maybe the answer lies exactly in acknowledging and respecting that the Bible holds different human opinions about God and the world and that it is our responsibility to listen to this discussion and take it for what it is instead of showing a blind and uncritical adherence to the upfront messages of its stories.[75]

No book in the Hebrew Bible comes to us from the past without problems. As a canonical book we are as "stuck" with the book of Esther as with any other biblical book. The Bible is indeed a problem for Christianity, to borrow a phrase from Carroll, but as biblical scholars it is our obligation to deconstruct it and keep discussing its messages in the context of our modern world. Such discussions, then, may serve as bases and guidelines for people of faith seeking the true authority of the Bible.

5. *Is Esther a Bedtime Story?*

The readings in the present volume have identified and pointed at, I assert, the many human and worldly incentives behind the book of Esther, literary as well as sociological and political. Those incentives were far more important for the narrators and translators than is normally expected from a pious narrative about the will of God. No wonder that its place in the Jewish canon was a matter of debate. But in the end, it was included, exactly because it was a necessary story about how to survive in the Diaspora. What does this mean for the modern reader of the book of Esther? Do we still need its carnivalesque humor, its imperfect heroes, and its close blend of carnage and festival?

Let me try to view the problem from yet another perspective. The fairy tale *Snow White* is a long story about betrayal and jealousy, but also, as many other fairy tales, of love that conquers all evil. At the end of the

---

74. I confine myself to mentioning only two recent volumes: William P. Brown, ed., *Engaging Biblical Authority: Perspectives on the Bible as Scripture* (Louisville: John Knox, 2007), presents short essays by sixteen biblical scholars of different faith and hermeneutical background; and Carolyn J. Sharp, *Wrestling the Word: The Hebrew Scriptures and the Christian Believer* (Louisville: John Knox, 2010), which offers as an introduction to the debate in biblical scholarship "to the readers who grapple with unsettling ideas they may have heard about the Hebrew Scriptures in the halls of their church, in the cafeteria of their seminary, or in the public square" (xi).

75. Maybe this is even a possible present-day mode of understanding Luther's exegetical principle of regarding the Bible as its own interpreter, *Sacra Scriptura sui ipsius interpres*?

story, Snow White's wicked stepmother stands in front of the talking mirror and ponders if she should go to the wedding between Snow White and her prince. In the end she decides to go, to make sure who the bride is:

> And when she saw her she knew her for Snow White, and could not stir from the place for anger and terror. For they had ready red-hot iron shoes, in which she had to dance until she fell down dead.

This is the dreadful end of the story—but is it a bed-time story? Does it incite the seeking of revenge and the paying back of evil with evil, or is its message rather the message of love that conquers even death? If the latter is the case, then why the gruesome end of the story? Why not let it end as so many other fairy tales with the young couple living happily ever after? From my perspective, this is a matter of cathartic revenge phantasy. If the child in bed is to be able to sleep after "Snow White" has been read to her, she will need the fairy tale's closing assurance that the wrongs done to Snow White—and to herself, hopefully in a minor scale—will be righted. The child has identified with Snow White and needs the comfort that the wicked step-mother—or the witch in Hansel and Gretchen—will never return.

The slaughtering of the 75,311 Persians at the end of Esther works in the same way. A delicate balance between the protagonists has been built over the story through mimetic doublings, peripety, and repetitions of motifs. Suspense has grown until the first release when Haman is hanged in his own gallows. But that is not enough. To fulfill its community-creating mission, the book of Esther must end in the double relief of total victory and blissful joy. This narrated joy of Purim, colored by the audience's familiarity with the carnivalesque celebration of Purim, relieves the narrative suspense and everyday anxiety among a people, struggling to survive as a minority in a foreign world. Along the way, the audience/community/reader is treated with a burlesque story about absurd luxury and bureaucracy, a buffoon king, a wicked courtier, a wise man, and a beautiful young woman, Esther the Jewish queen of the Persians.

So, what do we do about Esther? Is Esther a bedtime story? In the book section of a major Danish newspaper, *Weekendavisen*, the question of what constitutes "appropriate" material for parents wanting to read bedtime stories to their children was raised. How gruesome can a story be before it ruins the child's nightly rest? The response was that the literary quality is the most decisive aspect of a good bedtime reading. If it is good literature, it is also good bedtime reading. The respondent recommended books by the Norwegian author and illustrator Stian Hole, whose children's books have been described as posing "a rare sentiment of serene insecurity." The respondent concluded: "Bedtime reading should not be idyllic or banalize reality, but at the same time is should always assure the child that all will end well. For I am sitting here right beside you, reading."

Somehow, this is how the book of Esther works. Once upon a time in a kingdom right around the corner there was a wicked vizier who threatened the lives of all the Judeans. But because of God's providence and through the shrewdness of the beautiful Esther and her wise guardian Mordecai the enemy was slain, and the Judeans lived happily ever after.

Bibliography

Texts

Biblia Hebraica Leningradensia
A New English Translation of the Septuagint and the Other Greek Translations Traditionally Included under That Title [*NETS*]. Edited by A. Pietersma and B. G. Wright. New York / Oxford: Oxford University Press, 2007.
Septuaginta: Vetus Testamentum Graecum Auctoritate Academiae Scientiarum Gottingensis editum VIII.3: Esther. Göttingen: Vandenhoeck & Ruprecht, 1966.
James B. Pritchard, ed. *Ancient Near Eastern Texts Relating to the Old Testament*. 3rd ed. Princeton: Princeton University Press, 1969.

Commentaries, Monographs, and Articles

Alexander, Jeffrey C. "Toward a Theory of Cultural Trauma." In *Cultural Trauma and Collective Identity*, edited by Jeffrey C. Alexander et al., 1–30. Berkeley: University of California Press, 2004.
Alexander, Jeffrey C., and Elizabeth Butler Breese. "Introduction: On Social Suffering and Its Cultural Construction." In *Narrating Trauma: On the Impact of Collective Suffering*, edited by Ron Eyerman, Jeffrey C. Alexander, and Elizabeth Butler Breese, xi–xxxv. The Yale Cultural Sociology Series. Boulder: Paradigm Publisher, 2013.
Almog, Oz. *The Sabra: The Creation of the New Jew*. Translated by Haim Watzman. Berkeley: University of California Press, 2000.
Anderson, Bernard W. "The Place of the Book of Esther in the Christian Bible." *The Journal of Religion* 30 (1950): 32–43.
Bakhtin, Mikhail. *The Dialectic Imagination*. Translated by C. Emerson and M. T. Holquist. Austin: University of Texas Press, 1981.
Bardtke, Hans. *Luther und das Buch Esther*. Sammlung Gemeinverständlicher Vorträge und Schriften aus dem Gebiet der Theologie und Religionsgeschichte 240/241. Tübingen: J.C.B. Mohr [Paul Siebeck] 1964.
Barth, Fredrik. "Introduction." In *Ethnic Groups and Boundaries: The Social Organization of Culture Difference*, edited by Fredrik Barth, 9–38. Oslo: Universitetsforlaget, 1969.
Beal, Timothy K. *The Book of Hiding: Gender, Ethnicity, Annihilation, and Esther*. Biblical Limits. London/New York: Routledge, 1997.
Beal, Timothy K. "Tracing Esther's Beginnings." In *A Feminist Companion to Esther, Judith, and Susanna*, edited by Athalya Brenner, 87–110. Feminist Companion to the Bible 7. Sheffield: Sheffield Academic, 1995.

Becker, Eve-Marie. "'Trauma Studies' and Exegesis: Challenges, Limits and Prospects." In *Trauma and Traumatization in Individual and Collective Dimensions: Insights from Biblical Studies and Beyond*, edited by Eve-Marie Becker, Jan Dochhorn, and Else K. Holt, 15–29. Studia Aarhusiana Neotestamentica 2. Göttingen: Vandenhoeck & Ruprecht, 2014.

Ben-Chorin, Shalom. *Kritik des Estherbuches: Eine theologische Streitschrift*. Jerusalem: "HEATID." Salingré & Co., 1938.

Berg, Sandra Beth. *The Book of Esther: Motifs, Themes, and Structure*. Society of Biblical Literature Dissertation Series 44. Missoula: Scholars Press, 1979.

Berger, John. *Ways of Seeing: Based on the BBC Television Series with John Berger*. London: BBC and Penguin Books, 1972.

Berlin, Adele. *Esther*. The JPS Bible Commentary. Philadelphia: The Jewish Publication Society, 2001.

Berlin, Adele. *Poetics and Interpretation of Biblical Narrative*. Bible and Literature Series 9. Sheffield: Almond, 1983.

Bickerman, Elias. *Four Strange Books of the Bible: Jonah / Daniel / Kohelet / Esther*. New York: Schocken, 1967.

Bickerman, Elias J. "Notes on the Greek Book of Esther." *Proceeding of the American Academy of Jewish Research* 20 (1950): 101–33. Repr. in *Studies in the Book of Esther*, edited by Carey A. Moore, 488–520. New York: KTAV, 1982.

Boase, Elizabeth, and Christopher G. Frechette, eds. *Bible through the Lens of Trauma*. Atlanta: Society of Biblical Literature, 2016.

Boda, Mark J., Daniel K. Falk, and Rodney A. Werline, eds. *Seeking the Favor of God: Volume 1, The Origins of Penitential Prayer in Second Temple Judaism*. Early Judaism and its Literature. Atlanta: Society of Biblical Literature, 2006.

Boraas, Roger S. "Purple." In *The HarperCollins Bible Dictionary*, edited by Paul J. Achtemeier, 902–3. San Francisco: HarperSanFrancisco, 1996.

Brown, William P., ed. *Engaging Biblical Authority: Perspectives on the Bible as Scripture*. Louisville: John Knox, 2007.

Broyde, Michael J. "Defilement of the Hands, Canonization of the Bible, and the Special Status of Esther, Ecclesiastes, and Song of Song." *Judaism* 44 (1995): 65–79.

"byssus." *Oxford English Dictionary* Online. March 2020. Oxford University Press. https://www-oed-com.ez.statsbiblioteket.dk:12048/view/Entry/25639?redirectedFrom=byssus (accessed April 3, 2020).

Camp, Claudia V. "1 and 2 Kings." In *The Women's Bible Commentary*, edited by Carol A. Newsom and Sharon H. Ringe, 96–109. Louisville: Westminster John Knox, 1992.

Carr, David M. *Holy Resilience: The Bible's Traumatic Origins*. New Haven: Yale University Press, 2014.

Carroll, Robert P. *The Bible as a Problem for Christianity*. Philadelphia: Trinity Press International, 1991.

Carruthers, Jo. *Esther Through the Centuries*. Malden: Blackwell, 2008.

Clines, David J. A. *The Esther Scroll: The Story of the Story*. Journal for the Study of the Old Testament Supplement Series 30. Sheffield: Sheffield Academic, 1984.

Cohen, Abraham D. "'Hu Ha-goral': The Religious Significance of Esther." *Judaism* 23 (1974): 87–94.

Cohen, Shaye J. D. *The Beginnings of Jewishness: Boundaries, Varieties, Uncertainties*. Berkeley: University of California Press, 1999.

Cohen, Shaye J. D. *From the Maccabees to Mishna*. 3rd ed. Louisville: Westminster, 2014.

Collins, John J. "Biblical Theology Between Apologetics and Criticism." In *Beyond Biblical Theologies*, edited by H. Assel, S. Beyerle and C. Böttrich, 223–41. WissenA schaftliche Untersuchungen zum Neuen Testament 295. Tübingen: Mohr Siebeck, 2012.
Collins, John J. *Does the Bible Justify Violence?* Minneapolis: Fortress, 2004.
Collins, John J. *The Invention of Judaism: Torah and Jewish Identity from Deuteronomy to Paul*. Oakland: University of California Press, 2017.
Collins, John J. "The Zeal of Phinehas: The Bible and the Legitimation of Violence." *Journal of Biblical Literature* 122 (2003): 3–21.
Columpar, Corinn. "The Gaze as Theoretical Touchstone: The Intersection of Film Studies, Feminist Theory, and Postcolonial Theory." *Women's Studies Quarterly* 30 (2002): 25–44.
Craig, Kenneth. *Reading Esther: A Case for the Literary Carnivalesque*. Literary Currents in Biblical Interpretation. Louisville: Westminster John Knox, 1995.
Crawford, Sidnie White. *The Book of Esther: Introduction, Commentary, and Reflections*, 853–972. The New Interpreter's Bible 4. Nashville: Abingdon, 1999.
Crawford, Sidnie White. "Esther and Judith: Contrasts in Character." In *The Book of Esther in Modern Research*, edited by Leonard J. Greenspoon and Sidnie White Crawford, 61–76. Journal for the Study of the Old Testament Supplement Series 380. London: Sheffield Academic, 2003.
Davies, Philip R. "Haman the Victim." In *First Person: Essays in Biblical Autobiography*, edited by Philip R. Davies, 137–54. Sheffield: Sheffield Academic, 2002.
Day, Linda. *Esther*. Abingdon Old Testament Commentaries. Nashville: Abingdon, 2005.
Day, Linda. *Three Faces of a Queen: Characterization in the Books of Esther*. Journal for the Study of the Old Testament: Supplement Series 186. Sheffield: Sheffield Academic, 1995.
Detienne, Marcel. *The Gardens of Adonis*. With an introduction by J.-P. Vernant. Translated by Janet Lloyd. Princeton: Princeton University, 1994.
Dietrich, Jan. *Der Tod von eigener Hand: Studien zum Suizid im Alten Testament, Alten Ägypten und Alten Orient*. Orientalische Religionen in der Antike 19. Tübingen: Mohr Siebeck, 2017.
Doane, M. A. *The Desire to Desire: The Women's Film of the 1940s*. Bloomington: Indiana University Press, 1984.
Doane, M. A. *Technologies of Gender: Essays on Theory, Film and Fiction*. Bloomington: Indiana University Press, 1987.
Dorothy, Charles V. *The Books of Esther: Structure, Genre and Textual Integrity*. Journal for the Study of the Old Testament Supplement Series 187. Sheffield: Sheffield Academic, 1997.
Durkheim, Émile. *The Elementary Forms of Religious Life*. Translated by Carol Cosman. Abridged with an Introduction and Notes by Mark S. Cladis. Oxford World's Classics. Oxford: Oxford University Press, 2001.
Emanuel, Sarah. "Trauma and Counter-Trauma in the Book of Esther: Reding the Megillah in the Face of the Post-Shoah Sabra." *The Bible & Critical Theory* 13 (2017): 23–42.
Exum, J. Cheryl. "Jezebel." In *Harper's Bible Dictionary*, edited by P. J. Achtemeier, 489. San Francisco: Harper & Row, 1985.
Feldman, L. H. *Studies in Josephus' Rewritten Bible*. Leiden: Brill, 1998.
Fox, Michael V. *Character and Ideology in the Book of Esther*. 2nd ed. Grand Rapids: Eerdmans, 2001.

Fox, Michael V. "Three Esthers." In *The Book of Esther in Modern Research*, edited by Leonard J. Greenspoon and Sidney White Crawford, 50–60. Journal for the Study of the Old Testament Supplement Series 380. London: Continuum, 2003.

Fretheim, Terence E. *God and the World in the Old Testament: A Relational Theology of Creation*. Nashville: Abingdon, 2005.

Fretheim, Terence E. "God and Violence in the Old Testament." *Word & World* 24 (2004): 18–28.

Fretheim, Terence E. "'I was only a little angry': Divine Violence in the Prophets." *Interpretation* 58 (2004): 365–75.

Fretheim, Terence E. "Is the Biblical Portrayal of God Always Trustworthy?" In Terence E. Fretheim and Karlfried Froelich, *The Bible as Word of God in Postmodern Age*, 97–111. Minneapolis: Fortress, 1998.

Fretheim, Terence E. "Theological Reflections on the Wrath of God in the Old Testament." *Horizons in Biblical Theology* 24 (2002): 14–17.

Fuerst, Wesley J. *The Books of Ruth, Esther, Ecclesiastes, The Song of Songs, Lamentations—The Five Scrolls*. Cambridge Bible Commentary on the Old Testament. Cambridge: Cambridge University Press, 1975.

Gendler, Mary. "The Restoration of Vashti." Pages 241–7 in *The Jewish Woman*. Edited by Elisabeth Koltun. New York: Schocken, 1976.

Gerleman, Gillis. *Esther*. Biblischer Kommentar zum Alten Testament 21. Neukirchen-Vluyn: Neukirchener Verlag, 1973.

Girard, René. *The Scapegoat*. Translated by Yvonne Freccero. Baltimore: The Johns Hopkins University Press, 1986.

Girard, René. *Violence and the Sacred*. Baltimore: The Johns Hopkins University Press, 1977.

Girard, René (with Jean-Michel Oughourlian and Guy Lefort). *Things Hidden since the Foundation of the World*. Translated by Stephen Bann and Michael Metteer. London: Athlone, 1987.

Glancy, Jennifer A. "The Accused: Susanne and her Readers." In *A Feminist Companion to Esther, Judith, and Susanna*, edited by Athalya Brenner, 288–302. Feminist Companion to the Bible 7. Sheffield: Sheffield Academic, 1995.

Goldman, Stan. "Narrative and Ethical Ironies in Esther." *Journal for the Study of the Old Testament* 47 (1990): 14–31.

Grossman, Jonathan. *Esther: The Outer Narrative and the Hidden Reading*. Siphrut 6. Winona Lake: Eisenbrauns, 2011.

Gruen, Erich S. *Diaspora: Jews amid Greeks and Romans*. Cambridge, MA: Harvard University Press, 2002.

Hancock, Rebecca S. *Esther and the Politics of Negotiation: Public and Private Spaces and the Figure of the Female Royal Counselor*. Emerging Scholars. Minneapolis: Fortress, 2013.

Herrmann, Wolfram. *Ester im Streit der Meinungen*. Beiträge zur Erforschung des Alten Testaments und des antiken Judentums 4. Frankfurt am Main: Peter Lang, 1986.

Holt, Else K. "Daughter Zion: Trauma, Cultural Memory and Gender in OT Poetics." In *Trauma and Traumatization in Individual and Collective Dimensions: Insights from Biblical Studies and Beyond*, edited by Eve-Marie Becker et al., 162–76. Studia Aarhusiana Neotestamentica 2. Göttingen: Vandenhoeck & Ruprecht 2014.

Holt, Else K. "'Let the Righteous Strike Me; Let the Faithful Correct Me': Psalm 141 and the Enclave of the *Ṣaddiqîm*." *Scandinavian Journal of the Old Testament* 33 (2019): 185–202.

Holt, Else K. "'The Stain of Your Guilt is Still Before Me' (Jer 2:22): (Feminist) Approaches to Jeremiah 2 and the Problem of Normativity." In *Prophecy and Power: Jeremiah in Feminist and Postcolonial Perspective*, edited by Carolyn J. Sharp and Christl Maier, 101–16. London: Bloomsbury T&T Clark, 2013.

Horowitz, Elliott. *Reckless Rites: Purim and the Legacy of Jewish Violence.* Princeton: Princeton University Press, 2006.

Hutchinson, John, and Anthony D. Smith, eds. *Ethnicity*. Oxford: Oxford University Press 1996.

Jacobs, Louis. "Purim." In *Encyclopedia Judaica*, vol. 16, edited by Fred Skolnik et al., 740–1. 2nd ed. Detroit: Thomson Gale, 2007.

Jensen, Hans J. Lundager. *Den fortærende ild: Strukturelle analyser af narrative og rituelle tekster i Det Gamle Testamente*. Aarhus: Aarhus University Press, 2000.

Jobes, Karen H. *The Alpha-Text of Esther: Its Character and Relationship to the Masoretic Text*. Society of Biblical Literature Dissertation Series 153. Atlanta: Scholars Press, 1996.

Jobes, Karen H. "Esther: To the Reader." In *A New English Translation of the Septuagint and the Other Greek Translations Traditionally Included under That Title*, edited by A. Pietersma and B. G. Wright, 424–5. New York/Oxford: Oxford University Press, 2007.

Jones, Bruce. "Two Misconceptions about the book of Esther." *Catholic Biblical Quarterly* 39 (1977): 171–81.

Josephus, Flavius. *Judean Antiquities* Book 11. In *Josephus Flavius: Translation and Commentary*, vol. 6A, 59–87. Translation and Commentary by Paul Spilsbury and Chris Seeman. Edited by Steve Mason. Leiden/Boston: Brill, 2016.

Kaiser, Susan B. "Toward a Contextual Social Psychology of Clothing: A Synthesis of Symbolic Interactionist and Cognitive Theoretical Perspectives." *Clothing and Textile Research Journal* 2 (1983–84): 1–8.

Kalmanofsky, Amy. "'As she did, do to her!': Jeremiah's OAN as Revenge Fantasies." In *Concerning the Nations: Essays on the Oracles against the Nations in Isaiah, Jeremiah and Ezekiel*, edited by Else K. Holt, Hyun Chul Paul Kim, and Andrew Mein, 109–27. Library of the Hebrew Bible/Old Testament 612. London: Bloomsbury T&T Clark, 2015.

Kellermann, Natan P. F. *Holocaust Trauma: Psychological Effects and Treatment*. New York and Bloomington: iUniverse, 2009.

Kratz, Reinhard Gregor. *Historical & Biblical Israel: The History, Tradition, and Archives of Israel and Judah*. Translated by Paul Michael Kurtz. Oxford: Oxford University Press, 2015.

LaCocque, André. *Esther Regina: A Bakhtinian Reading*. Evanston: Northwestern University Press, 2008.

Lang, Bernhard. "Joseph the Diviner: Careers of a Biblical Hero." In Bernhard Lang, *Hebrew Life and Literature: Selected Essays of Bernhard Lang*, 93–109. Farnham: Ashgate, 2008.

Laniak, Timothy S. "Esther's *Volkcentrism* and the Reframing of Post-Exilic Judaism." In *The Book of Esther in Modern Research*, edited by Leonard J. Greenspoon and Sidnie White Crawford, 77–90. Journal for the Study of the Old Testament Supplement Series 380. London: Sheffield Academic, 2003.

Laniak, Timothy S. *Shame and Honor in the Book of Esther*. Society of Biblical Literature Dissertation Series 165. Atlanta: Scholars Press, 1998.

Larsen, Kasper Bro. "Fan Fiction and Early Christian Apocrypha." *Studia Theologica: Nordic Journal of Theology* 73 (2019): 43–59.

Levenson, Jon D. *Esther: A Commentary*. Old Testament Library. Louisville/London: Westminster John Knox, 1997.

Levenson, Jon D. "The Horrifying Closing of Psalm 137, or, The Limitations of Ethical Reading." In *Biblical Essays in Honor of Daniel J. Harrington, SJ, and Richard J. Clifford, SJ. Opportunity for No Little Instruction*, edited by Christopher G. Frechette, Christopher R. Matthews, and Thomas D. Stegman, SJ, 18–40. New York / Mahwah: Paulist, 2014.

Levenson, Jon D. "The Scroll of Esther in Ecumenical Perspective: ('How can we sing a song of the Lord on foreign soil?' Ps. 137:4)." *Journal of Ecumenical Studies* 13 (1976): 440–52.

Linafelt, Tod. *Surviving Lamentations: Catastrophe, Lament, and the Protest in the Afterlife of a Biblical Book*. Chicago: University of Chicago, 2000.

Lipschits, Oded, and Manfred Oeming, eds. *Judah and the Judeans in the Persian Period*. Winona Lake: Eisenbrauns, 2006.

Luther, Martin. *D. Martin Luthers Werke. Kritische Gesamt-Ausgabe, Tischreden*, 1. Band, Weimar: Hermann Böhlaus Nachfolger, 1912.

Lyons, Malcolm C. *Arabian Nights: Tales of 1001 Nights*, Volume 1. Translated by Malcolm C. Lyons, with Ursula Lyons. Introduced and annotated by Robert Irwin. London/New York: Penguin, 2008.

Mason, Steve. "Jews, Judeans, Judaizing, Judaism: Problems of Categorization in Ancient History." *Journal for the Study of Judaism* 38 (2007): 457–512.

McCutcheon, Russell T. "Introduction." In *The Insider / Outsider Problem in the Study of Religion*, edited by Russell T. McCutcheon, 15–22. London: Cassell Academic, 1999.

Middlemas, Jill. "The Greek Esthers and the Search for History: Some Preliminary Observations." In *Between Evidence and Ideology: Essays on the History of Ancient Israel read at the Joint Meeting of the Society for Old Testament Study and the Oud Testamentisch Werkgezelschap Lincoln, July 2009*, edited by Bob Becking and Lester L. Grabbe, 145–63. Leiden: Brill Academic, 2010.

Moore, Stewart A. *Jewish Ethnic Identity and Relations in Hellenistic Egypt: With Walls of Iron?* Leiden: Brill, 2014.

Morrow, William. "The Affirmation of Divine Righteousness in Early Penitential Payers: A Sign of Judaism's Entry into the Axial Age." In *Seeking the Favor of God: Volume 1, The Origins of Penitential Prayer in Second Temple Judaism*, edited by Mark J. Boda, Daniel K. Falk, and Rodney A. Werline, 101–17. Early Judaism and its Literature. Atlanta: Society of Biblical Literature, 2006.

Mulvey, Laura. "Visual Pleasure and Narrative Cinema." *Screen* 16 (1975): 6–18.

Neyrey, J. H. "Clothing." In *Handbook of Biblical Social Values*, edited by J. J. Pilch and B. J. Malina, 21–7. Peabody: Hendrickson, 1998.

Niditch, Susan. *A Prelude to Biblical Folklore: Underdogs and Tricksters*. First Illinois paperback ed. Urbana: University of Illinois Press, 2000.

Niditch, Susan. *War in the Hebrew Bible: A Study in the Ethics of Violence*. New York: Oxford University Press, 1993.

O'Connor, Kathleen M. *Genesis 1–25A*. Smyth and Helwys Bible Commentary. Macon: Smyth & Helwys 2018.

Paton, Lewis Bayles. *A Critical and Exegetical Commentary on the Book of Esther*. International Critical Commentary. Edinburgh: T. & T. Clark, 1907.

Petersen, Anders Klostergaard. "Rewritten Bible as a Borderline Phenomenon: Genre, Textual Strategy, or Canonical Anachronism?" In *Flores Florentino: Dead Sea Scrolls and Other Early Jewish Studies in Honour of Florentino García Martínez*, edited by Anthony Hilhorst, Èmile Puech, and Eibert Tigchelaar, 285–306. Leiden: Brill, 2007.

Pike, Kenneth L. "Etic and Emic Standpoints for the Description of Behavior." Reprint in *The Insider / Outsider Problem in the Study of Religion*, edited by Russell T. McCutcheon, 28–36. London: Cassell Academic, 1999.

Pippin, Tina. "Jezebel Revamped." In *A Feminist Companion to Samuel and Kings*, edited by Athalya Brenner, 196–206. Feminist Companion to the Bible 9. Sheffield: Sheffield Academic, 1994.

Radday, Yehuda T. "Chiasm in Joshua, Judges and Others." *Linguistica Biblica* 27/28 (1973): 6–13.

Réage, Pauline (Anne Desclos). *Story of O.* Translated by Sabine d'Estree. New York: Random House, 2013. (Translated from French: *Histoire d'O*. Paris: Jean-Jacques Pauvert, 1954).

Reuss, D. Eduard. *Das alte Testament*, vol. 7. Braunschweig, 1894.

Rubinstein, Ruth P. *Dress Codes: Meanings and Messages in American Cultures*. Boulder: Westview, 1995.

Schwartz, Avraham, and Yisroel Schwartz. *The Megillot and Rashi's Commentary with Linear Translation: Esther, Song of Songs, Ruth*. Jerusalem: Feldheim, 1983.

Shapira, Yona. "A Postmodernist Reading of the Biblical Book of Esther: From Cultural Disintegration to Carnivalesque Text." PhD diss., State University of New York, 1996.

Sharp, Carolyn J. *Irony and Meaning in the Hebrew Bible*. Indiana Studies in Biblical Literature. Bloomington: Indiana University Press, 2009.

Sharp, Carolyn J. *Wrestling the Word: The Hebrew Scriptures and the Christian Believer*. Louisville: John Knox, 2010.

Siebert-Hommes, Jopie. "'On the third day Esther put on her queen's robes' (Esther 5:1): The Symbolic Function of Clothing in the Book of Esther." http://www.lectio.unibe.ch/02_1/siebert.pdf.

Smith, Anthony D. *The Ethnic Revival*. Cambridge: Cambridge University Press, 1981.

Spasić, Ivana. "The Trauma of Kosovo in Serbian National Narratives." In *Narrating Trauma: On the Impact of Collective Suffering*, edited by Ron Eyerman, Jeffrey C. Alexander, and Elizabeth Butler Breese, 81–105. The Yale Cultural Sociology Series. Boulder: Paradigm, 2013.

Stein, Stephen J. "The Web of Religion and Violence." *Religious Studies Review* 28 (2002): 103–8.

Stern, Elsie R. "Esther and the Politics of Diaspora." *Jewish Quarterly Review* 100 (2010): 25–53.

Talmon, Shemaryahu. "Wisdom in the Book of Esther." *Vetus Testamentum* 13 (1963): 419–55.

Thiel, Winfried. "קָרַע *qāraʻ*; קְרָעִים *qerāʻîm*." In *Theological Dictionary of the Old Testament*, edited by G. Johannes Botterweck, Helmer Ringgren, and Heinz-Josef Fabry, 7: 175–80. Translated by David E. Green. Grand Rapids: Eerdmans 2004.

Thiel, Winfried. "שַׂק, *śaq*." In *Theological Dictionary of the Old Testament*, edited by G. Johannes Botterweck, Helmer Ringgren, and Heinz-Josef Fabry, 14: 184–9. Translated by Douglas W. Scott. Grand Rapids: Eerdmans, 2004.

Troyer, Kristin de. *The End of the Alpha Text of Esther: Translation and Narrative Technique in MT 8:1-17; LXX 8:1-17, and AT 7:14-41*. Society of Biblical Literature Septuagint and Cognate Studies 48. Atlanta: Society of Biblical Literature, 2000.

Turner, Victor W. *The Forest of Symbols: Aspects of Ndembu Ritual*. Ithaca: Cornell University Press, 1967.
Volkan, Vamik D. "Transgenerational Transmissions and Chosen Traumas: An Aspect of Large-Group Identity." *Group Analysis* 34 (2001): 79–97.
Wagstaff, Bethany Joy. "Redressing Clothing in the Hebrew Bible: Material-Cultural Approaches." PhD diss., University of Exeter, 2017.
Watts, James W. "Ritual Legitimacy and Scriptural Authority." *Journal of Biblical Literature* 124 (2005): 401–17.
Wetter, Anne-Mareike. "How Jewish is Esther? Or: How is Esther Jewish?—Tracing Ethnic and Religious Identity in a Diaspora Narrative." *Zeitschrift für die alttestamentliche Wissenschaft* 123 (2011): 596–603.
Wetter, Anne-Mareike. *"On Her Account": Reconfiguring Israel in Ruth, Esther, and Judith*. Library of Hebrew Bible/Old Testaments Studies 623. London: Bloomsbury T&T Clark, 2015.
White, Sidnie Ann. "Esther: A Feminine Model for Jewish Diaspora." In *Gender and Difference in Ancient Israel*, edited by Peggy L. Day, 161–77. Minneapolis: Fortress, 1989.
Williams, Linda. *Hard Core: Power, Pleasure, and the Frenzy of the Visible*. Berkeley: University of California Press, 1989.
Williams, Linda. "Why I Did Not Want to Write This Essay." *Signs: Journal of Women in Culture and Society* 30 (2004): 1264–71.
Wills, Lawrence M. *The Book of Judith: Introduction, Commentary, and Reflections*, 1075–83. The New Interpreter's Bible 3. Nashville: Abingdon, 1999.
Wills, Lawrence M. *The Jewish Novel in the Ancient World*. Ithaca and London: Cornell University Press, 1995.
Wolde, Ellen van. "Texts in Dialogue with Texts: Intertextuality in the Ruth and Tamar Narratives." *Biblical Interpretation* 5 (1997): 1–28.

Index of References

Hebrew Bible/Old Testament

Genesis
1:28-29	11
34	89
37–50	2, 7
37:3-4	88
37:31-33	88
37:34	79
39:11-18	88
41:14	88
41:41-42	88
41:43	88
45:22	88

Exodus
2	119
2:11	119
3:5	119
7:9-14	91
11:3	119
12:33-35	120
17	95
17:8-16	140
17:8-14	95, 125, 130
17:8	95
17:9-14	95
17:9	95
17:14	95, 125
24	121
34	121
34:6-7	152
34:6	152

Numbers
14	79
25:10-15	154

Deuteronomy
25:17-19	94, 125, 143
25:19	103

Joshua
2	26
2:9-13	33
7	79

Judges
11	79

1 Samuel
4	79
15	91, 94, 95, 140–3, 150, 152, 153
15:1-9	94, 125, 130
15:1-3	140
15:2	141
15:7-8	140
15:8	94
15:9	140, 142
15:15	140, 142
15:17	142
15:19	142
15:21	140, 142
15:22-23	140
15:24	142

2 Samuel
3	79
11	62
13:19	79
16:20-23	99

1 Kings
16:31	67
18:16-46	67
19	79
21:23	67

2 Kings
9:36-37	67
18	25
18:37	79
21:30-37	67
23	124

2 Chronicles
34	79
35:1-19	124

Ezra
9	79

Nehemiah
8:1-12	124
8:1	13
8:9-12	13
8:10	14
8:12	14
8:13-18	13
8:14-15	13
8:17	13

Esther
1–8	118
1–2	51–3, 55, 59, 93
1	28–30, 55, 64, 78, 103, 114

Esther (cont.)

Ref	Page	Ref	Page	Ref	Page	Ref	Page
1:1-5	72	3:1	94	5:3	1, 130		
1:1	109	3:2-5	41	5:5-9	27		
1:3-4	114	3:2	100	5:5-6	130		
1:3	53	3:4	76, 77	5:6	130		
1:5	103, 114	3:6	77	5:14	33, 124		
1:6	72, 77	3:7	11	6	26–9, 101		
1:7	73	3:8-11	76	6:6-11	85		
1:9	74	3:8-9	98, 115	6:7-10	85		
1:10-12	72, 73	3:8	96, 100, 107	6:8	78		
1:10	53, 59	3:9	77	6:10	25		
1:11	53, 59, 78	3:10-11	86	6:11-12	86		
1:12	60	3:10	76	6:11	86		
1:16-18	60	3:15	78	6:13	26, 27, 33, 37, 86		
1:19	75, 93	4	12, 26–7, 36, 37, 41, 42, 55, 68, 79–81, 88, 125, 130	6:14	86		
1:22	60, 109			7	28, 29, 37, 38, 99		
2–3	27			7–8	27		
2	15, 28, 29, 39, 51, 52, 60, 62, 76, 78, 80, 84			7:1–8:2	27		
				7:1-10	130		
				7:2	44, 130		
		4:1-17	78	7:8-10	86		
		4:1	79, 114	7:8	85, 98		
2:2-3	59	4:3	12, 80	7:47-49	46		
2:3-4	53	4:4	81	7:50-52	46		
2:5-7	94	4:5-16	82	8–9	109, 152		
2:5-6	101, 108, 111, 114	4:5-9	81	8	28–30, 38, 45, 78		
		4:5-6	82				
2:5	114	4:7-9	82	8:1-17	24		
2:6	111, 114	4:8	81	8:1-2	38		
2:7	59, 60, 64	4:10-17	81	8:2	76, 77		
2:8	64, 102	4:10-12	82	8:3-8	77		
2:9	60, 64	4:11	83, 84	8:6	39		
2:10	115	4:12-14	81	8:7	39		
2:11	64	4:13-14	25, 82	8:8	93		
2:12	65	4:14	9, 37, 119	8:9-14	39, 77		
2:15	39, 60, 64	4:15-16	82	8:10-13	115		
2:16	64	4:16	12, 37	8:11	93, 98, 99, 152		
2:17	54, 72, 75, 78	4:17	41, 82				
		5	26–30, 37, 37, 41, 68	8:13	148		
2:21-23	45, 76, 101			8:15-17	77		
				8:15-16	78		
3	25, 27–9, 78, 121	5:1-5	27, 43	8:15	77, 78		
		5:1	82, 83	8:17	25, 27, 115		
3:1-11	76	5:2	84				

Index of References

9	15, 27–9, 39, 98, 107, 148, 152	*Job* 1–2 1:20 2:7-8 2:12	79 79 79 79	*Revelation* 14:10-11 14:20	6 6
9–10	86			APOCRYPHA	
9:1-19	118			*Judith*	
9:1-18	102	*Psalms*		8	89
9:1-12	44	50	142	9	89
9:1-3	45	137	144	9:2	89
9:2-3	117			10:1-5	89
9:2	93, 98	*Song of Songs*			
9:4	119	4	66	*Esther LXX and AT*	
9:5	98, 122	4:13–14:16	66	A:4-10 30	30
9:9–10:3	118			A:5-9 LXX	136
9:10	95, 124, 152	*Isaiah* 13–23	131	A:5-10 A:9 AT	136 136
9:11-15	39, 103, 117, 148	36 38	33 26	4:11 LXX C:1-11	43 41
9:13-15	78			C:12-30	41
9:15	152	*Jeremiah*		C:12-13	41, 83
9:16-19	45	7	142	C:14-28	42
9:16	95, 152	8:23 MT	79	D:1 AT	83
9:18-19	103	9:9	79	D:2	43
9:19-32	102	29:5-7	7	D:3-4 AT	43
9:19	14	38	26	D:5-7 LXX	43
9:20-28	45	40:2-3	33	D:6 LXX	84
9:20-26	46	46–51	131	D:7-8 LXX	44
9:20-23	121			5:12 AT	44
9:21-24	117	*Ezekiel*		7 AT	47
9:22	123	27–28	79	7:13 AT	77
9:23-26	102			7:14 AT	5
9:26-28	117	*Daniel*		7:15-17 AT	45
9:26-27	102	1–6	41	7:18-21 AT	45, 46
9:27	14			7:18 AT	46
9:29	122	*Amos*		7:33 AT	45
9:29	45	5:1-3	79	7:42-45 AT	45
9:29-32	40			7:45-46 AT	45
9:31	12	*Zechariah*		8:11 LXX	22
10	28, 29, 40, 86	1:7-17	151	8:14 AT 8:18 LXX	45 116
10:1-3	46	NEW TESTAMENT		9 AT	44, 45
10:2	87	*Galatians*		9:1-15 LXX	45
10:3	87, 93, 109	2:14	116	9:3-11 AT 9:16-19 LXX	45 45

Esther LXX and AT
(cont.)
10 LXX	45
10:3	86
F:3-6	30
F:3-9	136
F:8 7	13

2 Maccabees
2:21	112
8:1	112
11:22-26	22
11:27-33	22
14:38	112

PSEUDEPIGRAPHA
4 Maccabees
4:26	112

MISHNAH
Megillah
7b	103

JOSEPHUS
Jewish Antiquities
11:184-296	20

Against Apion
2:24 §201	47

CLASSICAL AND ANCIENT CHRISTIAN LITERATURE
Aristotle
Poetics
1452a, 24-26	25

Plutarch
Moralia
140 B 16	74

Xenophon
An Ephesian Tale
1:6	31

Index of Authors

Albright, W. F. 141
Alexander, J. C. 128
Almog, O. 138
Anderson, B. W. 6, 94

Bakhtin, M. 131
Bardtke, H. 4, 31
Barth, F. 110, 112, 114
Beal, T. K. 2, 4, 6, 7, 32–4, 55, 59, 60, 69, 74, 93, 103, 114
Becker, E.-M. 128, 129
Ben-Chorin, S. 6, 94
Berg, S. B. 10–12, 25, 36
Berger, J. 58, 62
Berlin, A. 21, 35, 44, 55, 56, 73, 74, 85, 92, 95, 102, 103, 114, 122, 143–5
Bickerman, E. J. 5, 22
Boase, E. 7, 129
Boda, M. J. 41
Boraas, R. S. 73
Breese, E. B. 128
Brown, W. P. 156
Broyde, M. J. 3

Camp, C. V. 67
Carr, D. M. 129
Carroll, R. P. 155
Carruthers, J. 3
Clines, D. J. 8, 23, 27, 81, 118, 122
Cohen, A. D. 9
Cohen, S. J. D. 47, 110–12, 116, 121
Collins, J. J. 112, 141, 153–5
Columpar, C. 59
Craig, K. 131
Crawford, S. W. 8, 11, 47

Davies, P. R. 90, 91, 95, 96, 100
Day, L. 23, 33, 35, 40, 43, 46
Detienne, M. 66
Dietrich, J. 71, 72
Doane, M. A. 59

Dorothy, C. V. 23
Durkheim, E. 123

Emanuel, S. 132, 133, 138
Exum, J. C. 67

Falk, D. K. 41
Feldman, L. H. 20
Fox, M. V. 6, 8, 19, 22, 23, 25, 26, 35, 37–9, 41, 73, 74, 90, 93–6, 102, 117, 141, 143, 148, 149
Frechette, C. G. 9, 129
Fretheim, T. E. 149–52
Fuerst, W. J. 6

Gendler, M. 36
Gerleman, G. 118–20
Girard, R. 92–4, 96, 97, 99–101, 123
Glancy, J. A. 58
Goldman, S. 25, 93
Grossman, J. 7, 130, 131, 145, 146
Gruen, E. S. 134, 135

Hancock, R. S. 2
Hermann, W. 6
Holt, E. K. 42, 69, 129
Horowitz, E. 32
Hutchinson, J. 110

Jacobs, K. H. 103
Jensen, H. J. L. 66–8
Jobes, K. H. 20–24, 30
Jones, B. 149

Kaiser, S. B. 71
Kalmanofsky, A. 131, 132
Kellermann, N. P. F. 138
Kratz, R. G. 122

LaCocque, A. 24, 122
Lang, B. 7

Laniak, T. S. 72, 108, 117, 121
Larsen, K. B. 20, 21
Levenson, J. D. 2, 9, 11, 23, 26, 39, 72, 74, 93, 108, 120, 144
Linafelt, T. 129
Lipschits, O. 122
Luther, M. 3, 4
Lyons, M. C. 54, 55, 61

Mason, S. 112, 116
McCutcheon, R. T. 111
Middlemas, J. 24
Moore, S. A. 110
Morrow, W. 41
Mulvey, L. 57, 59

Neyrey, J. H. 72
Niditch, S. 38, 51, 141, 154

O'Connor, K. M. 129
Oeming, M. 122

Paton, L. B. 7, 18, 74
Petersen, A. K. 18, 19
Pike, K. L. 111
Pippin, T. 68

Radday, Y. T. 26
Réage, P. 61, 63, 65
Reuss, D. E. 94
Rubinstein, R. P. 71

Schwartz, A. 60
Schwartz, Y. 60
Shapira, Y. 131
Sharp, C. J. 146–8, 152, 156
Shulman, D. 154
Siebert-Hommes, J. 72
Smith, A. D. 110, 111, 113
Spasić, I. 127
Stein, S. J. 149
Stern, E. R. 21

Talmon, S. 9–11, 40
Thiel, W. 79, 80
Troyer, K. de 20, 22, 24, 44, 47, 116
Turner, V. W. 62–5

Volkan, V. D. 126, 127

Wagstaff, B. J. 87
Watts, J. W. 124
Werline, R. A. 41
Wetter, A.-M. 112, 113
White, S. A. 38
Williams, L. 59, 68
Wills, L. M. 22, 25, 26, 31, 35, 51, 87, 136
Wolde, E. van 53

www.ingramcontent.com/pod-product-compliance
Lightning Source LLC
Chambersburg PA
CBHW070641300426
44111CB00013B/2204